Kidnapping,
Murder,
and
Management

Kidnapping, Murder, and Management

THE READING

Lynn Dorrough

ISBN: 978-1-4120-5177-4 (sc)
ISBN: 978-1-4669-7818-8 (e)

Library of Congress Control Number: 2011900109

Trafford rev. 01/18/2013

Trafford PUBLISHING® www.trafford.com

North America & international
toll-free: 1 888 232 4444 (USA & Canada)
phone: 250 383 6864 ♦ fax: 812 355 4082

Dedicated to the memory of my cousin

Preface

Murder, kidnapping, and management all transpired in relation to the following series of letters and thoughts. Except for those involved in such matters as kidnapping, the cousins always used composite characters to represent actual events that occurred across the many industries and locations in which they worked. No actual individual, innocent of any crime, is depicted at any time or manner in their correspondence. However, it should always be remembered that events discussed actually transpired. The text may be read as a process of management theory in action, management of interpersonal relations, or more deeply within the very plan itself. In many cases, the locations in which the events occurred and the organizations in which they were employed were metaphors. In other cases, the time sequence the events transpired was also shifted. The correspondence between the cousins was edited to comprise professional and family lives over the course of fifteen years, roughly from 1974 to 1989. The totality of their personal history is not represented as being included for this period, but the forty-plus letters included provide a definitive outline of their existence within American business culture and the plan. This text was held by an independent third party for six years to allow the fulfillment of some of the actions which were foretold therein. Crime, business, and cultural changes bearing on the shift from the historical nation-state; to the dominance of world wide cultures are central topics within "the letters".

It is hoped that through your reading of this book, you may be spared a good deal of the learning experience of management the cousins endured on a daily basis. One cousin went on to serve on the board of directors of several corporations. Both cousins learned that the academic education in management, marketing, finance, history, economics, and math they received at such institutions as Vanderbilt University and Knox College was priceless but only the beginning of their valuable management education. Each cousin started with a negative net worth and found great value not just in financial success, but much more importantly in the intangibles accumulated along the way.

The impossibility of expressing thanks to all who made this book possible is self-evident, when compiling an overview of more than a decade. The "novel" cousins themselves were shaped by the different types of persons they met over the approximately fifteen-year period. The patience of wife, editor, and others involved can never be fully repaid, but for which I will always remain profoundly grateful. *Fas est et ab hoste doceri!* (It is right to be taught even by an enemy; you may get a hint from the other side!)

Chapter I

October 19, 1975

Dear younger cousin

My first kidnapping went rather well; as such matters are patterned on prior experience, and I was very naïve, I am endeavoring to view the experience as part of my graduate education in management. Returning home for lunch, I parked in the basement garage. The attraction of this particular building was the superb view from the ninth-floor corner apartment and the underground parking. The auto was only one year old and stood out among the vintage vehicles used by other graduate students. In retrospect, it occurs to me that while appearances ease the way when dealing with those of similar or greater social stature, to set a style above that which is customary for any place and time clearly produces risk. For one to have the most current vehicle in the parking lot clearly distinguishes the owner and vehicle, making it easier to track, anticipate, and approach.

As this day developed, it revealed a weakness—of anything becoming a habit—a management trait I will continually work to avoid. For the creation of a habit by any individual or organization, even if the purpose is exemplary, produces a sequence of events subject to prediction. In the management of our very life, or any endeavor, this acquisition of "habit" allows other individuals (competitors) to predict your efforts. This sequence of events permits the opposition to easily nullify your efforts and perhaps even use your very acts to their purpose. However, as this was my first kidnapping, perhaps the events should just be viewed as a learning experience.

After parking the auto and walking toward the elevator, a finely dressed gentleman walked out of the elevator and in my direction. I distinctly remember focusing on the fine quality of his suit, for it was exceptional for a university campus, and I thought that after graduation, I should dress in much the style of this fellow. These thoughts represented another almost-fatal error in this sequence of events. Unusual circumstances, whether by happenstance or design, are often associated with times of risk. To be weary of the unusual is prudence, not paranoia, and represents a well-balanced view of the potential events existing in any environment. If we believe that man is a purposeful being, then being mindful of the probable purpose of those around yourself and doing business with you is a most reasonable behavior in both business and personal matters.

As our paths bisected, the trim stranger reached into his coat and produced a chrome-plated revolver. In an instant, the muzzle was pressed into my side. Beyond any question, anticipating the unexpected became another emphasis of my worldview as a result of this incident. Having never experienced violence in a civil setting prior to this, I had come to consider my personal surroundings to be a most civilized environment in which reasonable individuals dwelled. Only now does it occur to me that reasoned individuals may also be involved in criminal enterprises. The extent of my personal ignorance was such that I was completely taken aback and was not prepared to deal with such an imposing individual while unarmed and surprised. Cousin, it is now clear to me that to carry any situation to success without regard to personal safety, it is necessary and even required to have an advantage of such magnitude that direct confrontation is not to be considered a viable approach by your opponent.

While most of us focus on the competitor, opposition, or criminal on the outside, it is now my belief that the vilest enemy most likely lurks within our closest environment. Due to my slight stature and lack of weapons, my focus was not on direct opposition in this incident but rather on sensing the opponent's intentions. So I started the game rather late, after the opposition had made an imposing first move. It appeared that mental ability would have to suffice and that the perpetrator was an individual with some specific purpose. In retrospect, I remember well our uncle warning me that individuals in these large cities were not the same as the folks back home.

When my opponent requested my car, I gladly offered the keys with the hope that car theft was his objective. The reasonable solution was to give him the keys and wish him Godspeed. Again, my failure was to not ascertain a most probable objective. Car theft by armed robbery was not reasonable for what appeared to be such a professionally attired individual. As a management tenet, always questioning whether the original request by a customer, vendor, or competitor is the objective or merely a means to the objective was an important lesson learned. These events have had a more profound impact on my business perspective than any single course I have yet to take at Vanderbilt University. Yet, without the concurring course of my business education, I would not have the same appreciation for the very events that have so affected my life.

As we walked to my car, with the gun in my side, I felt truly alone for the first time in my life. For another car to drive into the garage another resident to appear from the elevator or for a security guard to stroll through to create some distraction and permit a remote chance of extracting me from the situaxtion was but a forlorn hope at best; not one individual appeared. It is odd, cousin, that despite being surrounded by family and friends, we never fully appreciate how truly alone we are in this world. Regardless of our personal situation, in private life or in business, I now understand that we are alone when it comes to producing results in any situation. In truth, our destiny is largely our own making. To create an opportunity is to manage a situation successfully; to be as uncreative as a dullard invites failure at best, and at worst, death.

I was not feeling very creative when the gentleman requested that I get into the trunk of the car. Given the choice of being shot at that moment, or perhaps being shot later, I chose the latter. Time is the greatest weapon; our family has used it to recover from the war we lost in '65 and the bank we lost in '32. I will always choose time over immediate adverse circumstances that are life threatening, unless I believe there are no options but immediate action against the opponent. Facing downward in the trunk, I realized the distinct possibility that I had made the incorrect choice and was about to be shot. The only positive thought was that the gasoline tank was directly beneath me and that the opponent might die with me as a result of the shot. However, it appeared that I had been abducted by a professional individual, as he closed the trunk and got into the driver's seat.

Cousin, as you have not spent any duration of time in the trunk of a 1974 model car, a necessary explanation is that a resident of the trunk can clearly hear the goings on inside the vehicle. It became apparent that my abductor had never driven a vehicle with a seatbelt interlock. The interlock prevented the auto from being started if the driver's seatbelt was not fastened. For a moment, I felt that the ignorance of my opponent might be my salvation, but unfortunately, he proved adept at adjusting to the situation and was successful in starting the vehicle. However, the moment gave me a feeling that whatever plan existed was not perfect and that in this very imperfection lay my hope for extracting myself from the situation. Remember, I gave him the initial advantage by parking in private underground parking, and this would not have existed if I had chosen to park in a more plebeian and heavily trafficked above-ground lot.

As we pulled out of the parking garage, I resolved to count corners to such an extent as possible so as to understand the general direction in which I was being taken. After a short distance the vehicle stopped, and my abductor warned me to be quiet or he would kill me. Then he left the vehicle. Another explanation might be added that it was impossible to open the trunk of this particular 1974 model vehicle from the inside, as it appeared to have been designed without any thought for the easy escape of any kidnap victim.

A lesson learned is to always plan for alternative ways of dealing with a situation, as any solution with only one entrance or exit can turn into a trap. Have you ever noticed that every room in our grandfather's home has at least three doors, and in some cases even four? His master suite walk-in closet even has a back door. In like manner, I will never propose an ultimate solution for any business problem but instead propound the use of tactics that create multiple favorable solutions, depending on the problem variables. I now believe that absolute faith in any single business cause, solution, or dogma produces single-door answers that can turn any situation into a trap of some type.

The driver's door quickly reopened and then slammed shut, and then he left a significant portion of my new tires on the pavement in a hasty departure. The vehicle began moving rapidly, and I heard the opponent turn on the car radio. The ability to listen to the radio from the trunk was an advantage. Within a very few minutes an announcer interrupted the music to bring the news that the Commerce Union Bank University Branch at 1313 Twenty-First Avenue South had just been robbed and that the police were searching nearby buildings (as it was believed the robber had escaped on foot). I felt reasonably secure the perpetrator had secured motorized transportation. From my experience, I believe one cannot count on the authorities, regulators, government, or others to know, understand, or even care about your personal situation except to such extent that it serves their own purposes. We, in our business and personal lives, must create our own futures before destiny is overshadowed by those of quicker wit. Unfortunately, during this afternoon, I definitely was not in the driver's seat.

An afternoon of driving around the highways of Nashville and middle Tennessee in the trunk of an auto resulted in utter confusion by this resident of the dark trunk in matters of direction of travel, or even the approximate location of the vehicle. In the darkness, points of reference became lost, and the situation did not appear hopeful. At this stage, I remember taking off my boots and settling in for the ride. The only hope appeared to be taking hold of the situation or confronting probable death at the end of the journey. Do you remember from your business readings that in most instances, decisions are never made that place the corporate existence at risk unless in those rare instances where the very continuity of the organization will be at risk without implementing such a decision? My existence was clearly at risk by allowing the event sequence to continue unfettered. It was time to belay the confusion of the dark and use those options available.

My business experience has trained me to strive to be the best in whatever environment occurred. The alternative business solution is to become the closest confidant of the leader of any situation, to actively seek such a close and personal role with my opponent was both unlikely and unseemly given his criminal endeavor. It was my solution to stand sufficiently above the actions of most kidnap victims so as to raise the probability of my survival. The trick was to take this course of action without creating undue animosity in my captor.

The vehicle stopped, and once more my abductor stated that I should remain quiet until he returned, or he would kill me. The matter-of-fact way in which he delivered his request strongly implied his sincerity in this matter. Have you ever noticed how we pick up on the tone of voice that others use in times of stress? I noted the lack of a southern accent in the voice, rather flat and mid-western. Yes, there was even a fleeting thought about when the carpetbaggers will ever leave the South

Starting to work on a plan, I released the full-size spare tire and obtained my objective: the metal rod meant to raise the jack. After a futile attempt to pop the trunk lid open, and considering much ill will against the auto designer who had thoughtfully covered the back of the taillights with sheet metal, I discovered the unhidden interior portion of the rear-side reflectors on either side of the trunk interior. Each was about five inches in length and one inch high. A selection was made of the side reflector on the driver's side of the trunk (to perhaps give me a view of his returning), and I began to pry it off with the tire tool, making as little noise as possible.

The question of available time was paramount, as the abductor had left the motor running with the seeming intention of a prompt return. If the reflector could be quietly removed before our journey was restarted, at least I would be more likely to determine my approximate location. Removing the side reflector revealed that the auto was parked in a rather large and unpopulated parking lot. Throwing caution aside, I tried yelling through the small gap created by the missing reflector but failed to attract attention. Have you ever thought that failure to attract attention to any product in a business situation may simply be due to an inadequate, low-visibility marketing campaign? So at this point, I decided it was time to raise the visibility of the product—me—with a better-focused campaign for visibility in the parking lot.

The thought occurred to me that I was now at risk from some potential car thief, as the motor was running and I had no way of knowing whether or not the doors were locked. The thought of being driven off by yet another individual gave urgency to my plan. To attract attention, I steadily and gradually widened the reflector opening with the tire tool. An obvious imperfection in the plan had been to overlook the removal of the tire tool before closing the trunk. I believe the day showed that any successful manager, given a stressful situation of little hope, should strive to search for and use any tools or options available, even if they initially give little promise of turning the situation around. Such a course of action is likely to be successful if he is blessed with an opponent using a static plan. Fortunately, most business opponents are fixated on a static plan—the annual budget or the annual plan—and take neither the time nor the energy to continually revise and adjust the plan to reflect changes in conditions.

As the reflector hole became larger, I continued to pry on the sheet metal, using leverage from the tire tool to my advantage. I was finally able to push my palm, my fist, and then my arm up to the elbow through the gap. Simultaneously holding the tire tool in my fist, waving it in the air, and yelling, I was determined to attract the attention of some individual, regardless of character. Yes, I was aware of the risk of attracting the very person who had placed me in the trunk, but felt the risk/reward tradeoff was more than balanced. I believe that I will remember this as my first multimedia ad campaign.

Cousin, there are times in our lives when exact words, along with their intonation, are impressed in the mind. For some individuals, it is the words of a speaker during a graduation, a wedding, or a funeral that create such a lasting memory. In my life, I shall never forget a young male voice, a teenager, stating, "Hey, man, workin' on your car?" After responding that I was not conducting some unusual type of trunk repair, I calmly mentioned that my keys had mistakenly been left in the ignition, and would he be so kind as to retrieve the keys and open the trunk. The young man actually did as I requested and opened the trunk. I believe that the calm and forceful tone in which I requested his assistance was of significance. Upon getting out of the trunk and putting my boots back on, I requested that he immediately accompany me to call the police, while explaining to him that I had not been in the trunk voluntarily. I will forever be thankful for a young man who was so helpful to a stranger and who had such a distinctive use of language.

After the arrival of the police and numerous news media, the FBI asked if they could dust my vehicle for fingerprints, and I urged them to take whatever actions were necessary. Their actions confirmed my opinions of our constabularies and made me clearly understand their focus is on apprehending the felon, not on mitigating the trauma incurred by the victims of the criminal acts. I did not mention to them that I was glad they had not found the criminal while I was in the trunk, for I had feared in such an event that any law enforcement officer would shoot at the fleeing thief without realizing that I was in the trunk of the car. I also wrongly believed the police and FBI would return my auto to its pre-examination condition. Again, from a business perspective I learned to clearly specify in any agreement all conditions for the fulfillment of any vendor's contract. The FBI simply finished with the vehicle and confronted me with a car having substantial portions of the interior covered with the residue of a black smudge used to search for fingerprints—which is not at all what I had imaged "dust" would resemble when I had so cheerfully told them to proceed with their work.

The usual visit to the police artist downtown was next, along with an FBI escort back to my apartment building, where I showed the location of my abduction to the authorities. The eventual viewing of the bank lobby camera tape confirmed my identification of the bank robber. My contribution being the revelation to the authorities that the Afro hair shown in the bank film was a wig and that in fact the robber appeared to be a Caucasian of Latin background, with a dark complexion. The wig had apparently been donned after my placement in the trunk and prior to the actual bank robbery. It was a good lesson that everything is not necessarily what it seems to be, and we need to question even the most obvious presentations of fact for actual content before making a final conclusion.

The authorities eventually located the bank robber's fine suit in a room at a nearby motel, within walking distance of the parking lot where he had left the vehicle and me. It is an interesting thief who dresses for work! I truly believe I was lucky to encounter such a professional, rather than some rank amateur who might have mucked the whole business. It is the dilettantes of the world who create the most havoc, and seasoned professionals in any field are seemingly never there when needed. I was fortunate! In business, I have seen an unending stream of newly minted undergraduates with little or no practical experience seeking to cover their lack of experience with the very latest technical tools. They have always seemed to illustrate a sure recipe for disaster, but their command of the technology always gives them some advantage.

The thief has not been captured, and no physical harm came to anyone as a result of his activities. One of the fellows from the FBI was kind enough to provide me with his business card, having a telephone number I can call if I ever see the individual again. The university has even been more helpful and kind, providing me with a new deadbolt for my apartment door. Sometimes it really is the small gift that is most appreciated. I have adjusted my behavior patterns and no longer park in the underground garage. Instead, I park above ground and almost daily vary the exact location. Additionally I attempt to vary my schedule so that I am not quite so predictable. To people who say an MBA is of little value, I can only respond that they have not lived the experience, or they would think otherwise. For an event that has encompassed only one day of my life, this little letter has turned into a bit of an oration. I trust you will have some patience with your desire to get out of the hills, for I can definitely attest to the fact that there is increased risk out here in the "real world." Yes, if I ever manage to buy a home of my own, it will most definitely have at least three doors to every room.

We trust your life is less eventful, but I know you are striving to be as productive as possible in that environment. Let me know how our kin are faring, for I have lapsed in my routine correspondence under the rigors of the academic schedule of a graduate education (no day was budgeted for a kidnapping).

Chapter II

Dear elder cousin,

We are thankful for your survival of the recent kidnapping incident and can report that we are merely focused on outwitting the visiting Yankees for their vacation dollars. I have obtained a wonderful opportunity to work underground as a cave guide and in the parking lot soliciting business for the cavern operation. It is a big step up (or is it down?) from days at the carwash.

The visiting Yankees expect real honest-to-goodness "hill folks," and we are trying to deliver a product that meets their expectations. I wear red, white, and blue striped overalls with a bright red shirt on underneath for effect. As their vehicles pull into the parking lot, I place my thumbs under my overall straps and holler out, "Welcome, you all come on out and stretch for a spell! For the mere sum of two dollars for an adult and one dollar for young ones twelve years and younger, you all can purchase an excursion beneath the surface of the earth to the subterranean marvels of nature beneath you feet!" I believe that my naturally bright red hair adds somewhat to the overall impact in the delivery of the sales pitch.

The next step is to guide them to the gift shop so they may purchase cavern tickets. The easiest way to move the traffic is to stress that there are clean restrooms behind the gift shop. We have been very pleased to have only killed one snake in the restrooms so far this year.

Once they are in the gift shop, we stress that the next cave tour is leaving in less than one half hour, so it is best to purchase their tickets as quickly as possible. As the entire tour takes only one half hour, another tour is always leaving in less than one half hour. About five minutes before the time for the next tour, we try to move the group down to the cavern entrance. Usually, the heat radiating from the parking lot warms up the group so much that they are thrilled just to feel the cool air once the door to the cavern opens and the previous tour exits.

As I start down into the cave, the other tour guide handles the business of hustling in the parking lot and the gift shop. We also have a lady in the gift shop to handle ticket sales. The other cave guide is a talented fellow who knows how to entertain a crowd. We are allowed to work six days a week, and twelve hours each day. Although the pay is less than two dollars per hour, it sure beats anything else I can get in these hills.

As we start down into the cave, we ask everyone to go single file so they can use the handrail until their eyes adjust to the dim light. In truth, this is just one of the techniques we use to ensure that the tour lasts an entire half hour. The entire cavern is less than three hundred fifty feet long and never more than about ninety-five feet wide, so slowing the tour groups down is a necessity to ensure they believe they received full value for their dollar. When the other tour guide and I started working, there was not a script to use, so we developed one on our own, and it seems to work pretty well. A basic geology book can work wonders if the public has not studied it.

As the departing tour guide has turned off all the lights in the cavern, I wait until the entire tour group (or as many as I can get on the first platform) are through the door and down the first staircase before turning on all the lights. Since the cave has little natural water on many formations (unless it has just rained outside), the developers have used colored lighting to add to the natural splendor. Some days I feel like I am working in a Christmas parade. Usually I can get up to a minute out of the surprise effect of all the lights going on at once and the tourists looking around before we proceed down into the cavern.

Again, the cavern is small (but of the highest quality), and it is best to keep the tourists distracted from focusing too much on their surroundings. To that end, the other tour guide and I have developed the ability to walk backward through the entire tour. In that manner, we always maintain eye contact with the crowd, and many focus on us and wonder if we will fall down the more than two hundred steps that exist on each tour.

The developers of the cavern have done a wonderful job of adding to the natural beauty, which would not meet the high expectations of many tourists today. We always have to remember to turn on the pump, which gets the underground river going every morning. For a little sport, one of us once dropped some dry ice into the river, and with the fog rising from it, we referred to it as a hot spring to the next tour group. At least the tourist industry provides some good clean entertainment for tourists and employees alike.

We believe we are doing a pretty fair job for the owners, as the crowds keep arriving. Our record so far is having two consecutive tours with more than two hundred on each tour! Yes, I know what you are thinking, and I too wish we had one of these on our family farm, but I have been unable to locate any trace of a cavern. As we bring the tour groups back to the surface, we always mention that we have available, "Genuine calcite formation chips removed from the cavern during pathway construction available in the gift shop for only one dollar!" I never believed you could sell rocks to Yankees, but it's all in the presentation.

My luck is just getting better all the time, as the other cave guide is kind enough to let me ride to work with him. The lack of transportation is really the only handicap to being poor, and I am blessed with a wonderful friend to bridge that small problem of getting to and from work.

After I get off work at the cavern in the evening, I go to another job I found in town at one of the older hotels that cater to the overflow tourist crowd. My night job is to run the front desk and check in tourists until the place is full. I am fortunate to have another friend running the chamber of commerce offices in the evening, and he guides folks down to the hotel after the other places are filled up. Once I sell out rooms, I get to close down the front desk and catch some sleep. Then in the morning, it is back to the cavern for another fun day underground.

There is not enough money for me to want to stay in these hills, but I believe I can make enough to get out. I am determined to go north to college as quickly as possible. My dealings with the Yankees have convinced me that they are not any more intelligent than hill folks; they simply have more money due to the resources, education, and economy that prevails in their locale. I am determined to earn the money that is required to buy the necessary education. I believe you have shown it is possible to combine scholarships, loans, and work to achieve the desired end!

I am searching for a college which does not allow cars and provides the highest quality education I can afford. By avoiding cars, I will avoid an unnecessary expense, and the relative state of my finances will not be so apparent to my peers. Cousin, we trust your MBA is just about in the bag, and that our grandfather will approve our continued quest for education. However, I doubt if either of us ever read Latin half as proficiently as he does today. The target for my exit from the hills is next year!

Chapter III

Dear younger cousin,

Your underground success in the hills is but a temporarily hidden victory, as I am sure you will yet emerge from the depths of those hills. As I view the back of the Touch and Glow massage facility from my new residence in Anchorage, Alaska, I wonder about my newly minted MBA and the time and effort to wrest it from Vanderbilt University. The gentleman who hired me during an interview in the Lower 48 specifically stated that he was not offering me a job because I had an MBA but in spite of it. That's another one of those phrases to be remembered for a long time. Although I had never ventured this far north before, he assured me I would not have any problem finding an apartment. The day after graduation, I started the drive to Alaska, and it took ten days to get from Nashville, Tennessee, to Anchorage.

When I reached the beginning of the Alcan Highway, the pavement ended and the locals referred to it as a gravel road, for the next eight hundred miles or so. Well, when you saw gravel, it was nearly as large as your fist, and when there was none to be seen, the mud was far deeper than our worst rural roads. For long stretches, there were simply two ruts through the mud and many miles between points of human habitation. The large trucks traveling to Alaska were another hazard, for they simply did not slow down. The best local product I acquired was a type of plastic headlight cover, which successfully prevented glass breakage when meeting oncoming trucks.

By the time I reached Whitehorse in the Yukon Territory, I was determined to drive to Anchorage the next day and find the pavement that the map promised existed at the Alaskan border. I stopped at the Alaskan state line just to walk on the pavement and tell myself the worst was over (I was wrong). Arriving in Anchorage about midnight, I crashed in the first motel, which actually had hot water. On the Alcan, several lodges had faucets clearly stating hot and cold water, but they were ornamental only, and all water was, in fact, cold!

The next morning, I arose early and purchased a newspaper, only to discover there were exactly two apartments available in this city of one hundred forty thousand inhabitants. Rushing out to the first one, I rented it immediately, even though the location overlooking the massage facility was less than perfect. The impact of the pipeline construction on this community is beyond my expectations, and I am simply glad to have lodging of any type.

Only one group of individuals has tried to break into my apartment as of this date. They were a simple group of drug purchasers who attempted to break my door down in order to get to me. It is really amazing how quickly one can stack furniture against a door while conducting a conversation to buy time to complete the task. When the Anchorage police arrived, the drug-oriented individuals were somewhat surprised when I asked that they be brought into my apartment for a discussion. To deal with unexplained violence and malice, I believe it is best to understand why someone is trying to do you bodily harm.

During our conversation, with the police present, it was learned that the three individuals had prepaid for some personal chemical stimulants and a seller had given my address, my very apartment number, as the designated pickup point. No, I did not lecture them about how a performance bond should always be acquired when prepaying for any significant services or merchandise from unknown vendors. Instead, I allowed the poor souls to look through my apartment while the police were there, stressing the extent of my poverty and my recent arrival in Alaska.

Much to the dismay of the police, I refused to press charges and urged the individuals to locate their irresponsible sales representative and retrieve their funds. I believe that in life and business, the creation of one enemy can overwhelm a hundred positive contacts, for individuals always focus on the negative and rarely remember the positive as being more significant. If I had pressed charges, the individuals would have felt assured that I was involved with the plan that had relieved them of their hard-earned capital. They would have simply posted bail, and, courtesy of the turnaround efficiency of the American legal system, would have been back in my face the next day. Residing in an isolated northern community will cause nontraditional solutions to become the norm rather than the exception.

Based on my experience, let me suggest that when you do graduate from college, take the time to make a personal onsite inspection of community housing before accepting that first job. Unfortunately, as I borrowed the money to relocate and will be making college loan payments for the next decade, I did not have an opportunity for an onsite inspection. No job offers were extended in the Lower 48 that gave much hope of repaying all the college-associated debt in a reasonable time and maintaining even a modest lifestyle, so Alaska is turning out to be my financial salvation.

My first assignment with the bank is as a new accounts representative; of course, my computer training has no immediate value except for the typing. I am learning that the local culture is slightly different from anything I have yet experienced. One day, a young fellow sat opposite me at the desk and asked to open a certificate of deposit for $20,000, a considerable sum. He asked if I minded if he smoked, and I responded that it would not be a problem and proceeded to type up the certificate and associated paperwork. I noticed a rather unique odor and the tellers on the other side of the lobby looking my way. It soon was apparent that the customer had lit up a joint and not the traditional cigarette I had anticipated. As I had previously indicated that the customer could smoke, and I wanted the deposit for the bank, I decided the best course of action was to simply type quickly and hurry through the transaction. However, for future reference, when someone way up north asks you if they can smoke, it is strongly recommended that the response be focused, as legal tobacco is the only type of smoking acceptable.

Meanwhile, at the main office downtown, there was a bit of a stir. One of our competing banks had decided to focus on attracting new accounts from new arrivals in Anchorage by exchanging up to $200 Canadian for $200 American as an even trade when opening up a new account. With the exchange rate for Canadian dollars around sixty-two cents per US dollar, this seems quite a deal for new residents. Unfortunately for our competitor, some of our employees at the main office heard of the deal and have used it to their personal advantage. Of course, there is nothing illegal about using the generosity of one's competitor against them, but I am afraid a number of our employees exceeded what could be seen as reasonable. We even had individuals going about during their lunch hours, visiting as many of the competitor's branch offices as they could, and making a tidy sum on the arbitrage between the bank's offer and the actual value of the transaction. Of course, our executive management has put out a memo to all employees stressing that they do not approve of this behavior, and it has all but ceased. It is interesting that the employees learned of this opportunity and used it before executive management, so perhaps market intelligence on the competition is more available internally than we realize.

At one of our regular trainee meetings, an astute senior manager told us about an event that occurred at one of our rural branches and warned us against using any bank property for personal benefit. One of our branch managers, in a locale without road access, apparently met a customer he wished to entertain on a more personal basis at a local fraternal lodge party. He invited the customer, of the opposite gender, to retire to his office in the bank building. Unfortunately, he was in a bit of a rush to illustrate how the couch in his office turned into a bed, and he dropped the end of it with such force that it set off the sonic alarm. Both the branch manager and the customer rushed to exit the building via the front door while trying to completely dress their persons. This strategy compounded their situation by turning on the bank camera system intended to record intruders. By the time they made it out of the bank building, they apparently were confronted by some local citizens concerned that someone was trying to rob the bank. Our senior manager never connected any specific names to his story, but it made a profound impression on all of us and the extreme consequences that may result from blurring the boundary between what is bank property and is to be used solely for that purpose and our personal presence on that property as employees.

Our bank is basically owned by one family, who have owned it since the gold rush days and resided in Alaska since that time. The return on equity is excellent, and I believe the organization will remain an independent bank for an indefinite time. The owner has a wonderful collection of Alaskan art and is planning a dedicated display area for it of some size in a new headquarters building they are considering building further out from the downtown area.

Your college search plan sounds logical, but please be aware of how it will affect our family. You know that until our generation, no one has lived outside of the South since we settled there in 1698. Our great-grandfather fought at Gettysburg, and some members of the family have yet to forgive the federal government for shooting at us during the War of Northern Aggression. By pursuing a private school with higher academic standards, you will successfully avoid at least a portion of the party-school nature of many public schools of higher education. However, I still believe it is possible to receive a solid education at any location, as the process of education is really within the individual and is more a matter of desire and drive than surroundings. I would suggest applications be sent to both private and public institutions, to postpone any family confrontations to such time as a final decision is necessary.

The bank reimbursed me for my transportation expenses to drive to Alaska. Did I mention that at the Canadian border, they asked my purpose, and when I said that I was going to Alaska to work, the border guard demanded to know how much money I had to make the journey? It seems that Canada does not want poor, stranded Americans only making it partway to this Promised Land. I did not anticipate the combination of the size of the security deposit for the apartment and the first month's rent, which is something for you to remember for future reference. Still, it is such an improvement to actually have a telephone in the apartment. At Vanderbilt University, I viewed a telephone as a luxury item. To receive or make phone calls, I used the public phone booth down on Twenty-First Avenue South. I still believe that the search for employment might have gone better with a phone in a private setting. Based on the budget, it appears that I will be able to repay our uncle for the loan I used to relocate up here within the first five months. The college loans are a matter of years yet to come, so I am resigned to not living in a manner consistent with my income.

The Alaskans have a very specific name for individuals which arrive in the spring of each year, but fail to make it through the winter. I am determined not to become one of those, as I simply cannot afford to leave. In history courses, remember how Cortes once prevented his men from dispatching him and returning to Spain? In effect, I have done the same for myself by eliminating any financial possibility of return, so success is the only alternative. The first snow on the mountains outside Anchorage, which you can see from downtown, is referred to as "termination dust" and is usually a sign when the fair-weather crowd head back to the Lower Forty-Eight.

There is a dire shortage of the opposite gender up here, which simply cannot be understated. One of my fellow trainees is going to use his first vacation to go home to Korea to interview a potential wife. The interesting thing about Anchorage is that there are so many different cultures and people from all over the world; the result is a feeling of a much larger city. The rural kids come into town to ride the escalator in the shopping mall, as it is the only such device in the entire state. At the other extreme, the over the pole, airline flights change crews in Anchorage, so you hear quite a number of different languages downtown. This letter is getting as long as our daylight; keep me informed on your progress and which college you select.

Chapter IV

Dear elder cousin,

The mountains of Alaska sound like such a wonderful degree of magnitude, greater in size than our hills, truly a location where you may be counted for what you contribute, rather than the economic situation of our family during this generation. I am settling into Knox College in Galesburg, Illinois, a community of about thirty-five thousand. While not large compared to your present location, it has far more folks than reside in our entire county back home in the hills.

The academics do not seem to present a problem, but as is usual for both of us, the finances will probably be a continual struggle. The total annual expense for this private school is roughly what a nice car would cost, but of course I don't have a car. The first job was to find some reasonable employment that did not interfere with my academic work. I ruled out jobs on campus for a number of reasons. First, the school seems to limit the number of hours that any student can work in a campus job to no more than fifteen hours per week. Such a limitation on hours, coupled with the minimum wage nature of the compensation, simply would not produce an acceptable amount of cash flow. Further, it is my opinion that getting a job in the cafeteria or on the grounds crew would just about rule out all chances of any social life by clearly announcing the extent of my financial distress.

To pursue employment, I walked downtown and tried several local businesses but initially had little luck. I walked past a building that housed a country western radio station. I entered the building, introduced myself to the receptionist, and asked to see a manager. She inquired about my purpose, and I simply stated I was seeking a position as an announcer. She looked somewhat amused and inquired about my experience in radio. When I stated I had none, she asked why I thought any manager would want to take the time to talk to me. I told her that not only was I from Arkansas and knew country music,

I stated where in Arkansas I had last worked. She said no such place existed. I simply produced my last paycheck, which had the name of the town—Dogpatch—clearly printed on it. After looking at the paycheck, she told me not to move and went to get a manager to talk to me. He was a pleasant fellow, and we spoke for some length. At the end of our discussion, he asked if I would cut a sound type for some other folks to listen to, and I had to admit I did not know the foggiest about how to cut a demo tape. He said it was not a problem and sent me upstairs with an engineer to produce the tape. Afterward, I was told to leave a phone number, and that they would get back to me if interested. They were getting ready to move into a new building.

The only phone number I had was the dormitory phone number, so I left it and went back to campus. I waited in the dorm for the next two days, and by luck, they actually called back and offered me a job. It is for somewhat more than minimum wage, so I believe it was worth all the effort. I am on the air from 6:00 PM until midnight, Monday through Saturday. Notice there is no conflict with my classes, which are all during the day. There were only two small problems. First, as you know, country music was never played in our family environment, and second, I needed a broadcasting license.

The radio station, WAAG-FM, was kind enough to lend me the necessary study book (watts, amps, volts, and the standard technical details about radio). I studied quickly and took the train to Chicago to sit for the broadcasting license. It was a day of many firsts: first time on a train, first time in Chicago, and first time to *pass* the broadcasting exam in the Federal Building in Chicago. Actually, I did not know I had passed until sometime later, but I felt reasonably confident. Yes, it was necessary to skip a day's classes for this endeavor, but cash flow is paramount.

To celebrate the day, I decided to live wildly and have lunch in the 95 Club on top of the Hancock Building in downtown Chicago. I had read about it in the *Wall Street Journal*. Yes, we actually receive daily copies of the *Wall Street Journal* on campus! One of the great benefits of our background is that we do not know what is possible, reasonable, or even allowed. So I took the express elevator to the ninety-fifth floor, located on the south side of the building, and waited in line with the others once we reached the top. Only when I reached the front of the line and was asked if I had reservations did I fully realize what little chance I had of being seated.

Again, I was most fortunate as the gentleman behind me in line asked if I would care to join him for lunch. I am sure he realized that this young country fellow really did not know exactly what he was doing and for some reason was thoughtful enough to limit my embarrassment with his invitation. He owned a factory in the Chicago area, and we had a good discussion on current business topics.

I must remember to return a similar favor to some young man in my later years. He owned a factory in the Chicago area and we had a good discussion on current business topics.

It was only after I started working at the radio station that I discovered the college offered training in radio broadcasting and actually had a five-hundred-watt campus station. Folks were actually going to school to learn broadcasting and public speaking to pursue this activity for a career! I keep a reasonably low profile but really enjoy the fifty-thousand-watt power of country music on WAAG. The programming manager is a great individual, with a degree in broadcasting from a public university in Illinois, and I am learning quite a lot on the job. It is the first job that I've ever had where the boss can actually listen to every word you say on the job. I talk about life in the country and comment on the music while being paid for it! This is exactly the type of opportunity that the north offers those willing to seek it. If I had chosen a public university in the South, this opportunity would never have presented itself.

On the negative side, getting off work at midnight reduces the opportunity for social engagements. By the time I get out of the station and walk down the alley beside city hall and back across campus to the dormitory, it is always close to 1:00 AM. As with most facets of life, this arrangement has positive and negative aspects, but I choose to focus on the positive. The radio station is moving into a new building with beautiful new studios, and I feel most fortunate.

On the academic side, I have decided to leave the field of physics and the beauty of math for the more practical fields of economics and business administration. Such a combined field will allow me to acquire the coursework required for a CPA, creating another career option, while still allowing some abstract thought and some math in the area of economics.

While the radio station job, scholarships, and loans have closed the negative flow of cash and actually turned it somewhat positive, I decided I needed some spending money and have found another part-time position. Only a few blocks further away from campus than the radio station, and only one block north of Main Street, I found a YMCA. I still had my Saturdays free, and Sunday afternoons as well, so I approached them about a job. I am now the front desk manager on Saturday and Sunday afternoons. The primary part of the job is keeping order among the young people in the lobby, and I am responsible for keeping the coal in the furnace bin filled at the beginning of each work shift. The total for both jobs is about forty-eight hours a week, plus such time as is required to walk back and forth. It is difficult to imagine what it must be like to actually go to school full time and focus entirely on the academic side of life.

I must confess I do not always attend every class session, but I never miss an exam or any class in my major. I would much rather spend time reading in the library. The college even runs a shuttle to the library of another school, Monmouth College, about twelve miles away, so I have two libraries to enjoy for the price of one!

As you know, my mental habit of drifting off while dealing with the details of daily life has always been a challenge. It is worse when I am tired, and I always seem to be a bit fatigued. This week I finished a meal in the cafeteria and left to walk back across campus to the dormitory. I was about halfway across campus, walking along, when I noticed people staring at me. At that point, I realized I was still carrying my food tray from the cafeteria, along with the remains of my meal and plates. The embarrassing part of this ordeal was turning around and walking back across campus to the cafeteria and properly placing my tray in the return area.

Rumor has it I make a reasonably good roommate, as I am never in the room. Remember that church college close to our home, where the women's dormitories were on one side and the men's on the far side of campus? Well, the Yankees certainly have a different approach to daily life. With the exception of freshman dormitories, which are separated by gender, the dormitories at Knox are coed. There are two suites on each floor, with one for men and the other for women. Each suite has its own bath, and a door separates them, but it rarely seems to be closed. Living so closely with the other gender does tend to take the romantic mystery out of the situation, and no one seems to date anyone they live very close to in the dormitories. I am sure there is a good psych project in the details somewhere, but I do not have the time to pursue it. I try to maintain good relations with all the folks I live with, but I also try to not get too close to any, as I realize more than they do that a substantial cultural and economic gulf separates us and our life experiences. In fact, I sometimes think I am the token conservative on campus. Stay busy and enjoy Alaska!

Chapter V

Dear younger cousin,

Your continued success in college is to be much applauded. Would it not be most interesting to have the resources to simply study and not have to worry about the financial details that seem to drive daily life? You are absolutely correct that the work is required to have such of the academic life that you are allowed to enjoy, but I truly hope the benefits and joy of knowledge exceed the personal cost. I am afraid that while both of us have attended college, we never have really "gone" to college; in the sense more affluent individuals immerse themselves in the total college experience of classes, sports, parties, and the enjoyment that may come from carefree years between high school and adult responsibilities.

Up here in Alaska, one of the great benefits of the pipeline construction is that banks cannot retain employees due to the higher wages from working for the oil companies. As such, I have been promoted again, this time to wage and salary administrator in the Human Resources department. They were having challenges budgeting, as each department always came in under their compensation budget due to the personnel turnover. I have simply tied the personnel turnover factor for each department to their annual budgets through a rather simple algebraic equation. As a result of this endeavor, they have allowed me some greater freedom to make suggestions in other areas. In order to increase profits, while appearing to provide a higher return to depositors, I have changed the method of compounding interest on regular savings accounts. It is now compounded continuously to provide the highest possible return on qualifying balances. This satisfies the customer's psychic need for a better return than the competition can offer. At the same time, the interest is calculated on their initial monthly balance. As most Alaskans' savings accounts grow during the month, the bank effectively does not pay any interest on that amount of growth in deposits until the next month. All parties seem to be quite pleased with the outcome, and my position appears more secure at the moment.

An opportunity has presented itself to teach part time on Elmendorf Air Force Base for Golden Gate University (from California). It seems the military is more likely to promote individuals who are pursuing more education, and business courses are needed. As the number of us who have graduate degrees in business residing in Alaska is limited, I have started teaching business classes in the evenings. The students are generally as old as or older than I and take the class work seriously. Have you noticed that it is the attitude of those around you who make almost any endeavor a joy or an endless task?

The fringe benefits of the job are also pretty good. I am a civilian card-carrying member of the officers club. The food is very good, and last week, the guys invited me to join them in the Cave on Friday evening. The Cave is in the basement of the officers club. I really did not know what to expect but went along and was greatly surprised at the entertainment. The floor show consisted of young ladies dancing in somewhat less-than-swimsuit attire. Apparently, this event occurs on one Friday evening every month and is most popular, given the scarcity factor of the local female gender. Obviously, this is not to be spoken of back in the hills but is yet another example of the wide range of human behavior. I truly do not think it would manifest itself if there were more females around on a daily basis.

In your psychology classes—blessed are the benefits of a liberal arts education—have you yet had the opportunity to teach lab rats to play basketball? I will always remember how, with positive reinforcement (food), the lab rats could be trained to initially roll the small ball into a hole. Then the "net" was gradually raised out of the base of the training ground until the rats had to actually pick up the ball and drop it through the net in order to score and obtain their positive reinforcement. To watch the human condition begs the question of how our society determines exactly what the net is and how high it will be set.

Our local winter conditions are a wonder to endure. I have had the great fortune of getting far enough ahead financially to afford the down payment on a small condominium unit. They call it a one-bedroom loft unit, but the reality is that it consists of one large room with a sleeping loft and a bath upstairs. The great benefit is the outside security door for the building, which places some additional distance between me and the outside. I have even gotten accustomed to plugging the engine block heater in on my car in the evenings so the oil will not freeze. The other detail is to always remember to unplug the vehicle before departing each morning. No, I do not have covered parking but have become adept at rapidly removing the evening's snowfall from the car before going to work.

To aid the process of getting about, everyone uses studded snow tires during the winter. They really do not harm the streets, as most of the time the streets have a protective coating of snow and ice. Another interesting detail is that whereas we are accustomed to snow melting prior to the next snow, up here the snow simply layers each time on top of the prior snow until spring. When the snowplows make a clean cut, the layers of snow remind me of the annual growth shown in tree rings.

Cousin, remember the customary annual sermon by the pastor on the problems associated with pride and position in life? A group of our assistant cashiers—the entry-level officer position—banded together to question why they were being compensated less than the cashiers in the grocery stores in town. Well, they knew very well that the grocery employees were union members, which is why the compensation difference exists. It always amazes me when folks complain about the inadequacy of their pay for work compared to someone else's. First, if they desire to have a career in the grocery industry, that option is always open to them. Second, if they would focus on exceeding their employer's expectations, the probability of higher compensation and promotion would be greatly enhanced. Nevertheless, the response of the Human Resources representative was priceless, when he simply pointed out that, while the grocery personnel were "cashiers," our personnel were "assistant cashiers."

Although my financial situation precludes the indulgence of most furniture, I have acquired a tropical type of tree and positioned various grow lights over it to add a touch of green during the winter. On the opposite side of the living room, a local artist fashioned a six-foot tall piece of driftwood into an indoor waterfall with the placement of well-designed metal foliage, giving a great patina effect. The living room has a sixteen-foot ceiling, and the fireplace is the only other item that breaks the open space. The lack of chairs or tables may seem somewhat of a negative, but with the waterfall running and resting beneath the green foliage with the fireplace ablaze; it is almost like having a private park in the middle of the subarctic.

Our retail manager had an unusual event to report at our weekly meeting: to explain why the police surrounded our branch in Spenard (a section of Anchorage). It seems a new loan officer had been shown his desk, and while getting settled in, he found a button under the top of the desk and presumed it was a convenient way to ring his loan assistant. He hit it the first time, and the loan assistant did not respond. However, the silent alarm went off, and the police called the branch manager to make sure all was well at the office. The branch manager assured the police that it must simply have been a malfunction in the system and reset the alarm.

Meanwhile, back at the new loan officer's desk, he decided that the loan assistant had probably been occupied and decided to ring her again. The same sequence of events occurred, with the branch manager and the police becoming even more perplexed. Finally, the loan officer decided that the loan assistant was simply ignoring him, so he really lay on the button for some time. The police, having received three alarm signals from the same branch, decided that the branch manager was probably being held hostage and was unable to divulge her true situation over the phone. The next event the branch manager noticed was four police vehicles in the branch parking lot. At about the same time, the new loan officer complained to the branch manager concerning the lack of respect his loan assistant was giving him when assistance was needed. Remember the old hill saying about respect being earned and not given? Well, the loan officer was given the opportunity to earn his respect by going out to the parking lot to explain to the police what had occurred. According to the retail manager, he almost made one final mistake by reaching into his coat pocket to obtain his ID, but fortunately, no shots were fired.

The point our retail manager was trying to make was that every new employee should receive a full and thorough orientation of their surroundings. While hidden, silent alarms were well known to the existing employees, and the poor fellow suffered a somewhat embarrassing training sequence. It was a point well made, and even though I have not met the loan officer, I imagine he will think twice before unknown buttons are pushed again.

We had a bank-wide competition on the sale of credit cards to customers. I determined that it would help my career to show that a staff individual, without any customer contact, could also sell and set about Anchorage touting the wonders of unsecured credit on his personal time. Some luck was had with individuals in the dental profession, as you have them cornered when they are cleaning your teeth. At the end of the month, I had placed the most approved credit cards of any bank employee at any of our branches in all four time zones. A meeting of officers was held in Anchorage, and I was as surprised as anyone when they announced that I had won the overall sales prize. Summoned to the front of the room, I was awarded a matched set of Ulu knives. These crescent-shaped knives remove fat from the skin of seals. Although I can not begin to think what kind of incentive management thought such an award would produce, it has a display with a small inscription indicating that I won! The objective, of course, was not simply to win but to help executive management remember that individuals are capable of more than the specific function to which they are assigned. Cousin, I am not sure I would ever give an employee a set of knives as a gift for exceeding expectations, no matter how well intended. Remember when we learned to throw knives on camping trips? Those were great days of innocent fun in the hills.

I made a significant mistake in a presentation to senior management but learned something in the process. At the end of a presentation, the executive stated that while he agreed with my analysis and with the suggestion for the resolution of the issue, "what exactly is this standard deviation thing" I had referred to? It was one of those moments of insight in which I realized I had better indicate that the issue was not of much importance, simply some odd bit of math from my notes that I should not have included in the presentation. The individual in question knows much more about banking than I do, and it was simply not the time or the place to focus on technique. Going forward, any math calculations will be shown in private meetings only, with the caveat that they are a crutch that I use to substitute for experience.

The one thing I will always miss from our southern hill culture is the manner in which we approach issues with other folks. Even if we disagree, it would simply be considered rude to bluntly state that the other individual is absolutely wrong in his thoughts. Instead, it is far more common for us to suggest slight adjustments in a civil way. In the north, I am convinced that they lost all need for civility when they won the war, and their entire culture is based on confrontation and force. They seem to believe that if they say something loudly enough, it will be correct, regardless of the facts. I believe we can learn to use their approach to our advantage through the use of understatement, which seems to be something they are unaccustomed to and do not know how to respond to in a professional setting. The use of the velvet glove over the iron hand of logic is probably the best approach.

I have now encountered my most challenging boss. A fine individual from Taiwan, he has adjusted to American culture far better than I might have ever survived in Taiwan. He still keeps a Taiwan/English dictionary handy for the odd moments when we both fail to get the language nuances between us. His request to arrange a Christmas luncheon showed ample understanding of the seasonal significance of events in our Western culture. However, the timing of his request on the morning before Christmas probably resulted more from a focus on business than seasonal good cheer. The staff appeared to enjoy the pizza provided by the department, although they were required to purchase their own soft drinks. I took great pains to point out to the staff that the boss had done a little something extra for them, and to please express their appreciation to him (I had even ordered toppings rather than the lower cost of plain cheese).

When confronted with a management directive, rather than a request for suggestions, the best approach seems to be using one's ears and not vocal cords. To do otherwise is to risk the boss viewing your initiative as something of a negative. I know you differ in this perspective and still believe the world really wants input, but my experience seems to show that actions (not thoughts) are most rewarded. The risk simply does not seem commensurate with the reward. Any public display of intelligence in my industry by those younger than fifty years of age appears to risk being pronounced as being an issue of vanity. The socially acceptable margin in the northern culture for individuals with little authority seems to be limited to issues of gradual improvement. Any sweeping change from the direct application of logic appears to provoke hostile responses from the guardians of the corporate status quo. I believe this is true not only in my present organization, but in business in general. The magnitude of human pride is such that none of us truly wants to be shown as incorrect in any public or business setting.

I have come to think of my new approach as "raging incrementalism." It is a preferred series of small, steady changes that create improvements to be jointly enjoyed by all parties through the guidance of humility in our actions. Enjoy college life, and perhaps radio is your future path! Just a suggestion, but striving for perfection seems to produce ill will in all parties.

Chapter VI

Dear elder cousin,

Your business experience seems interesting, but I must ask: to what purpose? I suppose the primary reason for any of our work is to provide the cash flow required for our daily existence, to repay our debts, and to enjoy that odd moment of personal pleasure. However, have you noticed that our lack of risk capital precludes us from ever really reaping the full benefits of our contribution to the capitalistic system? Ratings at the radio station are up, and the station manager has been generous to provide raises in compensation to all employees, but is a raise all the return we are to expect from the investment of our human capital? It would seem that without risk capital to invest, we are trapped in the class of wage earners without an obvious exit. Yes, I realize that Small Business Administration loans are available, but what sane individual would layer the risk of business loan repayment on top of the repayment risk we have already incurred for education loans?

On campus, I have been asked to work part time as a tutor in the Economics department for a senior who is having a bit of a problem with his final year. It is yet a few more extra dollars and provides some assistance for an individual who seems to appreciate the help. I can understand you part-time teaching, for it is rewarding if the student actually wants the assistance.

The stress of seniors at Knox is related to their senior seminar in their chosen major. The seminar is basically a cursory review of an individual's major during the spring term of their senior year, followed by an exam on the entire subject matter of the major. If a student does not pass, he simply does not graduate and must return in the fall to retry the process. I have seen folks find out they did not pass after four years of college and face the unpleasant reality of calling their families to tell them they will not be graduating. However, simply getting passing grades and paying tuition should not guarantee a degree. It is the mastery of the subject material and the entire liberal arts process of learning that is required before the awarding of a degree.

Knox still has the tradition of the annual "Flunk Day" on an undetermined day each spring term. The student leaders ring the Old Main bell at 7:00 AM to proclaim that we simply will not go to classes on that day. I have no idea how long this tradition has been going on, decades at least, and perhaps the better part of a century. For the entire day, everyone simply does whatever they choose to do, all of us nerds on the loose, and a generally good time is had by all parties.

Have I ever told you about our marching band? To be blunt, we did not have one, as the symphony folks just cannot adjust to the "marching" concept. But the football team felt somewhat slighted, and a number of individuals decided to simply create a marching band. In short order, the Knox College Marching Kazoo Band was created. We will always remember with pride of being told of their first performance in the Knox Bowl. They proudly marched to midfield and lined up on the fifty-yard line. The announcer then stunned the crowd by proclaiming that the marching Knox Kazoo Band had formed the complex "flag pole" formation on the field. Several other similarly challenging designs were formed on the field before the band yielded to the football team for the second half. To the best of my knowledge, the football team has not requested any additional musical entertainment. As you know, the Knox Bowl does not actually have seats, except for a few added to the top rim of the earthen bowl of the field for an occasional lost alumni and a few faculty.

I have finally met an academic challenge, a foreign language. Most of my classmates had the benefit of taking a foreign language in high school. As three terms of any language are part of the graduation requirements, I am currently addressing the issue. It is yet another lesson in humility. Simply because we are blessed with the types of memory which are well suited for most academic work does not mean the same type of intelligence is used for grammar in a foreign language. I have great difficulty reconciling English grammar with that of another language and concurrently speaking any sort of fluent conversation. Fortunately, my grade point average can stand this speed bump on the way to graduation.

Remember the old maxim of land, labor, and capital being factors of production? I believe that capital should be divided into the economic factors of financial and human capital. The human capital would be defined as the creative aspect that a human brings to a job, which is something quite different than the labor aspect associated with the job itself. In that way, the human would be rewarded for labor as a base compensation and separately rewarded for creativity brought to the job to increase productivity. Under the present system the owners of capital reap the rewards of creativity, unless labor forces the reallocation through some direct action.

Along those same lines of thought, someone was successful in reallocating some capital from the college toward tuition, thereby reducing the amount of loans required from this point on. This person simply went into the registrar's office and requested that a copy of his transcript be sent to another institution. The registrar actually came out to the front desk and asked for the reason behind the request. The individual mentioned that the cost of the education was beginning to be a burden and that he was seeking a more economical school. Less than a week later, the individual received notice that his scholarship had been increased. It did not seem appropriate to thank the registrar, nor to mention to others what had transpired. It may simply have been one of those unique coincidences in life, but I will always remember that it is at least possible to reallocate capital to some degree if the individual is perceived to have some value.

Grandfather is ill, and I imagine this will be his final decade. I do not know what we can possibly do for him beyond always remembering him as the model we have tried to emulate. I believe few of our generation have had the honor of being brought up in homes where the mastery of the language was paramount, education and knowledge were considered a necessity, and honor was a requirement of the very lifestyle. He will be sorely missed but never forgotten for his efforts on our behalf. I believe that I was almost twelve before I noticed that there were not anywhere near the number of books in our friends' homes relative to those held dear by our family. As to curse words, I remember having to ask friends in junior high exactly what these words meant and in what context they were used, for I can't remember even one being uttered in his presence. His world and ours are continuing to change, and I do not necessarily believe that progress in technology equates to progress in the fabric of our society.

Cousin, I pose a question. If knowledge is the very basis of economic wealth, and the speed with which knowledge is diffused through the society continues to increase as technology erases the friction caused by distance, language, and governmental boundaries, is the marginal value of knowledge over time less to each generation? The very enhancement of the transferability of knowledge seems to decrease the duration of its benefit to the recipient.

We have a rifle range in the basement of Alumni Hall, and I have now had the experience of indoor shooting. I never knew such a thing existed prior to coming to this school. Of course, only .22 caliber is used, but it is interesting to shoot at targets rather than squirrels in the trees like we did back home. This may be an equal-opportunity world, but my accounting classes have only one female student compared to about thirty of us males. Until there are more females trained in the details of business, I doubt if equal opportunity will exist in little more than words.

A campus record may have been set for the shortest date in school history. I met a young lady over at Williston Hall, and we walked across campus to attend an event on a Sunday evening. By the time we reached the event, we both agreed that we really were not suited for each other, and I walked her back across campus to her dorm. The best that may be said is that little damage was done to either of our egos, and humility is best never forgotten.

Recently I felt somewhat fatigued and went to a doctor in town. The receptionist asked for my name, and when I gave it, she told me I was not that person. It seems that she listens to "that person" on the radio on a regular basis, along with his stories from the hills, and that she believed him to be a much older individual. After producing identification to prove that I actually was myself, I assured her I felt as old as she thought I was on the radio. The usual medical advice of slowing down, resting, and pacing myself was received with the usual thought of *what world do you live in?*

I have lined up a Christmas break job, working construction on a ski lift. The radio station will let me have the time off, and the construction combines good exercise with good pay, plus a change of pace from the academic environment. It is probably not exactly what the doctor had in mind, but it is as close to it as I can get at this moment. Enjoy springtime in Alaska, but always remember the warning in that country song about Alaskan women in the spring. I believe our uncle will take over the family farming operation from Grandfather, so it will continue much the same as we remember it. He is already talking about purchasing another two hundred acres under the hill to take the eastern boundary to the Des Arc creek. At least we will have a moat!

Chapter VII

Dear younger cousin,

Yes, I share your concern about the adequacy of the return we are earning on our human capital versus the benefits we provide to our employers. There is no doubt that part of the return on invested capital is from the creativity of those employed. However, I do not currently know how to address the issue to any degree of satisfaction. To risk even $10,000 or $20,000 in an investment is as yet not a matter of comfort to me, as I always remember how difficult it was to accumulate the sum to be invested.

Another promotion was received, this time to the position of financial analyst for the bank. I am beginning to take more risk in my work and am attempting to do what I actually believe is the right thing, rather than just blindly following orders. Otherwise, I might as well be at Auschwitz, always proceeding with little regard for the consequences. That I am more willing to risk my very job and sole source of revenue on the matter of principle than to risk some amount of money is a risk-oriented investment.

My new boss received an official request on letterhead from the US military at Subic Bay in the Philippines. He confirmed the authenticity of the letter by placing a phone call to the Philippines at the phone number shown on the letterhead. They were requesting an original blank copy of the bank's official check for use in an investigation. When the boss requested that I fulfill the request, I indicated that I would do as requested. However, rather than sending the military an actual blank official check as requested, I copied one and forwarded the copy. I knew full well that the copy did not show the actual color of the official check, or some of the details, and I also realized that my actions could at best result in a rather harsh reprimand, and at worst the loss of my employment. However, I just had a very uneasy feeling about the entire request, so I took the risk of doing something slightly different than I was requested to do.

About two weeks went by, and the boss came down the hall to my desk and stated that he had received a call from the Philippines and was aware that I had not done exactly what he had requested. I indicated that it was an oversight and stated that I would address the issue at once. The phone call struck me as odd, as the military I deal with on the local air force base seem so paper bound, and I resolved to tactfully postpone the issue to a later date. In retrospect, I truly must have loss my senses to have placed my job at risk over such an issue, for there is no financial reserve of significance to fall back on in this far-off place in the event of unemployment. At this stage, my very career was at risk for simply failing to follow specific directions.

Another couple of weeks went by, and the boss again came down to my desk and asked if I had taken action on sending the military the blank official check that they had requested. I confessed that I had forgotten the matter and would immediately get it in the mail. He stated that he had received another letter from the military warning banks that criminals in the Philippines had for some time been soliciting US commercial banks in attempts to obtain actual blank official bank checks to forge and that it was just as well that I had forgotten to send it. He and I both knew full well that I had not forgotten to send it, for I am most thorough in my work, but the way we resolved the situation saved him face and me my job. The point is that I apparently was willing to risk a job on principle, yet my conservative nature with money makes investing an even greater personal challenge.

The only good thing that has resulted from this entire chain of events is that the boss has recommended me for yet another promotion. One does wonder exactly what his real motivation might have been, but I don't question such issues too closely. Now, as head of the bank's Economics department, I have one employee, and a view that faces the mountains to the east of town. Previously, my desk simply faced the wall behind a door, so it appears as progress of a sort.

Did I mention that we have moved into our new bank headquarters south of the downtown area? I was asked to draft part of the annual report, and in it I referred to the new location as "midtown," and it appears that folks are actually starting to use that description for the general area.

The chairman's secretary came in and said I was invited to attend the monthly board meeting, which was already in progress. She said I should simply go in and sit in an empty chair along the back wall of the boardroom. I thought the chairman was trying to give me some training, which again shows the extent of my naïve nature. Ever I tell myself, always look for the motive behind others' actions. I went in and was really enjoying the meeting when the chairman announced that I would now give a report on the economic prospects for Alaska. It was all I could do to keep a straight face, but I stood up and gave lengthy discourse on the volatility of natural resource, extraction-based economies, such as Alaska's. The idea was to keep the presentation on a broad sweeping level, for which I knew the fundamental answers, and to buy myself time to study more of the details of the State before the next monthly meeting. Up until now, I have been more concerned with how the bank is planning its future in relation to the Alaskan economy, but an adjustment is in order. It appears to have worked, for I am still employed in the same capacity as the banks economist.

Office shoe customs in Anchorage are somewhat different than in the Lower Forty-Eight. During the winter, we leave our office shoes, the professional looking ones, at the office and wear what we jokingly refer to as "moonboots" back and forth from home in the snow, slush, and ice. The winter boots have about a two inch thick sole, which raise your feet above the cold surface of the ice and snow and seem to endure the salt and water slush reasonably well. The added benefit is that your trousers legs are raised up above a good portion of the mess, but they still end up with snow on them. Anchorage has an extensive system of bike trails, more than twenty miles, within the city limits. For those of us without the luxury of a bicycle, they also make great hiking trails. During the winter they are also used for cross-country ski trials. This is truly a wonderful city set on the very edge of the wilderness, but with many more creature comforts than any of our rural communities in the hills back home. The oil money keeps pouring into the State coffers, so there is no State income tax or even a State sales tax. The increase in take-home pay from the reduced tax burden is continuing to allow me to make progress on paying down the education debt on a regular basis. The city does not have a country club, but frankly, I view that as an asset. The lack of such a facility means I do not need to worry about the expense of joining and deal with the country club social events that create class distinctions in many communities.

The economics department also has the responsibility of completing branch office applications to the regulatory officials when the bank wants to build a new facility. I am trying to add a little more structure to the process by focusing more on traffic patterns and the probable growth of the Anchorage road system in the future, rather than just where the business is at this time. While I believe that the community will suffer temporarily after the completion of the oil pipeline from the North Slope, in the long run, as long as sufficient natural resources exist to extract I believe that Anchorage will be a reasonably sure bet for the bank. A completed application exceeds fifty pages and is somewhat like the old college term papers. Most of the bank office expansion is currently planned for the Anchorage and Fairbanks markets. Our offices in southeast Alaska appear more than adequate to serve the timber trade and governmental functions in Juneau (the State is a major deposit customer).

I have been asked by management to go down to Seattle and spend some time with Rainier Bank, one of the largest financial organizations in the Pacific Northwest. I was asked to learn anything that I thought was useful about the new subject of asset/liability management. Remember those thoughts about the fleeting value of knowledge? It seems that all it takes is for management to hear that another business in the same industry has a new idea, and they immediately set about ferreting it out. The marginal value of knowledge surely seems fleeting when it is so easily transferred around an industry. In commercial banking we have always had regulated pricing of our deposits. This wonderful deal, which caused all banks to have about the same cost of funds (otherwise thought of as our cost of raw materials) is nearing an end as the government has now deregulated the $10,000 and over six month certificate of deposit (CD). Previously, the only area where bankers really had to compete for deposits was in the unregulated $100,000-and-over CD market.

The challenge with this deregulation of deposits is that it opens the issue of how to manage our gross operating margin, which in banking is the net interest margin (gap) between the cost of funds and the interest earned on loans and deposits. Under the historical regulated system, as all banks had about the same cost of funds, all banks tended to charge about the same interest rate on loans of equal credit risk. This produced a pleasant, low stress industry in which competition was not based on pricing to any extent and there was little if any drive to become more efficient in the deposit function. As all good things do come to an end, the beginning of deregulation in our industry is causing material concern to management. Everyone is referring to the new management of the deregulated cost of funds as asset/liability management.

When I made it down to Seattle, I checked into the Seattle Athletic Club for a week. This was the most economical sleeping facilities available (though I would not recommend it for a vacation), but it was within walking distance of Rainier Bank. These people live in a world that is far above the standards of what we consider normal banking in Anchorage. The executive dining room on one of the upper floors actually has a jade-surfaced fireplace. I suspect that eventually the deregulation of our industry will end such lifestyles, but these folks are certainly enjoying it now. While it is a large institution, they actually do not seem to have much of an idea of exactly how to address the issue of asset/liability management. I believe there is a misconception in business that large organizations automatically know how to handle complex issues better than smaller organizations. The reality appears to be that they simply have more people and resources to throw at the issues. Everyone seems to believe that by tracking the maturities of previously issued certificates of deposit and comparing these category totals to upcoming pricing opportunities for loans; we will be somehow to better manage the gross operating margin (net interest margin in banks).

The problems with this approach are boundless, as it supposes that the possibility of repricing our deposits and loans are equal. This is simply not the case in the real world, as the supply and demand for deposits does not remain constant in any local market, versus the supply and demand for loans. As an example, while the price of unregulated money is determined by both the national trend in the level of interest rates and the local demand for deposits by banks, the demand for loans does not exactly track the same course in the same local market. I believe this issue will be an area of concern for the banking industry for a long period of time and may offer an opportunity to reap some economic profits in working as an employee to help the industry resolve the problems.

Well, banking is not just analysis; we actually had a bank robbery! This is somewhat rare in Alaska, as most thieves realize that getting out of town is not easily done due to our isolation. Down at our Juneau branch, near the Alaska state capital, an individual came in and robbed the bank. Fortunately no one was hurt, and the robber was recognized (one of the many benefits of small, isolated communities where most people know each other). The police simply gave him sufficient time to get back to his home and went over, knocked on his door, and arrested him. It was not exactly a massive manhunt but did generate some excitement in a town of about twenty thousand residents. The area of the city of Juneau is really larger than the area of New York City. By annexing everything even remotely connected to the city, Juneau is able to claim a far-larger population than the city proper could ever hope to have due to the constraints of ocean in front and mountains behind downtown. Juneau does not have any road connections to the outside world, only ferry and air service.

Anchorage is continuing to boom, as the pipeline construction continues, with housing going up everywhere the ground permits. We have a bit of a local problem with permafrost in a few areas of town, which restricts building. If you build directly on the permafrost, the heat from the building will simply melt the frost and the structure will just gradually sink into the ground. We built a new branch on permafrost in Glennallen (between Valdez and Fairbanks). It was necessary to place the office on pilings, which supported it above the permafrost; the pilings have flanges at right angles to the ground between the building and the soil to dissipate the heat from the building. It is amazing to realize the oil fields of the North Slope are providing the money to develop this wonderful state and allow so many people to enjoy the natural beauty.

The family that owns the bank fully realizes the temporary nature of this economic boom and are looking forward to understanding what the economy will be like after the construction workers and their associated money have left the State. They have a good long-term perspective, as their family was here when the original gold boon occurred and the bank was headquartered in Skagway. When the railroad was built connecting Seward to Fairbanks through Anchorage, the current bank president's grandfather moved the bank's main office to the new city of Anchorage. They clearly understand the need to diversity the economy of Alaska, to even out the huge swings from boom to bust. One side benefit of all the oil development is the construction of many new motels and hotels in south central Alaska. Presently, they are fully used by new arrivals, local residents out exploring the state, and by relatives of the newcomers up to visit; but after the boom is over, these businesses will be a resource to help the state expand the tourism industry. So many people up here associated with the pipeline development have now had a chance to experience Alaska, and we are sure they will want to come back to enjoy the natural surroundings after they have moved back to the Lower Forty-Eight. At least that is the future we are hoping for in our community.

I have joined an athletic club with an indoor swimming pool in downtown Anchorage. It seems like a long way from swimming in the creek downstream from Blanchard Springs back home in the hills. The flight crews from the over-the-pole flights stay in the downtown hotels and frequent the same athletic club. They seem like nice folks, but the language barrier is difficult to overcome. The athletic club has separate facilities for men and women to work out in, but the swimming pool is a shared facility. The exact details of this arrangement were apparently unclear to a couple of Nordic stewardesses. They simply ran out of the ladies side and dived into the pool sans suits. There was some minor embarrassment by all parties involved, and now the club has placed signs in languages other than English to reduce the probability of any repeating of this incidence. Again, the splendid nature of this place is the wide range of people you meet and the different perspectives they bring to the community.

My good friend from South Korea finally selected a bride from his hometown. I was pleased to be invited to the wedding. He has adopted the Christian faith, as he is committed to becoming fully integrated into our culture, and he planned a formal church wedding. He even selected a western-style wedding dress for her (no Korean attire whatsoever), and it is very different from the traditional dresses worn by brides in his country. It was a great event, with a beautiful bride, even if she did not speak or understand English. She had learned the appropriate two words—"I do"—and pronounced them perfectly when the pastor nodded toward her at the appropriate time. The groom also selected the wedding cake and went all out, as it was the first such creation I have ever seen that had a fountain inside the cake between the tiers. I wish them the best of futures in this land they have chosen for their home.

I have been so fortunate to find the combination of a great organization to work for in such a beautiful state. I have even become accustomed to the minor earthquakes. The first one I experienced happened before I moved into the condominium, and I was doing my laundry at a public facility. I felt strange, and I noticed that the trees were swaying without any breeze. Everyone just looked at each other and went about their business as if it was nothing unusual. I have only had to hang on to my desk at the office once during a tremor that was about 5.0 on the scale.

We are both working too much. If you cannot take the time to develop a relationship with the opposite sex, or if you perceive the risks are too great, perhaps you should buy yourself something outrageous as a testament to your success in escaping the hills of our youth. Take care and enjoy the stable ground in Illinois.

Chapter VIII

Dear elder cousin,

Good news from the home front! One of our female cousins has wedded, and I was actually invited to the wedding. She had completed some of her college education, when a ski holiday to the Rockies was arranged. By some good fortune, she met and made quite an impression on a young Yankee. Well, the customary courtship ensued, and they entered into wedlock. I am so pleased for her, as their branch of the family has suffered even more setbacks than ours in some regards.

It was the most American of weddings, with her family being members of the Church of Christ and his being of the Jewish faith. I believe one of the keys to the success of our generation of the family is our ability to be flexible and have an open mind about others in society. It may be debatable about whether all members of the clan, in particular the older generation, share that perspective.

At the rehearsal dinner the night before the wedding, the relatives and friends of the bride were seated on one side of the hall, while the relations of the groom sat opposite. I truly believe the greatness of our country is enhanced by our ability to blend cultures to create the unique American outlook on the world. To observe most members of the Church of Christ crowd choosing to not partake in wine (they instead made a mass order of iced tea) reminded me so much of our hill culture. Meanwhile, the groom's family also remained true to their culture and supported the vineyards of this country. As the groom's family is responsible for the organizing and payment of the rehearsal dinner, they had also hired a band, which I thoroughly enjoyed. Of course, our side of the group does not dance, as it is not condoned by the creed of the Church of Christ.

Our cousin simply looked stunning, and I believe she has selected a very good fellow. His family owns a business, and I am sure that he will operate it once his education is completed. I do not imagine that we will see much of her ever again, for she will have little need for poor country cousins.

Remember the old joke the pastor once told about the difference between the Methodist faith and the Church of Christ? He said that a Methodist fellow passed away and was blessed with going to heaven. As Saint Peter was giving him the obligatory tour, he asked the Methodist to please be very quiet as they passed through the next section of heaven. Afterward, the Methodist asked why more than the customary reverence was required in that particular section of heaven. Saint Peter responded with a wry grin that they had just passed through the portion of heaven reserved for those belonging to the Church of Christ, and quietness was required, for they believed they were the only ones present. It is a wonder that we share the same cemetery, with members of both faiths in the same patch of ground when they cannot agree on the path necessary to ensure a proper course from that ground to whatever lies ahead.

It was the first Jewish wedding I had ever attended, but if one will just focus a little less on the particulars of the faith and a little more on the happiness of the young couple, it really makes small difference about the details of the faith. I know you and I disagree on the matter of religion, but the more history courses I take, the more I find the entire subject disagreeable. It seems that religion is the very catalyst for violence between humans and has been used for that excuse over a number of millennium. Should it not be possible to be a person of faith in the beautiful design of the universe, to recognize that the very math involved invokes the recognition of an extremely skilled practitioner, without being bogged down in the details of doctrine? It seems of the utmost human conceit to believe that so new a species was selected as the one single highest purpose of any great designer. While not an agnostic, I do not hold that any single nail in the vastness of the great structure is, or even might be, the sole purpose of the structure itself. That said, I confess I will always enjoy the spirit of a rural congregation joining in one of the old hymns of the Christian faith.

Here at Knox, we have experienced the fad of streaking, which seems to have taken the campus by storm. If it was not the depths of winter, I imagine it would even be more of a circus. Does each generation need to take such pride in doing what the prior generation cannot even reconcile with normal behavior? The oddest thing to see is a group of college students tearing across campus en mass, wearing only shoes and ski masks! A few have even dared to participate without the ski mask. No, of course I have not been involved with this activity as a participant. It is difficult not to notice though, as when I was typing a term paper a great commotion arose outside, and I peered out to see a coed group leaving the quad and rounding the corner of the furthest building. Even though I only observed them from the back, there was no doubt about the mixed gender of the crowd. I doubt if this is one fad that will ever catch on in the hills.

One of my colleagues was recently injured in a physics experiment. Using classical hands-on experimentation to ascertain that for every action there is an equal and opposite reaction, in the application of the force, he was injured to such an extent that stitches and a trip to the local hospital was required. It seems that although he understood the concept well enough, he failed to fully grasp another variable in the equation. When one passes a 110-pound female student to someone else standing in the shower, one should always remember the force is not directly transferred to a solid floor when the floor is wet and soap has been applied. Instead, an individual's body is shoved in the opposite direction with considerable energy until it encounters a wall. He will always have a scar to remind him of this particular experiment. The rest of the residents in the suite may be somewhat more subdued in their physics inquiries in the future.

Physics is such an interesting subject; I truly wish I could see a profitable future in it. Regrettably, it would seem that the most likely career from such a course of study would be either teaching physics or working for the government in some capacity. Either of these outcomes could have been achieved at a much less expensive public university, so it will probably remain just an interesting hobby. Still, the fact that sufficient mass can actually bend light is a thought that I will dwell on, for it is most interesting. You are correct; the benefits of a liberal arts education are not so much the exposure to any particular discipline but rather the intertwinement of the ideas that creates a new perspective on the world.

As you most assuredly know, long hair is now the fashion, and I have adopted it. Most of our football team also has long hair, some even with beards. I believe they are all going to trim their hair a bit or place it more securely beneath their helmets. I will make the observation that the close cutting of the male hair, both of the beard and head, most probably developed as a result of the violence that has shaped so much of our society. Given a decision between looking dapper with long hair and giving your opponent yet something else to grab during a conflict, I believe our ancestors chose the logical alternative of short hair. Remember, it was the Roundheads and not the Cavaliers who won the last great conflict between those of different hair length in our culture. Although it would be a sign of a much more peaceful society if this phase of long hair would prevail, based on the overall culture it most likely is only an odd aberration of short duration.

Did I tell you that Knox does not rely strongly on athletic scholarships? It is a joy to see folks participate in a sport because they enjoy it, instead of being the equivalent of paid performers. Of course we rarely win when competing against schools that place an emphasis on athletic scholarships. Nonetheless, the principle is sound, and if adopted by more schools it might change athletics from a Roman circus to more of the older Greek perspective of the joy in competition. In our current society, it would seem in the interest of all governments and most university administrations to advocate the use of athletic scholarships. The process allows the schools a reason to rally alumni on campus and provides a great backdrop for fundraising activities. To the extent of the entertainment involved, it also allows individuals in the surrounding area to develop a connection with any particular university through the athletic program and is one more distraction from the mundane, dreary daily life that most must endure. To that extent, it could be said that athletic scholarships are a public service and that they provide an outlet for aggression other than against the government. As you probably are thinking, this liberal arts educations leads to entirely too much thinking and more doing would be best! However, I continue in all of my various jobs and believe that I am a productive member of the society and not just an observer.

I had an opportunity to go back to the hills for a few days during spring break. It always amazes me that folks with money go to the mountains or beaches during this time, but wealth does have its privileges. I actually found an underclassman that had an unauthorized car stashed away in a rented garage across town, and she lived not more than 150 miles south of our home. She was most gracious and offered me a ride, both down home and back. I awoke in an unnamed state south of here, to notice the obvious sound of a police car. She stated that she had been going over the limit as she pulled the car over to the side of the road. The local constable approached our vehicle, tapped on the window, and mentioned that he had clocked us at more than 110 mph and had to turn around as he was going in the opposite direction. Well, this is the fastest I have ever driven in a car, and I managed to sleep through the experience! He requested that we follow him to the local courthouse, and I firmly believed that an awkward situation would most likely develop. I noticed that my traveling companion had adopted the most genteel of southern accents when addressing the law enforcement officer. I was told to stay in the car, and she was requested to accompany the officer into the courthouse. After a lengthy wait that seemed like an eternity, she emerged from the courthouse with a grin, and we departed. She did not even receive a warning ticket! It reminded me of our mentor suggesting that in many jurisdictions, it makes far greater difference concerning who and how the issue is stated than the matter of the facts.

More thoughts on the diminishing marginal value of knowledge over time to successive generations due to the steady removal of barriers to the rapid movement of knowledge to competitors, both individual and business. It would appear that there are only two logical means to address the issue on a personal level. One may consistently arrive at the next logical step in the progression of a system, idea, or concept applied to a business situation. This appears to be an extremely difficult and unlikely route to success. Even if it is feasible to build on your concept of "raging incrementalism," you must continually be more creative than the vast majority of individuals around you in your particular industry and specifically in whichever company employs you. With this approach you will need to forever attempt to nudge individuals and companies toward change. As you know, the typical human abhors change in their environment.

May I suggest an alternative to this focus on continual improvement, for with your approach I fear that you will most likely reap "raises" and no permanent benefit to your condition in life? Should we not use our combined educations to try to anticipate the general trends of the future, and somehow strive to allocate risk capital toward these trends to achieve personal benefit? In this manner, if we are successful in anticipating the probability of large, general future trends, the benefits will accrue to us instead of some corporate entity.

As an example, take the investment in land near metropolitan areas that are likely to grow at greater than the overall rate of increase in total population. If our country continues to attract immigrants due to the combination of opportunity and freedom, the limited availability of land near these metropolitan areas is likely to drive the price of land in these markets higher and at a far faster pace than the general increase in the overall price level. Yes, there is substantial risk, for if we are incorrect about the demand side of the equation, the price will not adjust as expected. However, I believe the two hundred acres that our uncle has added to the family farm will eventually prove to be a wise investment. Please give the idea some thought, at your convenience.

Chapter IX

Dear younger cousin,

Yes, I have given your letter some thought on diminishing marginal utility of knowledge over time due to the incessant removal of structural barriers, and I fear you tread on dangerous intellectual ground. Have you thought that the very manner in which the society is structured is based to large degree on the premise that an individual will have the means to support himself and his family based on the skills obtained in his youth with only minimal additional updating? There is simply no economic means for the vast majority of workers to take a few years off mid career and go back to school to learn completely new methods of generating cash flow, without disrupting their families and personal lives greatly. Prior to our usual discussion of possibilities and trends, which is typically hidden in the chatter of daily life, allow me to digress to an Alaskan event or two.

First, I finally felt like I had to get out of the city, even if it is the dead of winter. Somehow in Alaska, the "dead" of winter has a very real ring to it, compared to the mild winters of the hills back home. I determined that I would drive north to get a better view of Mount McKinley, or as some of the Alaskans refer to it, "Denali." We can actually see Mount McKinley from downtown Anchorage on a clear day, for it is only about 160 miles by road north of our part of Cook Inlet. You just drive north to Palmer, fill up with gasoline, and take a left on the road to Fairbanks. I had never driven this route before, and I was unprepared for the vast valley and plain of swamp going north parallel to the Susitna River. It is not the most scenic of drives, but I was on a mission, and determined to reach the objective. Actually the objective was primarily just to get out of town, for a touch of cabin fever seemed to be setting in as the winter dragged on relentlessly.

Far up the valley, after crossing the Chulitna River, I managed to get a flat tire. To put this event in perspective, imagine a horizon of endless snow, with a fine view of Mount

McKinley (the highest peak on our continent) looming to the northwest. It is somewhat obvious to state that the temperature was extremely low and there was no other traffic in sight. In other words, no sane individuals had ventured out during this season for sightseeing purposes. The tire jack was removed from the trunk without difficulty, and I kept the motor running to ensure I would not be stranded. However, by the time I got the vehicle elevated, the tire changed, and the flat stowed in the trunk, I discovered that another more serious problem had arisen. The jack itself had frozen and would not release to lower the car back to the road. Again, it is an absolute feeling of stupidity to find oneself in a situation for which you are simply ill prepared. Some type of portable heater was all that would have been necessary to loosen the jack and allow me to beat a hasty retreat to the warmth of Anchorage. Even if I had felt that another vehicle would arrive shortly, I would not have been concerned. But during this season, the road is not heavily traveled, and the thought of running out of gasoline and the associated heat did not seem attractive. Therefore, I resolved to rock the car off the jack without turning the vehicle over or having it crash back on me. Physics in action proved successful, but I would not recommend it for entertainment when the temperature is below zero degrees. Going forward, I will probably try to find something to relieve the winter blues within the Anchorage city limits and not venture far out into the Alaskan winter so lightly dressed or ill prepared.

I recently had reason to think about your perspective on the labor factor of production actually being composed of the base of routine labor and the more valuable creative inputs. Due to time constraints, a bank analyst and I recently had to spend the entire night at the bank completing a presentation. We were successful but did not finish until after 6:00 AM, and we simply both went home, showered, changed suits, and returned for another full day's work. The fact that we were successful was simply presumed to be part of our job, and the unfortunate loss of sleep is viewed by management as nothing out of the ordinary. Corporations appear willing to use our thoughts, bodies, and youthful determination to succeed with little regard for the long-term future. It is absolutely focused on what an individual is capable of contributing now, without any regard for the health or well-being of the individual. Never have I felt so much like a "factor of production" and not an individual. No problems were found with our output, but neither was there a "by your leave, we appreciate your efforts."

If I may turn to your proposal to focus on general trends to achieve larger future gains, rather than running with the mob of other rats, beware that you are describing to some degree our uncle out of the mob of runners. He was successful in judging the pent-up demand for travel after WWII and correctly invested in gasoline distribution and service stations. This is an example of an individual correctly judging the trend and directly joining in the specific course of events, not just standing above them and investing with the mob. He was also successful in judging that rural families would flock to the convenience of liquid petroleum gas for heating, as opposed to the drudgery of firewood, and invested directly in the distribution of the raw material. However, he also serves to illustrate your opinion of how difficult it is for any individual to correctly anticipate the details of developments by his investment in a national motel chain location in his community when it was not on a tourist venue. Yet, he did get the family back into the banking business by trading a service station for stock in a small community bank. In most respects, his timing has been beyond reproach. Do you suppose he would agree with your proposal to anticipate general trends and invest in the overall trend rather than specific risks?

I believe our grandfather would agree with you, for that is somewhat the course that he has taken. It is a matter of whether one chooses to stay in the background and ride the course of events, or whether you wish to engage in the highly risky course of always trying to be more creative with the use of limited personal financial capital. Our uncle has chosen the more highly visible route of personal involvement, but frankly, our grandfather would just as soon have the forty acres back that he gave to our uncle and which was sold to start our uncle's ventures. Grandfather shares my view of the transient nature of most facets of city life. From the constantly changing business of most success, to the very neighborhood that is deemed most seemly to reside in, the only stability is knowing that nothing is stable. I will attempt a middle ground of combining work for corporations, with a foothold in the country. This is somewhat consistent with your expectations for rural property appreciation, which is reasonable with the anticipated population expansion and the American dream of owning such property as to provide both privacy and some semblance of scenic beauty. Yes, it would seem far better to ride the wave instead of being pummeled by it.

Have I ever mentioned that glacier ice is blue? It seems that the pressure under which it is formed causes it to diffuse the short wavelength of blue light even more so than the atmosphere, giving it an almost otherworldly shade of blue. The easiest glacier to get to from town is Portage Glacier, just thirty-five miles or so from downtown, east down the Turnagain Arm of Cook Inlet. The icebergs calf off of it into a lake, which is several hundred feet deep and float down to an outlet where a small steam flows a couple of miles to the Arm. After the tourists are gone in the fall, the lake freezes solid to a depth of six feet, and it makes a great surface to go hiking on, when properly attired. You can see the Chugach Mountains soaring thousands of feet on each side of the lake and a sky that is so blue, it appears like something off a postcard. The other nice detail about hiking during the winter is that the bear population (of which there are a considerable number) are all hibernating for the winter. No, I do not engage in this activity alone.

The natives sell walrus ivory, of which I have acquired a handsome piece. When first it was offered to me, I presumed it was an oddly shaped tusk of a large walrus, but I was wrong. Referred to in the native tongue as an "oosik," it is a bone from the male walrus. I have designed a display base for it which consists of an elongated pyramid, being perfectly aligned on three sides at a forty-five-degree angle, but having a thirty-degree angle of assent on the fourth side. The oosik is displayed by placing it into the elongated ridge of the fourth side of the pyramid, which is done in copper facing. Those who cannot work with their hands create with their thoughts, and a local artist was kind enough to build my display stand. It seems everyone has some aspect of Alaskan culture displayed in their homes up here, so this is my tribute to the local practice. To put the oosik in proper perspective, it is nearly two feet in length.

On your topic of gauging general trends within the culture, and investing to take advantage of the trends, two possible developments appear as most probable. It has been necessary, even in the public interest, to highly regulate specific industries, since the debacle of the 1930s. Those that I have in mind consist of public utilities, transportation, and commercial banking. The result in all of the examples is a fragmented industry structure, with many competitors having little distinction from one another.

The three industries differ from one another in that the utilities are heavily capital intensive, but all seem to adapt similar technologies in short order of their development. The airline industry, while also capital intensive, is greatly dependent on highly skilled labor that can manipulate management to the detriment of shareholders. Finally, the banking industry, of which I am most familiar, combines capital intensity with a largely unskilled (or at best lightly skilled) workforce that management views as being mostly interchangeable. While all three industries are likely to consolidate as the experience of the 1930s grows dimmer in our collective memories, the banking industry is most likely to consolidate in a most steady manner. The multitudes of commercial banks in this country are relatively small, with concentrated ownership in the hands of leading families within their communities. The burden of the estate tax is likely to cause many such families to view the sale of their local bank as the best way to meet their tax obligations. Mergers with larger banks would also allow them to retain their after tax capital within the same industry with which they are familiar. The problem with this avenue for investment is twofold, first the difficulty of locating small banks with older owners in a small town business culture that is an extremely closed environment, and secondly finding individuals willing to sell us shares in those same institutions as long term investors. It would need to be a most patient approach, not concerned with business cycles as much as the longevity of the owners. We would need to select banks with capable managements, who could manage larger organizations resulting from mergers, and who would also be willing to take a very long term perspective to investment. Too many bank managers view the world from quarter to quarter, rather than from decade to decade.

So to your initial suggestion of well located rural land as a long-term investment, I would add small, well-managed commercial banks. The key will be to avoid managements who are focused on selling for short-term gains rather than growing the business as one of the surviving entities in the industry.

On another of your points, the potential reallocation of capital, in reference to the increase in the scholarship, may be sheer coincidence. Occasionally in life are instances that are actually unplanned, where synchronicity brings forth events that are not of our own doing.

On the land issue, you may not be aware that two of the parcels acquired by our grandfather during the first part of this century support your thesis of investing for decades instead of years. One three hundred twenty-acre parcel was originally acquired for ten dollars per acre, while another forty-acre parcel was acquired for two dollars per acre. In both cases, I believe the increase in the value has far outstripped the increase in the general level of prices during the same periods (supporting your perspective). However, part of the value change must be connected with the improvements in economic infrastructure, the paving of the primary roads and electricity becoming available in the countryside. These factors have added to the allure of life in the country. In the city, I raised a concern once to our uncle over development of a parcel due to zoning issues, and he simply laughed. It seems that zoning is another illusion for the masses, easily changed to their advantage by those with the political will to make it happen in at least small, rural communities. Along those same lines, remember that our home state has absolutely no rural zoning whatever. To achieve the value trend that you believe is possible would require a parcel of such considerable size that unsuitable developments in the near vicinity would not have an impact on the investment. This appears to be another risk to your plan.

Do not mistake my small concerns for disagreement, for I believe the general plan is reasonable. In addition to the two parcels that I mentioned above, I believe our grandfather paid somewhat more for other pieces of land that he has accumulated over the years. The other defining characteristic of the acquisition trend of our grandfather and uncle is that the land has always been contiguous to their existing holdings.

I most definitely agree with your analysis that continuing as only a wage earner will definitely not produce sufficient financial results to sustain reasonable retirement or even an adequate reserve for the unforeseen bumps along the career road. One of the many problems with a professional career in business is that it appears that it will require a number of relocations and movement from one company to another across the country. Based on my experience in moving to Alaska, I can bear witness that even with obvious relocation expenses paid for by the companies; you will lose out on the equity trend in your residence due to the transaction costs of selling it (yes, I have considered leaving Alaska, but the finances simply are not right at this time). In the banking industry, these transaction costs are not paid for by the employer; it is the employee who ends up paying the real estate agent for their services.

My financial situation, and I daresay yours, precludes either of us from going into the land acquisition mode as of this time. While land is a good long-term investment, it is not a liquid asset. Looking forward, I believe that the core family farm is a most suitable site for expansion, but we must do something that the prior generations have not thought of in their acquisitions. While our grandfather and uncle have acquired land solely for the agricultural purpose, first cotton and now cattle, they have failed to acquire any road frontage. Without road frontage, the value of the land will be much reduced to future generations, as who would want to own land that looks into the back of some other rural home or farm? Even if the front of rural domiciles looks reasonably good, the back often contains everything from cars on blocks to decaying barns. I believe that road frontage is the key. Your graduation is near; brace yourself for the "real world"!

Chapter X

Dear elder cousin,

Yes, you are correct. My days at Knox are numbered fewer and fewer, and it is both a wonderful feeling and a sad one. At the end of last year, when my parents came to pick me up, they offered to take me out to dinner to celebrate the conclusion of another successful year. While my mother changed clothes, I laid down on a bed in their motel room for a moment of rest. When I awoke, I was the only person in the room. I went outside and it was broad daylight, so I thought they might have gone on to dinner without me so I could get some rest. Well, it turned out that I had slept more than twelve hours and it was now the next day. They had simply rented another motel room. They told me they had tried to wake me, but I seemed to be in something of a comatose state, so they went to dinner themselves. I apologized for turning into something of a vegetable, but they now seem somewhat aware of the stress of working one and a half full-time jobs while attending college at the same time.

The radio station has offered me a full-time job as an on-air personality, but I do not believe that talking about country music daily for an indefinite period is exactly the career path I will choose. Did I tell you I had the opportunity to interview Tom T. Hall on the air for the radio station? He was doing a concert in the area, and we are the largest country radio station in western Illinois. His speaking voice sounds much the same as his singing voice, but he seemed so tired. The look in his eyes and the manner he carried himself spoke of a person who is pushing himself both touring on the road and searching for the next hit tune which is necessary to continue the great success that he has enjoyed. I know that fans never appreciate the poised appearance of performers onstage and the tremendous effort required to appear relaxed and well rested when exactly the opposite is true.

I was also offered the position of a teller in a bank for about $10,000 per year, which I have also declined. The liberal arts education gives us a broad understanding of the world but little to offer employers in the way of immediate return on their investment in us.

I will miss the all-night diner down at the train station and the seemingly unending all-night poker games that have developed during this last year in the dormitory suites. By the way, never play poker with math majors who toy with probability in much the same way that the athletic crowd dapples in the dating game. In that regard, I have managed to complete an undergraduate education and remain single. Actually, I have had far less interaction with members of the opposite gender than I would prefer. To progress down that route, I believe we need the combination of time to shower attention on the possible center of our affections and the money to deploy in the pursuit of the same. To be fair to them, it is difficult to imagine what a poor working fellow, with no family connections and seemingly poor prospects other than a boundless optimism could offer in the way of definite prospects for the future. While we all speak of the wonders of a world with equal opportunity for women, I doubt if many actually believe the details of the same. Rather, it is probably a search for someone who can offer them the opportunity to pursue a career if they so choose, while providing the security they need to pause to raise a family if they decide that option is most enjoyable.

I will also miss "steak night" at the cafeteria. As you know, the cafeteria has three entrances, and on the rare (no pun intended) nights when steak is served, a fair number of us try to consume at least two and sometimes three steaks by getting to the cafeteria when it first opens and then using the other lines for seconds. With me this was always balanced with the need to rush down to the radio station for my shift. Obviously this has been a slight bending of school policy, but perhaps some donations later in life can make amends for enjoying food to such an extent.

The tedious week of final exams at the end of each term will not be missed, nor will the consecutive all-night study sessions that I have come to associate with them. I will miss term papers, strangely enough, for I doubt there will be many chances going forward to frankly state what is believed on any particular subject without regard for the ongoing political ramifications of what is said in any organization, either government or business. Even the teachers and their approach to their disciplines will be missed. How could I ever forget my economics professor, and the times he became so involved in his presentation that he forgot his eyeglasses had been pushed up on top of his bald head? I was blessed to have an economist from the Chicago area come out and speak to us while I was a freshman, and he made a convert to his theory before his presentation was finished. Today he has a Nobel prize and everyone is a monetarist, but I will always remember Milton Friedman as the articulate gentleman who spoke as strongly about the opportunities capitalism had provided to his immigrant mother (from the Ukraine) working in the garment district sweat shops of New York City as he did about the obvious connection between changes in the money supply and the economic cycle. His discourse had a profound effect on my outlook; it is one of the few discussions that I just have to look at the room where he spoke to see it vividly in my memory. I will miss our history professor, who combined decades of teaching with a willingness to share the excitement he still felt when a subject was addressed from a slightly different perspective. Of course my physics professor not only taught classical physics but retained a genuine interest in the possibility of ideas that lay beyond the known rules. These great instructors were what made the Knox experience so personal to me. I have kept a suitable distance between myself and them throughout college, as I do not believe it is best to become personally known to instructors. In fact, I can count on one hand the number of times I have visited an instructor's office, outside the classroom, over the past four years. This omits the required meetings with academic advisors to obtain approval of coursework for upcoming terms.

I regret hearing of your mother's passing. She was a fine lady who carried on the family tradition of teaching as her mother did before her. To pass at such a young age, sixty-two, is most distressing. You said that the cancer was inoperable, having spread from the brain to the lungs and elsewhere. It seems that even if we do not smoke, it still is possible to suffer the ill effects of aging at so young an age. I honestly cannot remember anyone else in our family passing away prior to the age of ninety.

Your good humor concerning the mishap at your mother's funeral was well received. Our disagreement in the prospect of any such wonder as a "hereafter" aside, I believe we are in complete agreement that life vacates the body upon death and that funerals are arranged for the benefit of the living. The trauma of losing a loved one is so great that we need a most solemn ceremony to have us, the living, cross over to the great vacuum of life without our most cherished family members. The sad truth is that no matter how great the outpouring of our grief, we lose more than a little of ourselves with the passing of each loved one, which can never be recovered.

If I understood your story correctly, the pastor was delivering the graveside service and the family was gathered under the customary tent when you noticed, out of the corner of your eye, the hearse beginning to move. Yes, I believe you made the correct decision. It was far better to silently watch the hearse begin to gather speed rather than interrupt the last prayer over your mother's grave by a leader of her faith. However, I do not know how you retained your composure as the hearse accelerated downhill without a driver, and a member of the funeral home staff trotted after it hoping to avoid the inevitable disaster. As I understand it, the hearse left the road inside the cemetery, crossed over an undeveloped part of the area, went through the low hanging chain link fence, crossed over the adjacent land and ended up in some poor fellow's backyard. I truly hope your vision of an afterlife is correct, for I know that your mother must have found great humor in the problems of the living at her final event.

Have you noticed that the family seems to be best illustrated by an inverted pyramid? With each successive generation after the War of Northern Aggression, there have been fewer and fewer members. It certainly makes one ponder the inevitable conclusion of this process, for I have no great desire to add to the multitudes of the world.

For the immediate future, I have arranged a job in an odd-lot grocery distributorship for the summer. They provide less than box load restocking to small grocery stores of none-food items. My responsibility will be to take flat, non-formed boxes from a pile, transform them into fully formed boxes, and hang them on an assembly line belt that will move in front of my work station. I am aware of your thoughts: *It took a college degree to do this?* I completely agree, but it is only temporary while I have the time to fully decide which career to pursue. By the fall, I hope to obtain some type of full-time professional employment. Besides, this will be the first time I have only worked forty hours a week since going to college!

Do you believe women truly make a home? I have come to that conclusion, and it is a wonder to just watch them as they go about a process for which we are so ill equipped. I do not believe our gender has the slightest possibility of making the private and personal side of life half as grand as they do simply by being themselves. Keep up the hunt, for I am sure that there are good ladies out there somewhere, less focused on money, with a southern perspective.

Chapter XI

Dear younger cousin,

Congratulations on your graduation and the successful attainment of an undergraduate degree! I believe it will be one of those days you will remember long after the commencement speech fades away. However, given your personal financial situation when you started the education (a negative net worth is such a motivator), I never had any doubt of your success. As for your summer job, it is easily understood as a break from the process given the amount of time your work consumed while you attended college on the side, so to speak.

Thank you for your kind words concerning the passing of my mother. I agree with all of your reflections on the joy she added to our lives, and I will add one other. Frankly, she was the best southern cook in the family! I only hope that some day one of us will find a lady with her style and good cooking ability. In Alaska, such individuals have been rather few and far between.

The pipeline construction is now winding down, and along with it the associated construction jobs along the route from the North Slope all the way to Valdez. The money that all those folks pumped into the Alaskan economy is being increasingly missed. Whereas only a few years ago the chief worry in banking was where to secure reasonable cost deposits to fund the unending demand for loans, today the problem is not just where to locate any potential new good loans but also how to ensure the outstanding ones are repaid. At the financial institution where I am employed it is obvious that executive management and the very owners are looking for ways to reduce non-interest expenses. In my business, unless you contribute to revenue in a very obvious way, it seems your work is highly valued while the economy is expanding and far less valued when the economy and bank earnings turn downward. I understand the practicality of the situation and if it were my bank I would definitely be thinking the very same things. Rather than waiting for the proverbial shoe to squash me, I have decided to take advantage of a lucky chain of events.

Our Human Resources director at the bank left some time ago to accept a similar position for a commercial bank in Idaho. When I came north to Alaska, I did not see Idaho, as North Dakota was as far west as the route took me before crossing over into Canada. He called me out of the blue and asked if I would be interested in coming down to Idaho for an interview with the executive vice president of the bank. It was January, and after a number of Alaskan winters I would have flown anywhere during January as long as it was warmer. My viewpoint is also that if someone is willing to purchase your airline ticket just to speak to you, it would not be courteous to refuse.

The Human Resources director arranged the flight, and all I had to do was show up at the airport, pick up the ticket, and board the flight. I landed in Boise after dark and the director was there to pick me up. He had arranged an introductory meeting with the EVP. He seemed a pretty decent fellow, and we spent the next two days getting to know our respective viewpoints on banking issues. He offered me a job as balance sheet manager on the last day. The bottom line is that I would be responsible for managing the net interest margin for the bank, which would include pricing all deposit categories. I told him that a day or two of thought would be required and would call him after I returned to Alaska. I left Boise after dark that evening and had a smooth flight back to Anchorage.

Boise has beautiful mountains to the north of downtown, and the bank occupies a twenty-story office tower downtown. I was shown my new office on the fourteenth floor that has a great view of the mountains. There are, of course, challenges with any opportunity. This will be a new position for the bank, as deposit rates have been decided by a committee up to this point. There has been no individual held accountable for deviations in the net interest margin to this point. I have decided to accept this position, so there will now be an accountable individual should any trend in net interest margin turn in an unacceptable direction. What I have not told them is that it will be necessary for me to somehow gain control of loan pricing if I am to be held accountable for net interest margin, for deposit prices are but half the issue. This opportunity prevents my probable unemployment in Alaska and gives me access to a bank structure more than three times the size of our Alaskan institution. Just from a résumé perspective, it had to be accepted. The HR director will always be remembered as a good friend who also is superb in his job. Good luck on your job hunt. I now must arrange to relocate back to the Lower Forty-Eight.

Did I mention that in Alaska we get the television network news one day late? I noticed in Boise the news was on the same day and it reminded me of our unique situation. Due to the distance and the small size of our audience, the networks fly their evening news up to Alaska from Seattle on tape, and it is broadcast on the local stations the next day. It is forever confusing to remember that the date shown on the newscast is yesterday and not today. I was also shocked to get off the plane in Boise and discover that there was not any snow on the ground in January. They said that it does snow in Boise, but the mountains to the north shield the city from most of the snow, along with the lower elevation. Of course Sun Valley is just about an hour or so from town. The higher compensation package they offered me was just a bonus for such an excellent opportunity. When I compare this interviewing experience with the variable fight to obtain a decent job when I graduated with the MBA from Vanderbilt, it really gives one pause. Today I am no more intelligent than when I graduated, simply the matter of a few years of practical experience and the one important connection with the Human Resources director for the introduction was sufficient to turn a job search upside down and enjoy the process of someone searching for me.

On a personal note, my health has taken a slight downturn, but it is manageable. The skin that surrounds me has become somewhat uncomfortable, with an apparent life of its own. When I visited a physician in Alaska, he ran some lab tests, and I thought he had struck gold when he came back to the exam room. It seems I am a very uncommon mutation, which he has never seen before; he stated that the odds of finding an individual with such a condition were more than 400,000 to 1. While it was nice to add a notch to his personal record book, I was more interested in finding out if there was any way the ill feeling could be decreased so I might more easily focus on work.

He referred me to the medical school in Boston, and I have made a flight to that city and allowed the physicians at a medical school there to get some academic enjoyment from my condition. They were also excited and asked if they could bring a group of medical students to see me. From an academic perspective I hardly could have said no, so I let the games begin. A group of young medical students were allowed to examine me to determine if they could correctly state my illness. None of the students were that insightful, and I believe the doctors enjoyed the exercise as much as their students. More importantly, they gave me advice to avoid humidity, overly hot weather, and excessive (any) exposure to direct sunlight. I also have a prescription for an occasional antibiotic if I succumb to scratching. My mental discipline is reasonably solid when to it comes to ruling over the conscious relationship with my body, so I don't imagine there will be much need for the antibiotic. So "medical oddity" may now be added to the list of academic initials after my name. I have paid cash for all of the treatments and opinions, for I do not want to have any medical record that indicates I am different than a perfect physical specimen. It has been my experience that in business, everyone speaks as if your physique is unimportant, yet I notice that I have yet to meet a professional individual in any high position who has any noticeable physical defect. I do not believe that this observation is a coincidence, and in Boston, on the other side of the continent, I will bury the record of being different.

Now arrangements must be made to depart Alaska, with the usual two weeks' notice to the employer. This time I will not be driving, for this bank is more generous in their relocation expenses. Besides, one time driving up the Alcan Highway is sufficient for any lifetime. Instead, the bank is going to pay for a moving company to ship my belongings down to Boise. They will probably be surprised at the relatively small size of the bill, as I have not accumulated so many belongings as an individual might living down south. On the matter of the car, they are going to transport it down by ship. It will leave Alaska four days ahead of me and I will fly down to Seattle, spend the night, and pick the car up at the port to drive on to Boise. You are supposed to deliver the car to the dock with less than one-eighth of a tank of gasoline in it. While I have been to Seattle, I never left the city proper, and I am really looking forward to the drive to Boise.

The fountain in my living room has been spoken for by the real estate agent who sold my condominium. Given the poor real estate market, I was simply glad to be rid of the residence at the same price that I paid several years before. I did not quibble with the agent on the price for the fountain, for she may well have sold the condominium just to obtain the artwork. Again, little was lost financially, but I imagine it will be some time before a suitable fountain is located as a replacement. Good craftsmen and artists are difficult to find. I would not trade my Alaskan experience for anything! Everything, from the start of the Iditarod dogsled race to Nome in downtown Anchorage, to the diversity of the people, to my experiences in so many facets of banking, this has been a period in my career I could not have duplicated down south. The financial rewards have been most helpful in paying off my college loans. Keep me informed of where you are heading!

Chapter XII

Dear elder cousin,

As you know, I am not completely following in your footsteps, but the allure of Alaska was simply too much to pass up, so here I am in Anchorage. My trip up was considerably easier than yours, as they have placed a significant amount of new asphalt over that gravel road that you endured. Yet the scenery is all I could have imagined.

I was offered a position as an entry-level economist with the State of Alaska Department of Petroleum Revenue, which is part of the State of Alaska Revenue Department. As a state employee, I have a benefits package I could not even come close to obtaining down south, including four weeks of vacation a year. However, I did make a significant mistake in accepting this job without first personally meeting my boss. I would wager that most individuals who expend lengthy periods of time selecting the significant other in their lives may also make the mistake of selecting the boss who comes with a new job as a result of a single interview (in my case by phone). At least that is what I am telling myself to justify how in the world I could have ended up working for this individual. When I interviewed for the job, he gave the impression of being a well-read professional. He seemed to have all the qualifications for a good boss in economics: an earned doctorate and years of experience working for the state of Alaska in the capacity of an economist.

When I first arrived at the offices in Anchorage (even though most of the state government is in Juneau, Petroleum Revenue is in Anchorage; most of the oil companies have their state headquarters here), the boss had the customary office-type family photos that appeared to frame a successful family life in midterm: a wife, children, and snapshots from a vacation in a warm climate. You are aware of how I try not to develop close personal relationships with those in my immediate surroundings, so I did not ask any personal questions that might have breached the line between business and the outside life. This appears to be a personal character flaw on my part, and I shall endeavor to correct it prior to accepting jobs in the future.

This experience has shown that a superior's personal conduct can have far-reaching effects on your professional and personal life. In the future, I think that it would be best to make oblique inquiries based on the office décor as a means of gaining insight into the real person I will be working for in any job. In this job, I did not ask any such questions and a nearly fatal chain of circumstances began to unfold. Even if I had made some purposely incorrect guess about the age of his children, as shown in the office photos, it might have revealed a great deal about the individual.

In this case, an offer of employment was simply extended, and it seemed so much better than assembling boxes in the warehouse, I jumped at the opportunity. It fit my training so well, to work on the econometric model for forecasting tax revenue from oil production (primarily on the North Slope, but also in Cook Inlet), that the personal situation of my soon-to-be boss was the last factor I would have even thought of as a point to weigh in the decision process. I now have a deep interest in the gap between the personal and professional façade that we all use daily. It has made me wish I had taken more than just three courses in psychology.

While I was enjoying the challenge of working on new projects with new colleagues, there was a gradual realization in me that there might be a lack of internal balance between personal and professional façades in the new boss. However, as the junior member of the department, and new to state government work, it was difficult for me to make an informed judgment without showing the cultural bias of an outsider. The boss had a suitable pride in his successful, well-educated professional wife (she taught at the local branch of the University of Alaska). However, I thought his perspective was occasionally overshadowed by a heightened expression of professional envy with his spouse. I did not believe this to be unusual, as I have often heard of spouses who have competitive relationships, and they are not assumed to be abnormal in any way. In retrospect, I now believe the need to compete is so great in much of American culture that many individuals may lack the discipline to hatcheck this emotion at the door of their personal lives. Again, in retrospect, I believe my new boss carried this emotion directly through the door and into the kitchen.

Going forward, I shall try to casually observe personal habits of superiors to attempt to gain some insight on their thoughts. The new boss went to female entertainment facilities, of which Anchorage has a multitude, but it seemed to be a customary expression of midlife rebellion against cultural norms and not an indication of any lack of balance. Something like that "Cave" facility you mentioned over in the officers club on the air force base up here. At the most, I thought of it as akin to buying a sports car at that age in life down in the Lower Forty-Eight. The joint income of my boss and his wife was that of a professional couple and certainly showed the advantages of a lifestyle beyond any that this young, single professional could hope for in the immediate future. The boss expressed strong displeasure at some common wifely expenditures, but I decided to simply minimize any personal contact with him as the best course of action.

After a relatively short period of time, I was summoned into the boss's office and asked to be seated. It was difficult to imagine the cause for the grave concern that showed on his face. He started a monologue of a series of mishaps that had occurred in his personal life since I had been hired and the incredible insinuation of some connection with me and possible clandestine motives on my part. The shock of his comments, the coldness of his voice, and the staring glare of his pale blue eyes were sufficient proof of the serious nature of his accusations (from his perspective). When he asked if I was or ever had been employed by the CIA, I responded directly and most strongly that I had no connection with that organization whatsoever!

I believe our southern culture has created a bias in us to continually look to the external as the most logical place for threats to our well-being and often fails to recognize that the greatest threats may lie within the unbalanced thoughts of those we may engage in professional relationships. Although I sound like I'm back in a management class at Knox, I now believe that no better argument can be made against the autocratic management style than the risk of illogical decisions being made by leaders who suddenly transition from the best and the brightest, into an unbalanced sequence of thought.

When I was personally confronted with the irrational, the unconventional, and the most unexpected line of discussion from my boss, I tried to not display any overtly harsh emotion or concern other than attempting to redirect his thoughts to more conventional modes. I tried to focus the discussion on the many and varied aspects of the boss's life and to stress that the distance between us was great on both a professional and personal level. I believe that it is not unusual for individuals to place blame for what they perceive as unjust personal circumstances on some outside entity, not on their own decisions and actions. Remember the religion courses? The dissident is always blamed for any gap in the doctrine, rather than the religious hierarchy addressing the situation and leading the faith forward. I assure you it is much less intriguing when you are chosen as the heretic and the casual factor for another's perceived misfortunes.

I will always remember that when an accusation of blame is made, the presenter is most likely to believe that there is little doubt in the accusations being true. For him to believe otherwise would mean confronting the reality that personal responsibility for such fault as may exist resides in himself! Not once did I make a vocal proclamation of the ridiculous nature of the accusations expressed, for to do so would have been to provide further credence to his irrational thoughts. I did remember from logic, that no rational argument can ever be successful when pitted against irrational, fanatical thoughts. To prevail in the moment, it is best to reframe the thoughts presented in a different light, so that just perhaps irrationality will be tilted back into a reasoned path. When the boss shifted his conversation toward the possibility of CIA involvement through channels other than me for his perceived troubles, I felt Anubis had passed his hand over me and on to another troubled soul.

The problem with private conversations is that they are private. The preceding discussion had thoroughly convinced me that my boss was either in or nearing a seriously unbalanced state. Yet publicly, he conducted himself with the most professional decorum and was unlike the person who had grilled me behind his closed door. I believe that if I had made any declaration of the reality I had encountered to anyone else in our department, I would have been possibly dismissed for trying to damage the professional reputation of a great mind. Who would have believed the new, young professional versus a seasoned veteran with a doctorate?

Hindsight is, of course, perfect, but I should have publicly presented unwavering professional support of the troubled figure and immediately commenced a search for new employment. However, I was relatively new to this job and with little professional experience; departure did not appear to be a viable alternative.

At this point, I had much greater empathy for your experience with the bank robber in Nashville. However, I do believe you were at least in the hands of a rational individual, regardless of his criminal intent. I am beginning to think that the irrational, while not normal, is not all that uncommon. It merely hides behind the tenuous face of normality that is presented to the world daily. My distrust of mankind has grown immensely; it will surely taint my perspective for a long time to come. Our American cultural framework allows the irrational and the logical to coexist in such a manner that generally contributions may be made by all parties to the overall benefit of the society. The flaw is that the framework does not guarantee personal safety or harmony and may in fact lead to greater personal risk.

While I no longer live in that academic ivory tower, I began a dedicated search for an alternative source of employment in Anchorage. The problem was that I probably waited too long to begin the search, but I felt every week worked was more experience to add to the resume. My personal financial situation prevented the search from being expanded beyond Anchorage, as relocation would be expensive, and I must continue to make my college loan payments without undue stress or risk possible default. The state did not reimburse me for relocating.

One Friday afternoon, the boss announced that we would not leave the office until the particular assignment given to me was completed. Even though I volunteered to complete the assignment over the weekend, the boss was unrelenting. I was uncomfortable being alone on the floor with this individual, so with a focus and dedication to task that was unusual for a government employee, the job was completed, and we departed for the weekend. It was an uneventful two days for one of us.

Arriving back at the office on Monday, a senior economist immediately inquired if I had heard what the boss had done over the weekend. I replied that the boss and I did not normally socialize, so I had not heard what the boss had done. His reply reaffirmed my belief in chaos theory, the normality of the abnormal, and the need to distance oneself from colleagues as all being perfectly reasonable. Apparently, the boss had left the office that late Friday afternoon and gone to the Anchorage airport to pick up his mother, who had flown up from the Lower Forty-Eight. He had not mentioned any pending family visit in the office. After arriving at his home and settling his mother in, it was alleged that he took his wife into the kitchen and murdered her with a kitchen knife. His mother was said to have herded the children to a neighbor's home and called the police. Perhaps it is just me, but the amount of blood that was said to be splattered about the kitchen seemed a bit too calculating, too well thought out, not a product of a truly deranged mind.

The police made the expected visit to the office and questioned all of us who had worked closely with the boss, asking the customary questions. It turned out I was not alone in believing that the boss had been acting a bit odd, but others had also turned a blind eye, for they had known him for a longer period and were aware of some eccentric behavior. The investigation by the police revealed that the boss had taken out an insurance policy on his wife prior to her death, with their children as beneficiaries. Of course the policy did not pay, otherwise I image there would be such an increase in death claims, insurance companies would not survive.

It was presumed by the authorities that the highly educated economist had not been aware that his alleged actions would make the insurance policy null and void. This was the same individual who would not leave a pebble unturned if he thought knowledge that would help his forecast of petroleum revenue be better might hide there. About the only thing that everyone at the office could agree on was that the boss had maintained a public presence of normality up to the very time of the death of his wife. He has been assigned to a psychiatric institute for a period of at least six years.

The postmortem discussion in the office focused on the fact that his wife had been pregnant with another child, which he is said to have not wanted, at the time of her death. The pregnancy issue was said to have driven him beyond the edge of sanity. What little faith I have had in the American system of so-called justice has been greatly diminished by this incident. The mental contrast of the dead wife's lovely face in the photo displayed in his office and the superbly calculating intelligence behind the cold blue eyes of the boss will remain with me for a long time. It is almost beyond belief that the sanctity of human life has been so belittled by the justice system that legal sanctuary can be given to those bold enough to publicly declare their abnormality with such conviction as to convince the system that they are not responsible for their behavior.

Cousin, when dealing with bosses and employees alike, I suggest credence be given to the normality of abnormal behavior and the potential of opening the floodgates to the perverse underside of the potential human condition. Please forgive the serious nature of this letter, but again, I now more fully understand the profound impact a single event such as your carjacking and abduction can have on your entire world outlook. I promise my next letter will find some good experience here in Alaska to share with you on the "outside."

Chapter XIII

Dear Younger Cousin,

I deeply regret how the incredible behavior of your boss affected your perspective, but I do understand your position on the issue of one person taking the life of another. If we define murder as the unlawful taking of the life of another person, with associated malice, prior thought, and planning, how can our justice system judge anyone innocent by reason of insanity? The very act of murder is almost by definition "insane," so are the courts saying the fact that some individuals appear more insane than others means they should not be accountable for their actions? Or as I fear to be the case, are some individuals clever enough, or have clever enough legal representation to effectively game the system? I do not know all the particulars of the case you have written about, but the general category of cases involving human life causes great concern.

Without sounding as if I hold to every letter of the "Old Testament," I believe our society has parted from the path set by the original founders who thought in the context of a society of equally responsible individuals. I still firmly believe in the separation of the secular and religious aspects of our lives, but until mankind can govern the secular with more rationality than we have displayed, retaining a certain standard of civility may require some religious insights. The problem is that while there may be many paths to religious enlightenment, some appear far longer than others. Of particular concern are those faiths that attach little value to the human life of those outside of their particular brand of enlightenment. I fear the American judicial process falls directly into the doctrine of these faiths by most probably indicating that these individuals are "insane" by definition! This country may need a great deal more insane asylums and even a few more jails. The case you described may adjust your perspective from the liberal bias toward individuals being reformed by prison (which I know has been your perspective) toward my more logical bias of prison simply being a waste of taxpayers' money for those involved in murder. A more cost-efficient solution simply involves the removal of those involved in such activities from the society permanently. At the very least, I would believe that you will be much less willing to divulge much about yourself to many around you, and conversely, much more interested in their actions and motives on a daily basis.

I have begun to mingle somewhat with the local residents and was even invited to a bachelor party. The fellow seemed to be drinking as if tomorrow was the last day of his life. One round even consisted of flaming drinks, of which I was not familiar, and a gentleman with perhaps a few too many spilled the drink. The flames went across his hand, down onto the table, and set the napkin on fire. The waitress quickly extinguished the flames, but it was a sight to see. When I attended the wedding the next day, there was some delay, for the pastor had misplaced his bible. It was eventually located under one of the groomsmen (who had been at the bachelor party the night before and probably did not know he was sitting on anything).

The new job is going well, but a learning experience occurred upon my arrival. While I am sure the timing of my arrival and departure for the job interview was a sheer coincidence, it prevented me from fully understanding the flora and fauna of the area. I now more clearly understand that the Boise River Valley is a magnificent oasis in the high desert, where irrigation has turned an unending sea of sagebrush into a lush agricultural haven. Going forward, I would recommend spending a few days without the escort of a perspective employer to familiarize yourself with the territory surrounding the locale of any employment offers.

In Alaska, I had become accustomed to a tree line on the mountains that indicated an elevation above which the weather was too harsh for trees to grow, indicative of temperature. Here in Idaho, the rules have been turned on their heads, for although there is a tree line on the mountains north of town, it is of a very different sort. It seems that below a certain general elevation, about six thousand feet above sea level, there is not sufficient moisture to allow trees to grow. Above that level, where a great deal of the moisture is in the form of snow, evergreen trees abound.

I am beginning to think of myself as a corporate migrant worker and feel more than a little kinship to the migrants that keep the Idaho agricultural machine running by moving the irrigation pipes and other duties. It is becoming increasingly apparent that middle-management individuals are really compensated to arrange the fruit of the corporate orchard be picked at a pace sufficient to satisfy the owners, but not so fast as to cause the unemployment of executives. You will not be rewarded if you pick the fruit too quickly, much the same as the over enthusiastic union worker, except in this case it is the solving of problems. An overtly quick solution may cast doubt and shine too bright a light on those who manage the orchard. The greatest challenge appears in attaining the proper balance so as to remain on the orchard crew.

Our uncle has purchased another ninety acres adjacent to the family farm back in the hills. For an individual who swore he would never again live in the country after WWII, he is definitely supporting the family through his land acquisitions. He has purchased the land at the upper end of the south valley and a pasture up on top. He was also reelected to the position of mayor in his community. As long as we stay out of his way, I do not believe he will be of any long term difficulty, but neither should we expect a great deal of assistance. In fact, he has recently given $40,000 to a college in the western part of the state where he was treasurer before WWII. Given the debt we both incurred for a college education, I view his generosity as a statement of displeasure with our chosen paths through life. I have invited him and our aunt to visit me in Idaho, and I will make no reference to his academic donation.

Do you believe that one lifetime is adequate? It is simply insufficient to correct the family financial situation and return it to the level that was enjoyed before the War. I view us as the fourth generation, including our great-grandfather who survived the War, to continue the struggle. Between the federal income tax and the death confiscation tax it is increasingly difficult for a family unit to view itself over a number of generations. The tax laws seem to conspire to turn us into a nation of self-centered individuals with no vision beyond our immediate lifetimes.

My new boss is a transplant from the academic world, having served as dean of the local business division of the public university. From serving in such a position his graciousness has been honed to a level required for the associated public presence and serves the bank well as a public figure. My job seems to be to support him in any manner advantageous to the bank. One thing they never did teach us in graduate school was diplomacy. My perspective is that gaining influence in any corporation requires building a base of widespread support among senior managers while not appearing to threaten the credibility or power of any individual. It is a tedious task, totally alien to the MBA perspective of reasoned success. At best, it is akin to carrying the water of executives to try to become a fulcrum for intellectual leverage.

A senior executive was approached about serving as an expert witness for a company in a hearing before a governmental commission. The format of the hearing allowed the testimony to be presented in writing prior to the actual event, organized in a question-and-answer format. At the hearing, an official would ask the expert a few questions from the document and inquire whether the witness desired to make any changes to his testimony. There being no changes, the commission would accept the testimony. I was asked to prepare testimony on the cost of capital, with preference for any original insights that I might add to the standard perspective. The testimony would be a critical factor in the commission's decision of whether to approve a rate increase for the corporation. The perception was that my level of academic achievement provided ample background for such a task (the MBA thing).

While this obviously had nothing to do with banking, and the expectation is that the details will be done on personal time, I have of course agreed to be of assistance. While the math required was simple, the format made me think of writing a play and exactly what the words would sound like in an official setting. I have tried to balance the presentation to gain governmental approval for the shareholder's best interest while dealing with the vexation of a slightly greater public burden in the immediate future. The executive officer approved the document and even made suggestions for changes in certain verbiage.

I believe the executive enjoyed the experience before the commission, as they approved the rate increase request and he was asked to serve as an expert witness for future hearings. He gave me a personal check for $1,000 as a gratuity, which makes me wonder what the corporation gave him? The executive has not volunteered to introduce me to any of the corporate officials we really worked for, nor is there apparently any hope of any acknowledgement of my efforts. As we have discussed this whole state of affairs, when we contribute intellectual capital to those with sufficient risk capital and status it borders on selling our very souls for money and I find it most disturbing. However, back on the subject of diplomacy, I appear to have gained credibility with another executive on an upper floor as a result of my efforts.

While I know you enjoy your governmental work, strange bosses not withstanding, I believe we both need to somehow shift from staff positions into some function that is more closely tied to the production of revenue. Rainmakers are always paid far more in respect and compensation than those who simply work the fields. As my physical stature, flaming red hair and all, appears to prevent me from getting a rainmaking type of position, I have decided to attack the objective from the direction least desired by those in rainmaking positions. The successful rainmaker personalities seem to seek the limelight; as the corporate input factors are the least glamorous, they will be my point of attack.

I have obtained an apartment near downtown, a couple of blocks to the south of Warm Springs, a street in the older part of town. It is a one-bedroom loft, just slightly larger than my old Alaskan abode, and I feel right at home. I drove up to Sun Valley to see how the other .1 percent lives, and it is a wonder! If the Sun Kings palace had been similarly placed, beyond the easy walk of the Paris mob, they might well still retain their position and pleasures.

Back to business, lest I wander into areas we strongly disagree on to no benefit to either of us. It appears my responsibility for deposit pricing provides an opening. Folks in charge of pricing seem to come up through the sales side of an organization, and are perhaps those who were not exceptional at sales so they are given the pricing function. I believe the application of math to deposit pricing may have a material effect on the net interest margin of commercial banks. In particular the concept of elasticity and segmenting markets by price seem to be unused in banking at this time. I am going to do my best to change that situation. To a great extent my profession is very dependent on personal connections for jobs, as that is how I actually got this opportunity. Another new individual was asked to join me in attending a few meetings and I asked him to attend one of my first asset/liability management meetings. After the meeting was over, he drew me aside and told me how much he had enjoyed the presentation but he had one question. He said, "Exactly what is this basis point thing you were talking about?" I explained that a basis point was one-hundredth of one per cent, and that seemed to clear up his confusion. I asked him about his background, and he said he had never worked in banking but had joined us as a vice president.

As you can see, it is a change from Alaska but in many ways a great opportunity. Please make the most of your time in Alaska!

Chapter XIV

Dear Elder Cousin,

You seem to be taking this new job of yours in Idaho much too seriously! After my experience with what I thought was a most reasonable boss up here in the north, I don't intend to take those around me lightly on a personal level or, conversely, my employment too seriously. Remember the idea on intellectual capital; it accrues to your employer, not yourself! I suggest you back off the strategy for a while and find some way to actually enjoy life.

I promised a lighter letter this time, and circumstances developed to make such a communication possible. After the exit of my boss, I was summoned down to Juneau to meet with various officials of the department of revenue, most notably a senior economist. A leading manager for the state suggested that to get better acquainted, we should go on a fishing trip the next morning and that he would pick me up at the hotel. This was my first time in Juneau, directly on the shore, and all I could see was a very narrow ship channel in front of town and a bridge over it to an island. The last time I had been fishing I was twelve, and my father took me out on a lake in the hills.

Regardless of my expertise, I was determined to do the socially correct thing and enjoy the Alaskan experience. As the Hilton was near the harbor, I presumed that his boat was kept there and that would be our point of departure. As we passed the harbor without stopping, I did not say anything, and eventually he mentioned that his boat was at his home. I simply thought that he had not wanted to haul it into downtown when he picked me up. As we arrived at his home, I still did not see the boat. When he said that the bass boat that he used was in his backyard and asked for me to help load it I realized I was in over my head (yes, pun intended)! I swear, the bass boat was a twelve foot model, and the mere idea that this was going to be our mode of transportation in the ocean left me speechless. I found myself in a situation so absurd, it defied reason, yet I felt my future employment decreed that this course of events must occur. I simply heaped praises on the fine condition of the bass boat and compared it to the condition of the old bass boats that I remembered from my childhood back in the hills. I believe this approach prevented anyone from losing face, and I made a personal connection that may have eased the transition after my previous boss had disrupted all of our lives and ended that of one of his family. Did I mention that the murdered wife was actually pregnant at the time of her death? We have been told that the apparent reason for his hostility was that he objected to another child. I believe they already had two or three children. Yes, this supports your thesis that the culture does not value the sanctity of human life.

When we arrived at the public access point to Lynn Canal, the stares of those putting larger craft into the ocean were vivid affirmations agreeing with my personal reckoning of the imbalance between risk and probable reward for this fishing venture. While narrow in width, not more than ten miles or so, and with no visible glaciers at the south end at tidewater, this body of water was undoubtedly ocean. As we proceeded into the ocean, my own misgivings were confirmed when an Alaskan State Ferry heading up toward Skagway passed us. I felt like a tourist attraction as the crowd gathered on the leeward railing to marvel and gawk downward from the two-hundred-foot craft. I have no doubt they thought they were seeing either two true native Alaskans or two insane persons, but I waved to lend a more assured stature to our presence. It was the first time I had removed either of my hands from a firm grip on the seat in which I had implanted myself.

Other than the minor detail of physical danger, it really was a beautiful sight, with the Chilkat Range to the west of us and Lynn Canal seeming to stretch endlessly north. I saw my first bald eagles as they hunted, and they are truly magnificent creatures. Back in the boat, my worst fear was that we might actually catch some fish. Even if the fish were of modest size, I did not feel comfortable trying to actually bring anything else into our little craft. The thought was comforting in the coldness of the water, such that any exposure to it as a result of capsizing would not make any difference for very long. The new boss caught the one fish of the day; it was a deepwater creature the likes of which I have never seen before. He made some remark about deepwater trash fish and threw it back in. Luck was surely with me throughout the day, for I managed to not even get a bite on my line! After returning to Juneau, I expressed appreciation to my superior for an experience that will be remembered for a long time.

Back in Anchorage, the next most senior economist has been promoted to the position that our mutual superior had vacated in such a horrible manner. In response to your statement on capital punishment, it remains difficult for me to agree. However, I no longer harbor doubts about what our fellow man is capable of and little would surprise me in that respect. Do you ever think of how thin this veneer of civilization is that covers countless millennium of savagery? Given the historical record, it appears we are blessed to reside in a rare moment of relative civil behavior in one of the most educated societies in history, and yet our personal safety is never absolutely sure, even from those around us.

You never did mention the Anchorage mud flats in your letters. Now that I am up here, I was most fortunate to have someone let me know of the danger involved. Although from the public outlook point in downtown Anchorage, they certainly look like beaches when the ten foot plus tide goes out; it seems like it would be a public service to let more folks know they are actually mud flats. They had to pull some poor tourist out last week who was stuck in what they probably thought was a very pristine beach before he sank too deep. However, the view of the sunset over Knik Arm of Cook Inlet, with Mount Susitna ("sleeping lady") in the background is worth the trip down to the public viewing area above the mud flats. I can imagine how, after a winter or two up here in the early part of this century, that mountain across the water actually looked like many a sleeping lady the fellows remembered back down south.

You also failed to mention that these wonderful summertime bike trails, which become wintertime cross-country skiing trails, are great habitat for moose! In the Lower Forty-Eight, looking out for the odd speeding bike is to be expected, but seeing my first moose inside the city limits of Anchorage was another surprise. I have made it up to the first foothills outside Anchorage to the east, the Chugach Range. The state park starts right at the city limits, probably at an elevation of about twenty-five hundred feet, and you can drive your car up to that level before hiking on upward. I feel more comfortable above that altitude, as it is not that far on up before you breach the tree line. Up above the trees, you can at least see if any bears are heading your way and not just stumble upon them. You know the old Alaskan joke, "Don't worry about outrunning a bear, it can't be done. Just concentrate on outrunning the fellow you are in the bush with." It is yet another good reason to never go hiking alone in the wilderness.

One of the guys at the office is a private pilot, and he asked if I would like to fly down to Homer with him for some sightseeing. Of course I said yes; you only get one chance to enjoy this beautiful world, and I intend to see as much as possible. He rented a plane, single engine, and we took off headed south. Chickaloon Bay, between Anchorage and the Kenai Wilderness area sure seems a lot wider looking down at it than it does from the south bluffs of Anchorage. The flight down was pretty uneventful, although the thought did strike me that there were few roads to put the plane down on in an emergency, compared to the Lower Forty-Eight. The ice-covered Kenai Range lay off to our southeast and Cook Inlet to our west.

After we landed in Homer, we asked at the terminal (a two-room building) if there were any cars we could rent. Well, at least we provided some entertainment for the locals. Compared to the normal for Homer, I realized we were overdressed and looked like we were from the big city. We decided to hitchhike our way into town, and a lady in a pickup truck stopped to haul us into town. Since her two children were in the cab and there was not any other space, we jumped into the back of the truck. He is a Harvard guy, and I am sure it was the first time he had traveled in this manner. As for me, you know it was just like being back in those hills.

Our transport was good enough to take us out to the end of the Homer Spit, which is really the local tourist attraction. It is actually an overgrown gravel bar five miles long and never more than a hundred yards wide and sticks out into Kackemak Bay. They have made a harbor on the sheltered side of the Spit, and the fishing boats tie up there. Down in Homer, the big fish, quite literally, is halibut! I don't believe I have ever seen an uglier creature pulled out of the deep. It can easily measure four feet across and just as long and reminds me most of an unusually large hubcap with two eyes on the same side. There is a motel at the end of the Spit, and we grabbed a bite to eat there before bumming a ride back to our plane. We split the expense for the day; planes are not really that expensive to rent, if you just rent a small one.

An opportunity for a part-time job in the late afternoons and evenings has come my way, and I have decided to take advantage of it. The private Alaska Pacific University in town has had a rough time of it over the past few years. First, most of the students and faculty quit to work on the pipeline or associated construction. Now they are trying to get the university going again, so it is somewhat like a startup operation. I met the new university president through a mutual friend. He is a man on a mission, and you cannot tell him the university was ever really closed (for that would have certain negative effects on their accreditation). The school was apparently once associated with the Methodist Church but now pretty much seems to be on its own financially. They really have a beautiful campus—several hundred acres to the southeast of downtown. Yes, you are correct; your "midtown" description of the area along Northern Lights seems to have caught on and is now in general usage. Anyway, you keep going east on Northern Lights until you see signs directing you toward the hospital, and the university is just to the east of it.

The university controller quit, along with the remainder of the accounting staff, and the university president asked if I could come out and reopen the books and hire folks to do the daily clerk work while he gets the school going again. He was not even in a position to get the payroll out! You were right about Alaska! Nowhere on the "outside" could I have hoped to have the opportunity to run a University accounting system as a part-time job. I clearly indicated that I did not have any experience in "fund" accounting for nonprofit organizations, but that did not seem to deter him in the least. He had found out that, although I was employed as an economist, I had considerable coursework in accounting. So I have accepted the position of acting controller of Alaska Pacific University under the leadership of the new president. I initially hired a lady in her late fifties who luckily had just arrived in Anchorage but was looking for employment, and together we are going to get the financial side of the university up and running. The president is arranging to have evening classes in the main building on campus, which also houses the administration, so I am able to work the books in the evening while other folks are in the building.

The campus also has private housing for the faculty along a secluded drive, a dormitory, and another large building for classes and such student union activities that exist at present. I really believe that if anyone can get this university going again, it is the new president. He moved up here from the Midwest and seems to have an almost missionary zeal to his daily activities. There is also a physical plant building, a dormitory, a student union building, and other structures. I believe the strategy is to build enrollment through the route of attracting part-time evening students, which will be served by part-time faculty drawn from local state government (a good number of which have graduate degrees). At the same time, an aggressive enrollment campaign is on for the fall term, to bring in full-time students to fill the dormitory. Do try to enjoy your more settled life in the warm mountains of Idaho. We both need to have more fun and perhaps a little less focus on career.

What do you think of our grandfather passing? I simply did not have the financial resources to fly back across the continent for just a funeral, and I believe he would have understood. Anyway, no one else in the family volunteered to loan us poor folk's passage back for the funeral, so perhaps I am viewed as a poor credit risk. Considering the amount of outstanding student debt I have, it would be difficult to disagree with their analysis. It would seem that legally we now are part owners of the family farm, but I don't imagine our uncle exactly sees it that way. As he has no children and our aunt has no brothers or sisters, I believe the best policy is that of patient waiting. Together they, our grandfather and uncle, have managed to amass 812 acres, unfortunately without road frontage to make it of any significant value.

Strictly from an economic perspective, I believe the overall value of the family place could be more than doubled through the addition of three hundred acres and about a mile and a half of paved road frontage. Given the probable population growth trends, and the convenience of road transportation to seven centers of employment (North Little Rock, Conway, Jacksonville, Cabot, Beebe, Searcy, and Heber Springs), I believe the economic value of the land will be equal to the personal value it has to each of us. A target of around eleven hundred acres should combine privacy, sufficient timber (about five hundred acres), and grazing land for cattle, and the place should be about self-sufficient. With the Des Arc creek for an eastern boundary and paved roads on three sides, it will almost resemble a small island. The key will be to minimize the number of small out parcels that may remain on our side of the roads. The additional advantage of two other small live creeks running through the place adds to both the scenic beauty and the value.

Our uncle is about sixty-five years of age, which in our family indicates that he has probably at most another good twenty years to run the farm. Now that he is planning to retire from local politics, he will only have the bank board to serve on and the farm to play with. Considering the sharp tongue of our aunt in domestic matters, I suspect he will spend a great deal of time out on the farm. Please do not press him about adding our names to the actual official record in the courthouse. It would simply remind him of his differences with grandfather on family matters. I plan to repurchase the forty acres that grandfather gave him, which he resold to finance his personal ventures.

Chapter XV

Dear Younger Cousin,

Our uncle and aunt have been out here to visit and do not seem to have mellowed with age. An entire lifetime without children and being somewhat estranged from our grandfather has left them extraordinarily independent minded. However, I still remember our aunt giving me those white sugar donuts when I was a small child. No one else would allow me that indulgence due to the thought that I was a slightly heavy child. So it is difficult for me to not believe that there is some semblance of normality buried somewhere in there. They have traveled the world—China, the Soviet Union, Europe, and just about anywhere they wished to go. At the same time, all they could manage for our grandparents was a one-room air conditioner in the living room at the farm. Oh, lest we forget, our uncle contributed one unused service station signpost to be used as a TV antenna on the farm. I know our grandfather would not have accepted any unusual gifts from our uncle due to the strain of their personal relationship, but I still believe that something could have been arranged if our uncle had truly wanted to help.

The latest development is that our uncle is not speaking to one of our cousins, for an apparent feeling that he has been slighted. Although we are the younger generation, I am continually amazed at the conduct of those who might have gained more wisdom through the years. Anyway, our uncle and aunt seemed to enjoy their visit, and I was pleased to entertain them (Sun Valley and the whole bit).

I approve of your long-term plan for the family farm. No, I will not force the issue of having our names legally attached to it, and I believe that the need for a daily escape from the finely honed tongue of our aunt should ensure that our uncle will not attempt to sell any portion of it. Still, the situation will bear careful watching as neither of us is back in the hills to be involved on a daily basis. Yes, given the population trends and location of the land, it is probably going to appreciate substantially more than the general rate of inflation if we garner sufficient paved-road frontage. As such, it would serve as the last bulwark against financial ruin if the careers turn into something less than stellar. In the interim, we will need to kowtow to most wishes of our uncle, as regardless of our education, he views his history of success as validation for any action he cares to take. I daresay that if we even ventured that we might be planning to live on the family farm someday, he would somehow take action to prevent it. His perspective is that family assets seem to exist solely for his enjoyment and not that of other relations. We are certainly well on the way to that independent society of educated barbarians of which we both have such trepidation. The sense of continuity in family over generations is being destroyed in favor of individual self-interest, and I believe society will be the worst for it.

My personal health has hit another minor speed bump. A lump developed on my wrist, and a doctor informed me that it was a ganglion cystic tumor. It seems it is not life threatening, merely an inconvenience. The surgeon recommended I have it removed, as it apparently will simply continue to get larger if nothing is done, and it was already affecting my ability to type. The surgeon was really a great fellow, for, as they say, "With a name like that, he has to be good." Honestly, it must take a gentleman of great character to pursue a career as a surgeon with the name of Gross. Given that this fellow had chosen to live with it for a lifetime, I felt that the burden alone spoke well of his ability and probable professional expertise. After they removed the tumor, it left a pretty good size hole, and I had to shower with my arm in a garbage bag to keep the wound dry until it healed. Of course, the wrist does not feel the same, and I suppose it never will, but it is just one of those minor inconveniences that we have to deal with as we age.

Speaking of minor inconveniences, I suppose you have heard that I entered into wedlock with a local girl. In retrospect, perhaps the emphasis should have been on the word "lock." Again, I do not believe it is the individual, for before we wed, she treated me with the utmost respect and kindness. That alone is probably sufficient to entice most men, as there is so little of it in our daily involvement with society. I believe that the problem is with the different expectations that each gender brings to the contractual situation. Whereas I believe most men view marriage as a final destination, the female gender may view it as a bridge in their plans along the way toward a home and family. Already I am under pressure to have children, while at the same time, college loans still must be repaid on a monthly budget. Can you image life without making those payments? It is one of my fondest fantasies. Let me stress, I am sure nothing is wrong with my new mate; she simply wants more than it is currently reasonable for me to give from a financial perspective. Then I find myself begging the question: are her wants unreasonable, or are my abilities the real inadequacy? At least in my household, marriage does not seem destined to be a safe haven from the turmoil of the outside world one hopes for in the evenings. I am beginning to have great empathy for our uncle, who has endured for decades what I am now confronting. It may have been this very situation that has driven him to acquire so much material success.

Let's talk business for a while. I have noticed that the academic training of most business individuals has been restricted, particularly if they did not obtain a liberal arts education that have given them greater exposure to different disciplines. We are blessed with that wonderful double major in economics and business administration that allows us to reach across a discipline for an idea. Such a leap of insight does not appear within the common grasp of the typical business practitioner, given the constraints of their training, and provides us with an advantage.

I have drawn from economics the concept of elasticity in pricing, the idea that not all raw inputs (in this case different maturities of money) are equally sensitive to pricing changes, and it seems to appeal to their common sense. After my Alaskan experience with "the standard deviation" and executive management, I have found it best not to dwell on the math involved and instead to focus on the results. They allowed me to experiment on one product line initially, interest bearing checking deposits. Applying the concept of price elasticity, I have shown that this product is not as sensitive to adaptive pricing (percentage change in price divided by percentage change in volume, adjusted for seasonality and time) as other product categories. As a result of this proof, executive management has transferred all deposit pricing authority in Idaho to me (as was originally promised). The initial delivery of my "green sheets" for deposit interest rates will ultimately be updated via computer, but at the moment I am just pleased to have added a little logic to what in most financial institutions is simply a game of copying what the other local market players are doing. In our organization, I am trying to drive home the point that money is our raw material and that it should be managed as to obtain the lowest cost over time.

As a result of this contribution, my office now has a wet bar, but considering that I do not condone drinking at work; it is just an ornamental feature. Different organizations certainly have different cultural values. We had our bank Christmas party, and the bank reserved a large banquet hall, provided dinner and a live band and a great speech from the chairman expressing his appreciation for the efforts of the employees. I probably enjoyed the event more than most, for I could not help but reflect back on another bank Christmas party where pizza was the main course, drinks were up to the individual to find in the soda machine, and the setting was the office. Both banks are very successful, dominant in their markets, and treat their employees well. The difference is simply in the local cultures and what is accepted as normal and reasonable.

We have moved out of Boise proper to an outlying community, Mountain Home. My superiors had started calling me at home concerning business matters, and it did not appear proper to tell them I did not wish to be disturbed. By relocating some thirty miles or so, it is now a long-distance phone call for them to reach me, and they seem less willing to spend their personal funds for the communication and more willing to wait until the next day. It seems to more clearly separate work and home, well worth the commuting time involved. They appear to believe that whatever you give during the workday is not enough, and in this business it is assumed you will become involved in the ongoing affairs of the community.

To that end I have managed to get myself appointed to the local draft board. Although the draft is currently inactive, the process and registration by youths of age eighteen is still required. As I never obtained a student deferment from the draft, they deemed me suitable for the position. My superiors have now backed off a bit about the need for me to become even more involved in the community. You never know when the draft might be reactivated, and everyone is related to some young fellow who could use a friend on the draft board. I personally wish government service was mandatory for all youth, with their choice of joining the military or working as labor on the highways. Unlike our youth, a great many young people never work until they get out of college. The country would be better for the work commitment it would require of individuals, and I suspect many young folks would benefit as well.

You are correct; I may have failed to mention the mudflats and associated hazards. I also did not mention that the highway south has a tendency to be closed upon occasion during the winter due to avalanches, and that ships dock in Anchorage at high tide; but these are minor inconveniences. I really enjoy the Alaskan perspective, which makes Texans look modest; it truly is "The Great Land"! Down here, we plod along, prosperous but never proclaiming that we are "The Great Potato" or "Great Sugar Beet." Enjoy the winter.

Chapter XVI

Dear elder cousin,

You are correct about the attitudes in Alaska; everyone is generally new to the state, and there are few bounds of restraint to your efforts. I was both pleased and disheartened to hear of your change in marital status. Do you think you might expect too much out of an institution that is as much a tradition as a necessity? As you said, the lady treated you splendidly prior to tying the knot, so did you expect such treatment to continue indefinitely? It is my opinion that personal moments of happiness are of the rarest sort, to be remembered on cool winter evenings, like a fine brandy. Back at Knox, where women actually lived (compared to Alaska), my fondest recollection of a happy moment with the opposite gender actually occurred in a public place! At the end of winter term, I was enjoying a final meal with some of the usual crowd when I noticed an attractive young lady enter and sit at the far end of the table. I asked the person opposite me who she might be and was told she had been studying in the Middle East for a while and had now returned to campus. In a moment of ill-judged hubris, I wagered my friend that I could arrange a date for myself with such an attractive beauty before she left the table. Never have I regretted a wager so much or so often! I simply went down to the opposite end of the table, drew up a chair, and entered into a conversation. Have you ever had one of those moments when you don't notice if there are any others in the room, and time itself seems to just stand still? Well, for me it was the first time I had encountered the experience. Her conversation was absolutely perfect, with a diction and style that spoke of background far away from our hills. It was amazing that such a beauty also appeared to be equally blessed with such a sharp and insightful mind.

Prior to getting up from the table, I asked her for a date after we returned from spring break. When she answered in the affirmative, I felt like there were no other concerns in the entire world, and I departed, oblivious to the fact that I had actually made a wager on whether this would be a successful conversation. Just as I placed my meal tray in the proper spot and began to open the door, I heard a yell from the table across the cafeteria. The person that the wager had been made with had heard of the result of our conversation and had felt compelled to share the details with the entire table, including the young lady. Obviously, there was no future beyond that single conversation, and the entire affair had lasted scarcely fifteen minutes. Yet I was happy in that moment and daresay it will be remembered for a long time. Which, full circle, brings me back to the point of this historical flashback. It may be best to dwell on those rare moments of happiness, rather than have expectations of similar events in the present, or future. I would hope your spouse and you share some few such moments, but I believe it is best to count the blessings of those you already have experienced; pray countenance that providence provides a few more yet to come.

Back up here in the frozen north, another opportunity has arisen that will distance me from the unpleasant memories of the Petroleum Revenue Division. An opportunity occurred at the Alaska Power Authority, for they were in need of an economist. The power authority is a state agency that has been given the charter to pursue avenues that will lower the extremely high costs of electrical power in rural Alaska. Most electricity in remote areas is generated locally using diesel fuel as the power source. The lack of a road network to tie the far-flung population together causes substantial amounts of fuel to be shipped seasonally by water, or in the direst situations, by air during the winter. Our two largest cities, Anchorage and Fairbanks, are not even connected by any transmission line and rely on local energy sources for electrical generation. The Anchorage area generates electricity using natural gas as a fuel for the turbines, obtained under long term contracts from oil wells in the Cook Inlet area. The Fairbanks area uses coal-fired boilers to produce the power, using coal from a mine not far south of town.

The state of Alaska has had sufficient foresight to realize that the revenue coming from the North Slope oil will not last forever and has decided to use a portion of the oil revenues to develop long term, environmentally friendly power sources. In Alaska, environmentally friendly means hydroelectric power, which I would debate anywhere in the Lower Forty-Eight, but the extreme nature of our environment makes everything relative it seems. The focus of my efforts is to be on determining which projects yield the greatest benefits to the taxpayers. This is somewhat akin to your focus on the cost of capital for that company you worked with to obtain a rate increase. Only those projects which return the taxpayers a positive yield relative to the current situation can be justified by the power authority. The engineering challenge is created by the dramatic Alaskan seasons. A hydroelectric dam will need to capture sufficient water during the warm, wet seasons to produce power during the frozen part of the year when water runoff is greatly diminished from the surrounding watershed.

The current project of note is lovingly referred to as the Hells Canyon site. It is located approximately midway between Anchorage and Fairbanks. My position has permitted onsite observations, and the helicopter ride to the remote survey camp was a bit of a thrill. Beyond the fact that I had never ridden in a helicopter before, I was unprepared for the initial landing site. The pilot took us down, we landed on the frozen river (I noticed the pilot kept the engine running and remained in the craft), and we all got out to survey the location. Next, we re-boarded the helicopter and traveled up over the canyon rim and stopped at the remote camp where most of the actual geology work is being done. There is no road to the site, and the expense of building one will be something only a wealthy state such as Alaska could even consider. It is my unofficial and off the record opinion that the combination of the remote site and extreme cost, even by Alaskan standards, of this project will forever prohibit development for the dam site.

The problem is the immense amount of natural gas that is sitting unused up on the North Slope. As the existing pipeline is only for petroleum, there is currently no way to transport the natural gas down to the two population centers to be used for electrical production. The apparent solution is for the State to use some of the current surplus to build an overly large natural gas pipeline down to Fairbanks for natural gas. Then when there is sufficient demand for natural gas in the Lower Forty-Eight to sustain the expense of a connecting pipeline, Alaska will have already predetermined its course by the construction of the first portion of it. However, everyone is focused on this hydroelectric dam dream as being environmentally friendly, so it is not for a public servant to rock this boat that has such a powerful financial engine at present. I am learning that when folks actually want my opinion, they will ask for it, and that the political types would rather economists speak only when spoken to. It seems that life never changes, only the authority figures one has to deal with daily.

However, I have stumbled on an economic rationale which will permit my full support for this project without any ill impact upon my conscience. As the most assured benefit of the project will be the construction of a power transmission line between Anchorage and Fairbanks, I have no qualms about signing off as a stanch advocate. The Alaskan spirit of self-reliance does not readily produce feelings of need to ship electric power off elsewhere, or to purchase it from another source. Yet the dam project will permit both cities to obtain something that is in the self interest of each, a more reliable power supply, through the construction of the power line to transmit power from the dam to both cities. From the political perspective the power line is just an afterthought; as it is hardly a grand project on the scale that Alaskans now wish to think. The economic perspective is rather different, for the power line is scheduled to be constructed first, followed by the dam.

The power line will provide each city with an alternative source of electricity, and going forward the fuels of natural gas in Cook Inlet and coal in Fairbanks will complement each other. Frankly, I can barely think about the environmental impacts of the aftermath of coal fired power generation on the pristine air of the Alaskan interior without putting pen to paper. Restraint is one of those things that does come gradually with age. I suppose that if an individual actually is fortunate to live long enough to reach retirement, and obtains sufficient retirement pensions, he may actually be able to speak his mind on the most important subjects with only modest fear of retaliation. This presumes that you are sufficiently fortunate to have a moderately intelligent mind left to speak upon the arrival at this intellectual nirvana of freedom and cash flow. I always try to remind myself that Jefferson penned that only the "pursuit of happiness" is deemed to be self-evident and never dared to broach the subject of the retention of such happiness as one might have at any given moment. I find this thought somewhat similar to guaranteeing a greyhound that he will always be able to pursue the elusive mechanical rabbit, without mentioning that only in the rarest of moments will he ever catch it.

So, I am publicly advocating the dam while privately knowing full well it most probably will never be built. If only we may manage to obtain construction of the connecting power line, it will be the beginning of a true south central Alaska Power Grid, and I believe that the marginal cost of power will be lower for both cities over the long run.

I really enjoyed your description of the Boise River Valley and the impact of irrigation. It would seem that living in such an oasis clearly shows the boundaries created by effort and the desolation which exists only slightly beyond where those efforts cease. It would appear very motivating to live close to the boundary where the visual perception of civilization ends, and the need to persevere is so self-evident. Okay, it would appear you have found the economic equivalent of Alaska in a remote corner of the Lower Forty-Eight! About all the motivation we need up here is to look outside at the snow, the mountains, and the cold, and it is quickly realized how thin a line we walk in this environment.

I find that the entire issue of materiality tends to be lost in the context of the Alaskan experience. Often new arrivals seem to focus on getting everything from float planes to fishing gear without regard for how long their jobs may last up here. For that reason, there seems to be a healthy market in used goods, when folks decide to head back south. The current scandal in state government concerns two wives of state employees who decided they had experienced more than enough of the frozen north, packed up two vehicles, and drove out over the Alcan Highway together. I believe they did leave appropriate notes in their respective kitchens. So you see, there can be far worse events than to be momentarily unhappy in your marital bliss. Try to imagine being left abruptly, without any warning whatsoever; by the individual you have trusted most in your life. These two fellows both look like they have been hit by a truck, emotionally speaking.

From your ongoing description of American business, the public sector does not look all that bad as a place of employment. It even permits one the illusion that we are providing a service to the general population. In your situation the group of corporate migrant workers to which you belong might be divided into two groups, hired guns and friends of management (FOMs). I am afraid that you fall under the category of a hired gun. I would suggest that when dealing with FOMs, steadfast support of their efforts is advised until you become financially independent. I would wager that one close friendship with a chairman has more internal value in any corporation than anything you learned connected with that MBA. As a hired gun, your designated function is to produce results within a narrow specialty. Generally, I imagine you will always be viewed as an outsider who can be replaced by another hired gun without substantial disruption to the informal, personal relationship network that exists within upper management ranks. The expansion of your hired gun status beyond your designated specialty (the very reason you were hired) would require widespread recognition of your abilities outside of the realm of your designated expertise. I believe that it is unlikely that any senior manager will knowingly open the door to a broader function for you. Guess what, cousin? I believe state government works much the same way.

I would suggest we both chart a course to higher visibility through the use of memos not only to our direct superiors but to theirs. In this way, we may claim we are trying to gain visibility for our managers who have led us to the proper course while at the same time gaining personal recognition for our efforts. I would suggest that the first memo be something so straightforward there can be no argument over the implementation of the idea. Then proceed to implement the idea as if approval has been granted. Either individual will presume initially that the other has given approval. I believe that success will create great forbearance for your sin. Please understand that such a course of action will put either of our careers at risk, but working in the bowels of either organization does not present any scenic view at present. I believe the American spirit prevents any gift of territory, in government or business, but rather than seize what you can best accomplish is perhaps the most unsettling aspect of success in our so-called civil society. I definitely do not remember any of this perspective being discussed in the old academic coursework.

Alyeska! The very name has such a ring to it, it sounds most Alaskan. I finally made it down to the ski resort southeast of Anchorage that goes by that name. The drive down Turnagain Arm of Cook Inlet is worth the trip alone, for it surely is a fair approximation of a fiord. I can believe Captain Cook most assuredly did think that he had found the fabled Northwest Passage at this point. He must have been extremely disappointed when he had to turn around again, giving the fiord its name. The resort is very nice, but as I have never been to any other ski resort, who am I to say for sure? I took the lift up to the lodge on the side of the mountain and the view of the ocean (Turnagain Arm) is something to see. As for the skiing, I never made it off of the beginners slope. It seems such an expensive hobby. It is about the same thrill we used to get skating as kids, but in a public setting. I did enjoy the jade carving facility that is adjacent to the ski resort and purchased a set of jade bookends. I could not help but remember those genuine calcite formation chips that I used to sell to the tourists in the hills and somehow feel that I have now been on the other end of the transaction. At least the jade is more attractive than the rocks we sold. Take care, cousin, and remember, even if you are in the Lower Forty-Eight, you are still on the "outside" in that town!

Chapter XVII

Dear younger cousin,

Of course, you are correct in your insight that happiness in the moment is not material in the larger scheme of things. I arrived at that belief independent of your suggestion, but your confirmation of the thought is most appreciated. To address the cash flow perspective, I have sought part-time employment. From a career perspective, this choice of actions borders insanity, for it removes precious time that might be given to thoughts on how to better the profits of the bank and at the same time improve my full time position. Instead, my spare time now goes into thinking about my part-time job. The idea is to produce a significant and material portion of what cash flow will no longer exist when my spouse takes whatever leave is necessary to have a child. Her focus is still on that idea, and I do not believe she can be dissuaded. The need in marriage is to support each other's goals and objectives without doing irreparable harm to the feelings of the other individual (it is far easier said than done).

Remember when my church back in Harrison, the United Methodist Church, blew up after I had gone off to college? Growing up in that church, it was always something that seemed so large (two stories) and formidable, I had presumed there was no risk of it disappearing. Yet according to what was said, sufficient natural gas accumulated in the building from a leak, a mere accidental spark was all that was necessary to basically level the building. It does not matter whether the accidental spark or the small gas leak was to blame; it is the incident that dominates my thoughts. No, I do not believe in signs or guideposts from a higher level. The point of this illustration is that I believe most marriages are very much like that formidable church building. While they appear incredibly stable from any outward inspection, the reality is, it may take but a single spark to destroy the most valued of all creations, a lasting and intimate relationship. For that end, it appears best to place the immediate creation of cash flow over the obvious long term advantages of creating lasting values for my employer. It appears that cash flow will be necessary to preserve the continuity of the marriage, but remember that is only my appraisal and that my partner may have an entirely different perspective. Finally, I always remember that the corner where the church once stood so formidably, only a block from Central Elementary, is still vacant today. Another reminder of how difficult it is to replace a structure that was so visible a sign of faith in the downtown area. I imagine marriages are much the same: difficult to replace, and most likely only through relocation to a more promising area due to the emotional wreckage left in their wake.

As you may have guessed, my new part-time job is teaching. My initial course was at Boise State University at their campus in downtown Boise. It is located within a half mile of where I park to work at the bank, and the course was near the noon hour, so my lunch was spent speaking in a classroom. My boss is really open-minded about these efforts and very supportive, probably due to his academic background and the fact that it may loosely be thought of as community involvement. The first day I reported to the assigned classroom, expecting something similar to my Alaskan college teaching experience. When I opened the door, it appeared as if I was in an auditorium! It even had a stage down at the front. In these situations, one simply goes on and adjusts expectations to reality. Whereas in Alaska, a class of forty would have been considered large and would have been a challenge to learn and remember individual student names, this would be a very different experience. There were nearly one hundred students signed up for the class, and the room was not even half full. I was accustomed to having students ask questions in class and having the time to answer them in full. In this setting, with the sheer number involved, the class became mainly a lecture. Although I tried to field questions, for the interaction with the student is the entertainment of teaching, in this setting I had to severely limit the interaction in order to finish the class in the required fifty minutes.

The students seemed to enjoy the course, so I am now teaching at Mountain Home Air Force Base. The class sizes are much more to my liking, usually thirty or less. By sheer luck, I have an advantage over most other potential instructors in getting assignments to teach out on the base. I reside in Mountain Home, with my house being less than ten miles from the classroom. The university saves having to pay mileage money that they would have to pay instructors driving out from Boise (a forty-five-minute drive from the base in the best driving conditions). For me, the extra miles are only the short round trip from Mountain Home to the base.

To produce the extra cash flow, I am now teaching nightly, Monday through Thursday. The courses start at 7:00 PM and end at 9:00 PM, with each class meeting twice weekly. In this manner, I can teach two classes, with one meeting on Monday and Wednesday, while the other meets on Tuesday and Thursday. The only negative to this arrangement is that I must prepare for the next night's class when I get back home each night, so it makes for some late evenings and also destroys Sunday nights in preparation for Monday classes. The victory in this madness is that I still apparently have sufficient energy to get my real job done during the day, and I believe that enough cash flow can be produced to support this quest called marriage. The college classes that are taught on the base are located in modular classrooms located not too far from the end of the runway. It takes a little getting accustomed to simply ceasing to talk when an F-111 cuts in its afterburner as it takes off. You certainly can not say that I ever seem to teach in a traditional college setting!

The insanity of my decision is that I am unable to have sufficient time or energy to devote to such study that might further my career, so I have probably reached a plateau for a while. From a marital perspective, however, it is most reasonable in that it supports the efforts of my partner and also provides me with such personal space that my focus is not on happiness but on getting something accomplished. I probably do not make the best of husbands. Do you ever notice that while we require training, experience, and testing to proceed with almost everything else in our society, for marriage the only requirement is sufficient cash for a license and you are granted immediate access to what may be the ultimate life-altering experience? I have adopted the loft overlooking the living room as my home office, complete with desk, typewriter, and chair. The living room has a ceiling of almost eighteen feet on the side where the loft joins it and a small spiral staircase going up to the loft, one upstairs bedroom and a bath. The master suite is downstairs, and this home actually has a garage!

If you have time on a weekend in Anchorage, there is a small native cemetery off the west side of the highway going north to Palmer. If you find a small Russian Orthodox Church, you are in the right spot. The interesting thing about the cemetery is the small burial houses over each permanent resident in the cemetery. I am unsure whether this is a native custom that was adopted by the church in the conversion of the locals, or a necessity given the probability of frozen ground when many deaths occurred. At any rate it is an interesting side trip. I always marveled at the insight of the Russians, in allowing the natives to retain their language and translating the Bible into the local tongue. It is certainly a contrast to our approach of sending the native inhabitants of the Lower Forty-Eight to schools where they were solely instructed in English. I know it must pain the Russians to this day that the largest Christian Church in the world, and by all rights what should have been their equivalent of the Vatican, is now the largest Mosque in the world. Without an understanding of the Russian history of relentless opposition to those from the East and South, who continually tried to seize lands, people, and change their religions, I do not suppose it will ever be possible for the typical American to understand their distrust for the outside world. In a real sense they have an Alaskan perspective, a sense of distrust that is not at all dissimilar to that of hill folks back home. Okay, you are correct; our liberal arts education leads thoughts far afield, and for what purpose but reflection!

My spouse enjoys visiting relatives in the Midwest for vacations with her family, but I do not choose to use scarce vacation time in such a manner. I offered to meet her at any city in the country for a day and night at the end of her vacation, but she indicated that she did not choose to use her time that way either. So I have adopted a new strategy to have independent vacations and have someone else pay for them. I had never been to Boston on pleasure, and I have often wanted to see the historical sights, but financing such a venture never seemed reasonable. So, I sent résumés to Boston commercial banks inquiring whether they would be interested in my employment. A large bank in downtown Boston responded and asked me to fly out for an interview (at their expense) to discuss my ideas on asset/liability management. I flew out early on a Friday and had meetings with the bank management for the remainder of the day, which was capped with a fine meal at the Harvard Club. I was unprepared for driving the narrow downtown streets, and for seeing how old everything back east appears. Anyway, they seemed to enjoy my intellectual perspective to managing interest rate risk and put me up in the Meridian Hotel for the night (top floor, corner no less). This country boy was impressed with the electric curtains; I guess my background will always show; it cannot be helped. The next day, I drove up the coast to Maine—the churches are really the most interesting thing to see—and it is apparent that the area has been prosperous for a long time. The next day I flew back to Boise and thought the experience was over.

In less than a week, I received another call from the same bank in Boston, and they wanted to know if I had time to come back to talk to them again about employment possibilities. Of course, I could not turn down such an idea, and the same basic course of events occurred again. I thought it was a reasonably fair trade for them. I brought new ideas on risk management from the west, and they provided me with an opportunity to enjoy the sights of the east. Frankly, after I drove in the congested traffic and saw the expense of living there, I would never have accepted employment regardless of the money involved. I enjoy the wide-open spaces of the rural settings and value them above the money the east has to offer. As a result of this venture, I believe I have found a means to an annual vacation, at little or no expense (as long as I have a new idea to sell).

I have a great fellow working for me as our financial analyst officer. He is almost twenty years my senior and has the most patience I have ever encountered in my business dealings. In most situations, he knows more than either I or executive management but is always respectful and listens as if he actually needs the instructions or suggestions being offered. I doubt that twenty years hence I will have the internal fortitude necessary to listen to either those considerably younger or older than me with the patience he displays.

Have I mentioned that our boardroom is on the twentieth floor and is the only floor without windows? I always think it is indicative of how difficult it is to be invited into that room. Our uncle is putting up a new tractor barn back on the farm, concrete floor and all. However, he is not taking down the old barn, so the place may look somewhat cluttered. He called and revealed that he had cracked the engine block on grandfather's old tractor and actually asked what I wanted him to do. I suggested he might want to replace the tractor; it seems so strange talking about personal responsibilities with our elders. He has arranged for one of our cousin's grandfather's nephew's son and his wife to bale hay for him. It seems that he really is settling into his retirement as a farmer. We know that it will be a constant adjustment from a life of politics and business. My father is also adjusting to life without my mother, but the adjustment process seems to be very stressful for him. My mother was truly what he had built his life around, and without her, he seems to continually need to search for ways to fill his days.

Take care in the far north, and if time permits, try to find that old cemetery I mentioned. However, I would suggest that one ocean fishing experience in a bass boat is sufficient. You did not mention Mendenhall Glacier just outside of Juneau, but I hope you had an opportunity to see it.

Chapter XVIII

Dear elder cousin,

I do not envy you the corporate or family position in which you are now burdened, but I do confess that your monetary success draws my attention. My six-month period of being acting controller of Alaska Pacific University has drawn to a close, and I will sorely miss being paid for two full-time jobs. Even in Alaska, such opportunities do not come along very often.

The economy up here is definitely suffering the aftershock of the ending of the pipeline construction and the declining population associated with the fewer available jobs. The university president seems to have managed to get the school back on track, but it is a small shadow of its former self. He has done wonders in fundraising to cover operating expenses, and I would hope that someday the university looks back and acknowledges the contribution he has made at a critical time for them. They now have a full-time controller and a real accounting department to keep the books for the university, so any need for my services has ended.

From your description, it appears that in corporate life, all that matters is the immediate value of your contribution. Over here on the other side, it seems that the production of routine reports, the regular analysis, and the expected performance of duties is all that is required. At quitting time each day it is almost like watching the salmon rushing upstream, while I notice the private sector individuals working past normal hours. Of course, my compensation will never be anywhere near what you may earn in the private sector, but the choice is a matter of priorities. Our normal workday ends at 4:30 PM sharp.

Yes, I located the old cemetery you described, and it is more than a little bit different. The key is to understand that the reverence for the deceased is shown differently in different cultures, but the one thing that seems to be consistent is a desire to honor their place of final resting. This seems to be common from Christian to Muslim to almost any religion that preserves the body intact. One day, this old cemetery may well become a tourist attraction, just as I imagine ours will be someday in the Lower Forty-Eight. I made it up to Palmer to see the Alaska State Fair and it was the most enjoyable state fair I have ever attended. The rodeo featured yaks, which do not buck so much as they spin and simply hurl the rider off with centrifugal force. There was one building with a long line, and I was most surprised to find out it was the "vegetable building." It seems that our long Alaskan days during the summer do some remarkable things to the size of vegetables. In particular, cabbage seems to get unusually large, but so do a lot of the other vegetables. Can you imagine anyone getting into a line for a vegetable building at a state fair back home? It is probably something they need to put in the tourist information for Alaska. They always have the fair over Labor Day weekend at the end of the summer.

We may have a slight divergence in our perspectives on the family enterprise, which we might as well discuss. I well may be a conservationist in a somewhat unusual way. I believe your long-term viewpoint may be more of a commercial or developmental nature. When you look out at Alaska, you realize the value of open spaces and the feelings that immense space can invoke in the human nature. I do not approve of simply locking great spaces away and pretending such actions will protect them forever. Even the greatest of human governments, such as Rome, rarely last more than a few hundred years before they change so much that the original purpose is lost. Could the Roman Senate have foreseen the change to a dictatorship a hundred years before the fact? I do not believe such vision is common within our kindred.

Yet our government locks up vast resources in Alaska and tells the common folk they will be preserved forever. What will happen after America is no longer part of the world of governments? I fear almost assuredly that the next government will not hold such a high respect for the environment. Would it not be better, as environmental Americans, to develop the economic resources of the land now while we have a government that will hold the developers to task if the land is not returned to its natural state after the resources have been removed? As you may be thinking, I might have difficulty in the private sector. But the point of this discussion is, what might be the long-term purpose of the family farm? I am well aware that in the capitalistic system, the long-term purpose of everything seems to be the sale of it to another party. The purchaser always sees some greater economic possibility than the buyer, or is forced to sell for economic reason of distress or other personal factors. In our case, the family farm now encompasses more than a square mile (albeit without the luxury of road frontage). Could we discuss a little bit what our long-term goals might be for the family assets?

From my perspective, the farm holds at least the possibility of being self-sustaining. I believe it might be managed so as to require little input of scarce monetary resources. Presently, it is about half timber and half pasture, along with all the creeks and water.

Our grandfather cut all the hardwood with a diameter of greater than eight inches from the land when you were about sixteen years old. However, he did plant some pine trees before he passed on, and they grow so much faster than hardwood. The pasture was previously cotton fields, and I am aware that the fertility of the fields was negatively impacted by a half century of cotton farming. On the positive side, grandfather did establish reasonably decent grass for the raising of cattle. In a sense, he diversified into cattle and tree farming in his retirement years and no longer needed all the hired help. He even tore down the old house down by the front gate, near the Ricket house, which he previously had used to house the hired help. The question would seem is it feasible from an economic perspective to use the farm as a retirement locale, and expect it to produce enough cash flow to support itself? Or conversely, is the primary family asset simply a large money hole, which will consume any who dares take on the task?

From an environmental perspective, I believe there is value in simply maintaining private ownership to limit public access to the land. As Arkansas has no rural zoning whatsoever, there is nothing to prevent someone from putting in anything from a church to a shooting range in so close proximity to the property line on any side of the farm that the overall value of the property would be greatly diminished. Once such usage begins, it is almost impossible to change the property back to a natural state. In the short and perhaps medium term, I believe our mutual interests are in agreement. The acquisition of any land that becomes available between the family farm and the three roads that surround it both preserves the environmental issue which I am most interested in and enhances the long-term commercial value in the back of your thoughts. It is in the long term I believe that perhaps we shall have some conflict.

I can only think of what excitement there must have been on the place when they drilled that oil well back in the '50s, before my time. It is my understanding that although they struck oil; it was not in commercial quantities. On the positive side, if they had found sufficient oil for development, none of the land surrounding the family farm probably would be available for sale during our lifetimes.

Did I tell you the location of our offices for the Alaska Power Authority? They are downtown on Third Street on the third floor of an office building that houses a post office facility on the ground floor, retail space on the side facing Third Street, and our offices up on the third floor. On a clear day, we can see Mount McKinley to the north. They say this was once the downtown location of a department store, before the big earthquake back in the '60s. Apparently, the site of our offices dropped more than ten feet, and all the existing property on the site was destroyed. I have noted that your old downtown bank office is close to my present location. Did you ever notice the lack of focus on Earthquake Park as a tourist attraction when you were up here? There is a parking area and a sign indicating that hundreds of homes were destroyed, but not much else. To me it looks like a wonderful location to focus on the temporary nature of the works of man, and the awesome power of nature. I believe such reflection is as much a part of the Alaskan experience as any of the standard tourists attractions and much more important in the context of our cultural perspective of conquering nature.

In your business environment, how do you cope with the constancy of change? If the purpose of any business is to build it up to such a degree that there is an economic profit, and not merely a financial one, from the sale of it, how do you reconcile that with the need for thirty year mortgages to procure housing and other personal commitments. I see the vast majority of business workers concentrating on doing something which will one day leave them unemployed, if they do it well. Does not the business owe the employee at least some acknowledgement of the probable destruction of their job at some time in the future, so that the employee could plan for it financially? Instead, I see employees who seem to believe that their job or one similar to it, will be available forever and go about their lives incurring debts and spending money as if the highest year of their earnings will be the year they turn age sixty-five. Even our religious leaders do not hesitate to ask for a tithe from individuals who already are forced to give a third of their hard earned wages to the government (either in the form of income, sales, or social security taxes). Out of the remainder it does not appear reasonable to expect anyone to save sufficiently for retirement and maintain the illusion of the American way of life. Write when you have time, and please respond to the issue of the farm!

Chapter XIX

Dear younger cousin,

Yes, I have been aware for a considerable amount of time concerning our different perspectives on the long term use of family assets. First, let me remind you that the last two times the family held onto fixed assets such as land and buildings for more than a century, all was lost. Either through war or national financial calamity the work, investment and sacrifice of generations vanished. In both cases, our family ended up either on the losing side of the war or in the financial backwaters deemed unsalvageable by the monetary authorities. By the time we both reach retirement age, the family will once again be nearing the century mark on an investment in fixed assets that have required generations of commitment. The obvious question is, "Are we feeling luckier than our predecessors?" I would argue that in the past the major error in the investment strategy has been the concentration of assets within one country, which has tied the future of the family solely to the whims of a specific government and culture. Successful international families have fixed assets spread across international borders, to diversify their interests and reduce the risks which have set us back time and again.

Further, there is the matter of the next generation and ones after that. Do we owe to them what has been preserved for our generation? Or do we succumb to this culture of individuality and view ourselves as the end of the chain? To some extent, I expect the answer to this question will be made by the next generation and whether they share the same values of education, honor, and family which have been passed on to us. So, in the immediate answer to your question, as that British economist said, "In the long run, we are all dead," so I see no need to address the issue in depth at this time. However, I believe the strategy of land acquisition, with eventual investment beyond our borders is the best long term strategy. The immediate concern on this end is not so much how to invest, but rather how best to take the declining state of my health into consideration. It is not of immediate concern, but I can foresee that it will be increasingly challenging for this body to be committed to what has become a traditional seventy-plus-hour week with the combination of full time and part time employment. It is this commitment to the unending endeavor of work which is creating the economic surplus in my life, not the specific rewards of any single employer. I doubt if the regiment is sustainable for more than a decade.

My marriage has ended, an emotionally wrenching experience, and most probably the blame may be laid at my feet. I simply do not believe it is possible for one person to make another person happy! The sense of happiness in the moment is either in the person or they are doomed to a lifetime of endless searching beyond themselves for what must be found within. I am blessed with the ability to perceive happiness in almost any setting where personal freedom and the ability to contemplate alternatives exist. Too late did I understand that this is apparently not a normal human condition and that the endless searching is more the norm. My ex-spouse has decided to condition her search elsewhere in her native Idaho, and I wish her the best in achieving what she may be seeking. For me, it is yet another learning experience that stresses my imperfections in this environment and the difficulty in intimate relationships when expectations differ on future plans and ideas. I would argue that the over whelming majority of individuals plan, if they do plan at all, simply for the next month or year; not the decades in advance which has been prevalent in our family.

Yes, I am still with the commercial bank, but there appears little chance for significant advancement and boredom reigns supreme. Brace yourself, on the side I have purchased a movie theatre. A family member suggested that the frustration of a career plateau might be relieved through the pursuit of an outside interest. I believe they were actually thinking along the lines of a hobby, but I tend to think always of cash flow. With that thought, I bought an entire theatre operation, the building, equipment and supplies. The total was less expensive than some individuals spend on autos, women, or drink, so I do not feel guilty about the venture. The pleasure I am getting from this theatre is determining how to turn a money losing enterprise, located about an hour from Boise, into the center of traffic for an acceptable number of cash carrying customers.

I believe in all business ventures it is most profitable to serve either the very wealthy or the very poor. To serve the poor seemed most reasonable, as the movie theatre is located in an old building in a poor community. There does not seem to be any means to serve the wealthy in such a setting (the building is more than a hundred years old and was once a vaudeville house). A narrow market focus appeared best, to serve those who can not access the products or services they desire because of distance or other obstacles. I needed to do more than simply improve, in a marginal way, the existing services and products offered. Marginal improvement only gains temporary market share benefits, until your competitor does your improvement one better. That is simply a long term losing game with little day to day pleasure, as any market is simply filled with predatory competitors looking to copy what you offer. The game then is to fit the new investment to an entirely new market segment which has not been served. Due to financial constraints, I am initially unable to upgrade the facility and such drawbacks as only one restroom to serve both genders will need to be used in their present condition for a while. The building has a usable balcony, with total seating in the building nearing three hundred. What passes for an air conditioner is really just a huge fan that blows air over a mat with water dripping down through it. Due to the dry desert climate, this type of arrangement will cool the building down about twenty degrees from the outside temperature.

In Idaho, large numbers of migrant workers arrive each March and April to do the manual work in the potato and sugar beet fields. The moving of irrigation pipe is hot, dirty work (which must be done twice daily), and the employees are a mix of legal and illegal migrants of Mexican descent. Some of the workers have become supervisors and permanent residents in the area with their families. It occurred to me, while driving past a migrant labor camp, that the required underserved market clearly existed and was a segmented portion distinct from the total population of the area. Societal and language barriers are unfairly preventing these people from having equal opportunity and access to recreational avenues open to the general population. In addition, although discrimination is said not to exist, speaking as an individual who shares the flaming red hair of our family heritage, I am very aware that large numbers of the population just do not like individuals who appear differently than their own clan. Given full consideration to all these factors, I made the decision to change the movie theatre from showing American films and serving a largely disinterested local population into an entirely Mexican movie theatre operation.

Although you, among many, have accused me of living in my own world, I am aware that this move will concentrate hundreds of the minority population in one downtown location of a small rural community, will not endear me to the Anglo population of the area. However, I have never played the popularity game well anyway, and I believe any venture that is in the public interest will succeed if it finds its market. As long as I adhere to all laws, regulations, and maintain a decent facility for family entertainment, I believe the locals will simply keep their distance from me.

The location of suppliers for Spanish language films was done through a search of telephone directories for Los Angles and Denver, which I found in the Boise State University library. The selection of two vendors was intentional, to avoid becoming totally dependent on any single supplier. I believe it is best to promote the wellbeing of several individuals or companies that you depend on in business. Dependence on any single entity risks the loss of all profits to unconscionable greed if the vendor believes there are no limits to pricing. Do you believe there is the same risk in personal relationships? I have made arrangements to ship film by bus, the lowest cost option, with my location being the last in the nation where most Mexican films will be shown. Being last is of no disadvantage, as my clients have no means to view the films any earlier.

Whereas the distributor of an English speaking movie requires at least a 70 percent cut of the ticket price for a small town operator, being the end of the line in the Mexican movie exhibitor business is enabling me to only pay the distributor 35 percent of the ticket (net of advertising expense). Of course sales taxes must still be paid. You see that a Mexican movie theatre can throw off twice the gross operating income from the same number of customers as an English-speaking theatre, just from the lower percentage of the gross revenue that must be paid to the distributor. I have also used the tack of pleading poverty when conversing with suppliers, which, considering the theatre has been purchased rather than upgrading my old auto or home furniture, is a pretty fair representation of reality.

To advertise among the labor camps and various locations where the clientele dwell appeared to be an insurmountable hassle at first. Then a more direct route was developed by using a one hour Sunday morning radio show, which is broadcast entirely in Spanish. They feature the schedule of the Mexican movies for the week. The key has been to target marketing only to my audience, delivering the full value of my message to the most likely group to purchase the entertainment. The less visibility my endeavor has among the Anglo population segment, the less likely there will be any backlash. Sunday morning is also the most economical time to purchase radio spots in this market, and you can often sponsor a small show built around the market you are targeting.

Exactly when to run the business was a bit of a quandary, due to my full-time employment at the bank and evening employment teaching for the university. You must, of course, time the hours of operation to when it will be most convenient for the target population to travel to the theatre. I believe too many business persons select the traditional hours for a business, when the world has become a very non-traditional place. In the movie business the norm has been to have evening shows in small town theatres. The migrant clientele was charged with moving the irrigation pipes every twelve hours, so the mornings and early evenings were their prime working hours and when they were least likely to be available for recreation. The solution was a midday double feature at noon on weekends, which has brought the Spanish-speaking population to town in large numbers. The theatre seats almost three hundred and is fully utilized. The customary visit by the local police chief occurred to determine that I was not overcrowding the building in relation to fire codes. In addition, someone had told him I was showing racy films, so I simply invited him to stand in the back and watch an entire feature to prove the decency of the offerings.

The operating hours strategy is the opposite of many businesses, who extend their hours throughout the week to try to attract all possible clientele, since they really do not have anything unique to provide their customers. As such, most American retail businesses are really in the commodity business, where they compete on convenience and price. I have no desire to enter that arena, as I see entirely too much of it in banking, and even the bankers do not seem to understand. My strategy of offering a unique product in my market, with limited hours, sharply reduces the variable expense of doing business and pushes revenue into the smallest time period possible.

The idea of a double feature is to increase cash flow. During the intermission, the concession area is packed. Placement of a fan to blow the popcorn smell out into the theatre also helps sales. I had never fully realized that popcorn has been the real blessing given to theatre owners. After calculating the fully loaded cost of a small popcorn bag (about a nickel), which sells for a dollar, or the cost of a retail two dollar bag (only a dime), it just makes intermission the best part of the weekend. Well, I guess you may tell the family that I now have a hobby and truly wish there would be a means to transform it into a long-term business opportunity. Yes, I know, for this it took an MBA! Note the difference in my little operation (single screen) Spanish house, and the typical multiplex that passes for a business today with its many screens. The single screen specialty theatre is structured to assist the customer in leaving every possible dollar in the theatre while providing an entertainment experience for the guest. The modern multiplex functions by focusing on maximum customer throughput (the largest number of customers that can be funneled through the facility). Next time you enter one of these businesses, tell me I am wrong; it reeks of efficiency, not a place of entertainment.

Of course, it is most efficient to place the concession area immediately inside the lobby, so merchandise is sold prior to the usher stubbing the tickets and entering a viewing room. Note that viewing room is more appropriate than theatre, a word which traditionally connotes a dramatic setting. I could sell tickets to my balcony just for the view of the theatre. By the time the customer enters the multiplex viewing room, it is a real hike back to a concession area for any impulse purchases. To compound the problem, the ushers commonly ask to see the poor customer's ticket stub to regain admittance to the viewing area. Pity the poor customer trying to part with his coinage, for the efficiency experts have made the experience into a challenge unsuitable for a pleasurable evening.

To add to the insult, and give proof the modern designer never operated a house of motion picture entertainment, the new structures are often built so that the departing customer exits the building without directly passing the concession area, and thus another sales opportunity is missed. I believe the design is most suitable for efficiency but not for maximizing the shareholders' wealth. To place the customer in front of the concession stand in some manner during the departure phase is to invite lingering, and a customer who extends his stay just a minute is one increasingly likely to spend his hard-earned dollar. It is my opinion that the wealth of efficiency experts exists only such that it is wrung from unknowing theatre owners, not from the theatre guests. I would design the operation so three quarters of the concession area was assessable by arriving customers and one quarter available to departing customers. As you may have guessed, I enjoy running a small business far more than being a cog in a large American corporation. I hope that I responded adequately to your questions on my long-term intentions with the family farm. Please let me know if you disagree on any matter of mutual concern. Be happy in the moment!

Chapter XX

Dear elder cousin,

Frost heaves dead ahead and I dare to mention personal matters, subjects we rarely discuss. One of the Alaskan things which you failed to mention prior to my arrival in "The Great Land" was frost heaves. I now understand the reason you never see anyone rational speeding down Alaskan highways is the hidden phenomenon of frost heaves. Due to the wild temperature swings we experience, during the warmer parts of the year, substantial sections of the roads simply subside by two to four inches as the ground underneath thaws. So for the newcomer, the empty roads appear as an invitation to speed, but the resident knows better. To come upon one of these frost heaves at much more than fifty-five mph simply invites losing vehicle control. So the frost heaves are most dangerous to those who do not see them but are instead focusing on the natural beauty of all that surrounds them. I believe you are heading toward a frost heave, and I should cross over into the areas of personal discussions to bring it to your attention.

Your last letter was great and deadly sad at the same time. Never have I heard you speak with such enthusiasm about banking as you did about your new little sideline of the Mexican movie theatre. It is wonderful that you have found something you actually enjoy. I would suggest it is not so much the Mexican movie business but the opportunity to actually make decisions and have an immediate impact. Yes, I know you make daily interest rate decisions, but these are intangible and have no immediate impact on your compensation. It also goes back to our family, where we will be the junior generation until midlife, and the elder generation makes all the decisions and does not request or accept input often. In our work lives, we serve the larger organizational structure, one public and the other private, and likewise have little or no actual control.

Do you remember when you were in college and always worked forty to fifty hours per week, in addition to carrying the normal course load while pretending to be a "normal" student? The reason for that particular course of action was to raise the necessary cash flow to maintain college expenses. We both know you overdid it and enjoyed the radio work far more than you would care to admit. Was it really necessary to work so hard that you were able to buy yourself diamonds? Or conversely, would life have been more stable to have worked less without cash flow required to acquire gemstones? Or, if you really felt such work hours were a must, would not the funds have been better deployed in the avoidance of college debt rather than conspicuous consumption of luxury items on even rare occasions?

You appear to have recreated your college experience in working not just one full-time job (the bank) but effectively creating another full-time job through the combination of teaching four nights a week and weekends at your movie theatre. By doing so, you managed to probably cohabit with a spouse without actually living with her. Adding in the time it must take you to commute from that small town into Boise; I can hardly see how you managed to devote time to any family life whatsoever! Yes, I know I am certainly not one to talk as I have not experienced marriage. Somehow I must believe that when or if I am fortunate enough to find someone to wed, I will desire to spend time with that individual. You will say that these are the words of a novice; I can hear you at this moment! At the least, dare I say that less devotion to your "real" job may risk turning that career plateau into a permanent "endless plain." I would suggest "frost heaves" exist in many different shapes and forms, and they may still easily throw you off the road even if you are not in Alaska.

Up here in Alaska, women are difficult to locate, and when you think fate has finally blessed you, you may be surprised. I reside in a very nice apartment complex with two-story units until I can afford to purchase a residence. A young lady, blond and very attractive, moved into the next apartment. I had just about worked up the nerve to ask her for a date when the unexpected occurred. Our apartments share a bedroom wall, and I have always been aware that in apartments, it is necessary to hold the noise down if you desire any privacy. Staying at home on a Saturday night has become the norm, as the alternative of drinking it away at some bar is both dangerous and unseemly. While reading in my bedroom on a Saturday night, sounds started coming through the bedroom wall that were most personal and unusual. It seemed that the two individuals on the other side of the wall were the same gender (not mine). I simply retreated down to my living room and marked it up as another experience that would unlikely have occurred back in the hills. However, you see the dilemma; women are scarce up here already, and apparently some of the few who reside here do not really care for the opposite sex. Of course I am not naïve enough to not be aware of folks who have different tastes than I was accustomed to in the dating area, but it sure makes one a bit more humble when it is brought this close to home and you realize there may be far fewer dating choices than you previously thought.

I took the train over to Whittier on Prince William Sound to see the other side of the mountain. It was quite an experience, as you are allowed to drive your car onto the train at Portage. You remain in your vehicle while the train goes through the tunnels and across Bear Valley, to finally exit the tunnel at Whittier. It was a military base during WWII, and the highlight of the town of about three hundred souls is a fourteen-story building. It was built during WWII to house troops guarding the port facilities on the fjord in front of the town. The halls are a bit narrow, but I imagine that someday the condos in the facility will be quite the rage. It is close enough to Anchorage and with train access; I believe that someday it will be discovered as a private place to get away from the crowds. The ground around the town is pretty barren, but there is a scenic little creek just back behind town. The locals suggest you watch out for the bears if you venture up the hillside too far. The Alaska State Ferry runs out of Whittier to Valdez and you are allowed to drive your car onto the ferry for the trip. However, due to budgetary constraints, I simply drove back onto the next train and went back to Anchorage.

Have you heard about our uncle? He has discovered the conservation possibilities offered by the US government. Since we have allowed one of our cousins to attempt to grow wheat on the worn-out land for a number of years, it apparently qualifies for a set-aside program. He may be paid fifty dollars per acre for ten years to agree to not grow wheat on the land. I personally have no objections to his actions. Moreover, I recognize that if I did have objections, he would simply ignore them anyway. The acreage involved is relatively small, about forty. He will retain the income himself, but this management fee is so small it is not worth a family disagreement. I am still troubled by his impact. When our grandmother passed away, instead of a normal obituary focusing on the great contributions she made as a teacher, wife and mother, I shall never forget the heading over her obituary: "Mayor's Mother Dies." I believe our grandfather shared the same displeasure that I did, but this particular uncle is not one to bother. Our uncle still retains his position on the board of directors of a local bank and has the respect of the community (if not his father). It is therefore more prudent to simply watch and wait. Do you imagine that other families manage their affairs across generations as we do, or is more interaction between generations the norm? I might add that I believe that our mutual isolation from family and the friends of our youth due to the great distances and financial limitations places our decisions at risk, as we lack any semblance of guidance, or merely suggestions from others that we trust. Cousin, please watch out for those frost heaves, for they may occur in the workplace or the home, and it may be expensive and time consuming to get back on the road.

I have somewhat followed in your footsteps by accepting a teaching position on Elmendorf Air Force Base for an outside college. Whereas you taught for Golden Gate University, I am teaching for La Verne University. Okay, I know the name is somewhat questionable, but I checked on it and it actually exists in a place called La Verne, California. I checked on the Cave at the officers club you had mentioned, and things have changed. Apparently a new base chaplin has degreed that the young females dancing on Friday nights must wear some minimum of clothing. To that end (no pun intended), they are now wearing g-strings and pasties. So you can see that civilization is coming even to Alaska, if in a somewhat belated manner. I have ventured onto the golf course and poorly play the sport. It is easy to see how those who are fortunate enough to have been born into the country club set could really enjoy the sport if they took it up at an early age. As a working fellow, it appears likely I will never have the time or money (the combination is really critical) to focus on golf. In Alaska, the golf season is very short, and one green is directly under the approach path to the runway for the military jets.

Alaska Pacific University has also rehired me to update an appraisal of the value of the fixed assets of their campus. Yes, I know that I have never done an appraisal before, but the nice thing about Alaska is that the lack of experience does not seem to bar one from almost any experience if you are willing to give it a try. The campus was last appraised in 1975 by some outside appraisers, and the president has asked if I might update it from an economic perspective. As long as I focus on the changes in the general price levels for Anchorage real estate from 1975 to the present, and specify that it is to be used for internal university use only, I believe I can present a fair and accurate idea of the probable value of the campus. It is critical that I clearly indicate I am not a certified appraiser but am merely applying economic perspectives to a valuation problem for a consulting client. As the appraisal is not to be used for the sale of the property, but merely for review by an accreditation association, I believe I am on sound footing as long as the valuation is conservative. The previous appraisal was for $19.85 million for 290.5 acres of land and associated buildings. The challenge, of course, is that the land is zoned for educational purposes, and any purchaser of a part of it would most probably choose to seek commercial or residential zoning. Perhaps becoming a certified appraiser someday would be an option. Take care and bring me up-to-date on your changing personal situation.

I would also like to discuss mineral rights on the family property. When you were young, I believe there was one oil well drilled, but all that I know is that no development ever took place. Are the mineral rights leased out, or was it determined that no probable reserves existed? I can assure you that seismic testing has improved significantly over the past twenty-five years and that one dry well does not necessarily mean no resources exist.

Has our uncle replaced any of the cedar fence posts that Grandfather used to keep the cattle in, or do we still have a vintage hill farm? My memory is that the barbed wire was actually holding the cedar posts up and not vice versa. I cannot imagine the manual work it took to dig the holes to place miles of cedar fence posts into the ground. Even a small forty-acre field has sides that are each one quarter of a mile long, so the single field has a mile of fence around it. I still remember Grandfather swinging an ax at age eighty far better than I might today. He was such a rare gentleman to combine intelligence and physical ability. Once, when he had to go into the hospital in his 80s, he took great pleasure when the night nurse requested he remove his false teeth, and he simply stated such action would be impossible as he did not own any (all his teeth were still natural). I will always marvel that he also never needed glasses, either for reading or distance. When you grow up around such a person, you sometimes forget just how unusual he is in the general population. I trust we will be able to recreate something he would have been pleased with during our lifetimes. Of course, that presumes we will be able to outlive the interim generation and that they do not take any actions that we cannot later reverse to achieve the greater objective. I always remember our great-grandfather, who survived Gettysburg and the trip home, only to die in the middle of a field when struck by lightning. That single event set the family back by twenty years, as the next generation had to come of age alone and in an economically hostile environment of the latter half of the nineteenth century in the South. Guard your health, for it will surely take two of us to succeed!

Chapter XXI

Dear younger cousin,

Sound words of advice and many are they who would dare not broach them to an individual with a temperament such as mine! I have taken them to heart and to some extent refocused on my primary employer, the Boise bank. Since I have already had some success applying the elasticity principle to the pricing of bank deposits, I have dared apply simple math to yet another area. On the lending side of the bank, I noticed that loan officers seem to focus on the credit quality of the individual and do not consider the value of the assets used for collateral in consumer loans. As an example, an individual with solid credit might qualify for a $20,000 loan and the borrower might choose to use the funds for such divergent purposes as several motorcycles or a single car acquisition. It occurred to me to research the probability of foreclosure on different types of assets used for collateral. Individuals are far more likely to be willing to lose their toys than their cars. As you can imagine, management was surprised to learn that loans with motorcycle collateral were much more likely to suffer losses than loans for the traditional automobile. Sometimes when you obtain compensation to illustrate the obvious you feel a bit like that Missouri lad who avoided whitewashing that fence.

As a result of this endeavor, my star has risen again at the bank and I now have the added responsibility of setting pricing guidelines for different lending categories of consumer loans. Yes, it is obvious that loans used for collateral which suffer higher losses will also have higher guideline rates. I have added these guidelines to the so-called "green sheet," which is now available in the branches on computer terminals. In the corporate headquarters, the pricing sheet is still produced in hard copy for the benefit of executive management. Note that computers, even the new IBM personal variety are still looked down on by executive management, who seem to view them as being suitable only for assistants and analysts. Another development of this additional responsibility is that I now have an assistant. The changes have further clarified who is really responsible for managing the net interest margin in our institution. Obviously, if it becomes messed up, I will also be the one kicked out the door. So, I am trying to be a responsible corporate employee and continue to add value for our shareholders. Your comments on the permanence of change in my corporate life, which you made some time ago, are in the back of my thoughts. Too wide a net interest margin and the net income grows too quickly and the risk of a set-back is increased. Too slow an increase, or even worst, a decrease and the risk of being replaced is heightened. So yes, it is insane to plan a proper life around thirty-year mortgages, marriage, and the responsibilities of children when you can not even guarantee that the job will be there next month to provide cash flow. The odd thing is that everyone seems to act as if the risk is nonexistent; the presumption being that you will always be able to provide for family and self in the style you wish.

I was thinking back on that funeral with the runaway hearse some years back. It was at this service that I first learned that pastors expect to be paid (cash in an unmarked envelope) for presiding at a funeral for a member of their flock. I was and am still so shocked at this custom that I wonder if a vow of poverty might be best for Protestant pastors. As an economist, you probably refer to this as the underground economy (never reported to the IRS, just buried away). Yet I definitely do not believe the process of putting someone underground should provide the opportunity for tax free income for anyone, pastor or not! Now that I have also experienced this custom through the formality of a marriage ceremony, with yet another unmarked envelope for yet another pastor, I question not the faith but the messengers who deliver it to the masses. How may we respect those who are blessed to provide guidance when there is so direct and obvious monetary benefit involved? This is a topic I have yet to resolve in my thoughts.

I observed a child and his mother in the park, and I suppose all children are a wonderful experience for their parents. To watch someone discover the world around him in the most basic ways is surely a wonder worth watching, and it was another moment of joy in my life. As you pointed out, small moments of happiness are interspersed with the tedium of daily life far too rarely. We should understand that it is the tedium that is the norm! From that perspective, reflections on those rare moments develops an appreciation for the fabric of life. Just as mass may bend light, those rare moments may shape our lives and send us on courses we would not have contemplated. So it would appear that the rare moments of happiness are critical nodules in the courses of our lives and how we manage those moments may affect the tacking into the wind for years to come. While the joy of the child is definitely a nodule, the weight of the mass is such that whether I will ever be successful in tacking through the course of a female relationship is questionable. Did your physics professor ever contemplate what happened to the fabric if the mass became so great that a great well was created? I sometimes suffer from such an emotional well, in which there is no way the light may be straightened back to the desired course. Do you feel as if you are responsible for the moments of happiness of those around you, and if such moments fail to occur that you are at fault? I am most assured the fault remains with me, but there is no apparent way to determine exactly where the mistake was made which has caused a cascade of personal events.

On a positive note, the monetary situation continues to be much improved on this end. I have invited our uncle and aunt to join me for a midwinter vacation in Arizona, at my expense. Even more astounding, they have agreed. This will be the first time I have been financially able to entertain family as I should. Remember that our uncle loaned me the money necessary to make that first jump to Alaska after graduate school, and although I paid him back promptly, it was still a loan that no one else volunteered to provide. He has a propensity to want his name on bronze plaques near the entrances of buildings, such as libraries and hospitals, but this may simply be a cry for attention. In any case, I wish you would give him more of the benefit of the doubt, rather than condemning all his actions. He has even started speaking with our other relative again.

Out on the family farm, our uncle has now felt it necessary to build a new farm road into the south valley. As there is nothing down there except an old field where our grandfather once grew corn in the bottom, I do not really understand what his motives are at this time. The old wagon road down the side of the hill may still be seen if one knows where to look for it, I am told. Even on the farm it seems that change is constant. The old farm house is falling into disrepair. I have volunteered to pay to place new siding on the house, as our uncle is unwilling to pay to have it painted. He has agreed to oversee the process, as long as I provide the funding. To the best of my knowledge, most of the furnishings remain in it, but it is not locked and anyone may help themselves to things when our uncle is not on the premises. Please try to think of the positive effect of having him there as an onsite grounds keeper when he visits the place, which is almost every day. Just having someone around the place probably limits vandalism and the fact that it is him most probably dissuades those in the county who know of him.

Back at the Mexican movie theatre, progress is also being made. I probably did not mention that the theatre did not have a functional heating system when I purchased it (a minor detail). The 1930s vintage boiler was beyond repair, but I had until mid-September before the cool season associated with the altitude of the town arrived. The day the new furnace was installed was significant for the clientele and this owner. Other repairs and improvements are being implemented as cash flow is permitting. A solid-state sound system has been installed, replacing a vacuum tube-based system that was a daily terror (as no spare parts were available). As you see, I did not so much purchase a movie theatre as the opportunity to create a movie theatre within a shell of a building. Heavy curtains covering the stage, footlights, and movie screen have also been repaired and now open and close electrically for the first time in more than a decade (according to locals who have looked in to check on the changes). As a banker, I am driven to break shells and ideas the numbers do not support. As a small-business owner, it is a constant joy to create something the public enjoys and supports. The enjoyment may be constrained within the Spanish-speaking portion of the public in my case.

Do you think bankers are driven into the profession because they have no creative vision to create a real business? If bankers had true creative vision, would they still be bankers, unless they owned the bank? The prosperity of my fellow bankers has traditionally been created by prudence and patience to such an extent that it almost seems like perdition. To try to sell the idea of simply mailing out loan applications to all large depositors currently without loans and inviting them to contemplate borrowing money runs against the grain of their experience. This is why credit card companies will eventually gain control of most consumer lending—they aggressively seek out the business. The bank waits for the consumer to come to the bank to specifically ask for the loan that the credit card company suggests is readily available through a much more dignified alternative. Dignity is in the privacy of the bankcard credit line, which may be expanded or contracted by the usage of the borrower. There is no need to make a potential borrower feel like a child seeking permission from a parent (a loan officer). In most cases, contact with a loan officer is really only needed if it is a borderline decision, the vast majority of the applications could be either approved or denied by a high level clerk. The response could be mailed if the application is rejected, or the funds simply deposited into their checking account if the application is approved. This concept would border on heresy in most financial institutions.

Just one example of the extent of the conservatism in my chosen profession should serve to drive home the point. Sun Valley is one of the most affluent communities in the west, with daily direct flights by private plane from California by the wealthy. I asked our chairman if we might consider placing a branch office there to see if we could capture some of the growth in the local community being driven by the visitors. He looked me straight in the face and informed me that Sun Valley was simply a resort community and it might be gone tomorrow if the skiing pastime went out of favor, or if the national economy took a bad turn. His perspective is that the risk of the resort community of several thousand individuals (including an adjoining community) is a bad long-term risk and not worth the potential rewards from investing in a branch office. If some bankers had been leading when the Rubicon was encountered, the ancient Senate might still exist today.

My old car, which has taken me to Alaska and on to Idaho, is nearing the end of its useful life. Driving home last week, I heard a loud noise and looked in the rearview mirror to discover my muffler bouncing back down the hill behind me. The vehicle has lasted for many years, has substantial six-digit mileage, and has some personal attachment, but it should not be expected to last forever. It will likely only give one more year of service.

I now realize that prosperity, or even the appearance of success, will attract notice from business competitors and the general population. The reactions seem to range from envy to contempt, for the tendency is to proclaim their ability to do what you have accomplished. They seem to attribute your success to luck more than to ability or effort. Some individuals even go so far as to make fairly obvious efforts to thwart your endeavors. This seems prevalent in both the corporate and small business environments. Very few are the friends who truly congratulate you on the success of your work.

Age does help when encountering insults, even if they are of a personal and most revolting nature. The point is that I now believe public displays of prosperity breed envy, and the animosity that ultimately confronts you should not be surprising. My opinion that it is far better to live a lifestyle that is substantially beneath your means is now further reinforced, although it runs counter to that of the typical American who borrows to live a lifestyle far above their means. The general public, friends and competitors alike, are not likely to understand that success lies within insight and effort, not within the structures you have built around it. As for discrimination, do you think it would have been likely for the police to visit an English speaking theatre operated by a local native if the crowds seemed so large. My distrust for the general population remains huge, but I trust the openness of Alaska keeps you in better humor. Oh, I discovered the owner of the theatre when the town put a sewage system in never connected to it, and I own a large septic tank. On the positive side, the city owed me the money they collected for sewage fees these many years. We will work out an accommodation that will show my generosity to the city, rather than what I actually think of those who question my business.

Chapter XXII

Dear elder cousin,

It was so good to hear you in a better humor about life. Do you suppose it is ever possible to have simultaneous success in business and personal matters? I regret the end of your marriage, but it may well be for the best as you seem greatly unburdened by the process. Obviously, your experience does not exactly push me to try such an endeavor at this time. Thank you for your kind words in support of my thesis that happiness is at best a transitory moment to be savored. The child you observed is an excellent example, as it has not yet encountered either success or failure in abstract thought and the joy is truly in the being for such an individual.

Another thought has occurred to me of an economic nature. As two thirds of our national economy is built on personal consumption, it is in the interest of the federal government to promote consumption to support the economy and placate the interests of the masses. Therefore the typical American uses short term cash flow to fund long term dreams. We have made investment in housing such a national priority, through the use of itemized tax deductions to make ever larger homes affordable, that we fail to realize that homes to not create wealth. Housing is, in fact, a factor of national consumption (overlook national income accounting) as other nations do not allow interest payments on housing to be deducted from taxable income. In other countries, individuals seek to enhance their financial positions through investments in earning assets (factories, ships, and other enterprises that actually produce something). Yes, I realize that in traditional national income accounting housing is treated as an investment due to the long life of the asset. However, I argue that anything that does not contribute to the ongoing creation of national income is simply an asset (very distinct from an investment) and not for the creation of true wealth. The problem is that Americans have come to see the leverage aspects of housing, small investment (large mortgage) as a means to financial profits through inflation.

On the top of my desk are a matched set of cattle horn weights Grandfather gave me. The weights were slid down the horns of a cow and then screwed into the base while the cow was still alive. The weights caused the horns to gradually turn downward, to the point that eventually the horn was parallel with the face of the cow and the poor beast could no longer use the horn to injure another cow or worse, one of us. They are on my desk to remind me that significant change may be accomplished gradually over time, without the owner of the assets even knowing what the end objective may be. Do you think we might slowly adjust American consumption by placing a cap on home interest deductibility, so that the public eventually realizes that other avenues for long-term investments actually create wealth for the entire nation and not just for the transient individual homeowner?

It would appear to be the American legacy to have promoted consumption to such an extent that we are creating real wealth throughout the world in the form of factories that produce the goods we crave. I am reminded of the Spanish, who thought they were wealthy from all the gold they carried home from the "new world," only to find a century later that the real wealth was in a small northern island nation that had factories. It is my fear that American housing is the equivalent of the Spanish gold—a foolish investment in an asset that does not produce anything of value that may be traded but to another fool for another home.

The national problem will lie with our generation, the baby boomers, of which there are far too many, and we are not producing sufficient successors (although I admit to little desire to add to the population personally). As our generation moves into retirement, I fear that the great illusion will become apparent even to the undereducated. They will realize that their perception of reality was but a façade that was necessary to provide a stable society. Their cash flows will erode with age, and coupled with their leverage and lack of significant equity, an awkward, even embarrassing unwinding of their leveraged positions will most likely occur. Such are the random thoughts of an underemployed economist.

I am considering dating an individual in the Lower Forty-Eight, although I know long-distance relationships are usually an invitation to disaster. In this instance there does not appear to be any local alternative. It will most probably be an error of judgment, but there have simply been too many long Alaskan nights this winter. I followed your precedent and obtained a job interview with a commercial bank in the Lower Forty-Eight which is seeking an economist. While I will admit that Pittsburg is not the Boston trip that you enjoyed, at least it was a paid trip to the outside for me. Mellon Bank was a good enough host; they are in the process of building a new headquarters in downtown Pittsburg. When you take a cab from the airport, the trip goes through a tunnel, and suddenly the town is directly in front of you at the junction of two rivers that join to form the Ohio River. The skyline is impressive; a wonder that the steel industry has wrought. While I did not get the equivalent of your dinner at the Harvard Club, I was treated to a very pleasant lunch downtown. The individual interviewing me stressed how the subway planned to have a stop in the basement of the building and the convenience that would add to the working environment. It would mean more money than I obtain as a public servant, but several factors argued against taking the position. They were seeking an individual who would definitely state the most probable direction of interest rates at any given moment, so as to more effectively manage the interest rate risk of their institution, and they really seem to believe that econometric modeling can provide the answers they are seeking.

Off the record, we both know that the type of econometric modeling that I have done for Alaska is most suitable for public policy types who are using public money. The business types want definitive answers, not the realization that chaos theory precludes certainty in all but the most obvious situations. They do not want to hear that the best long term investments are offshore, and most certainly they will find someone who will tell them what they want to hear. However, it will not be me! On the bright side, I actually managed to combine the trip with a dating experience and had an enjoyable evening. At least this time we exited Pennsylvania without the bullets that great-grandfather encountered with Lee. The bank paid for the trip, for which I thank the capitalist system with which we are blessed.

I desperately need an original economic thought I can sell at a premium. The value of knowledge is so fleeting, that unless the thought breaches new territory, one cannot hang a career on it. Anyone may master the math of those who have gone before, and there is no satisfaction in regurgitating theories to those who have not had the benefit of the prerequisite education. Original contributions to the base of knowledge are the only salvation for sanity. You have been troubled by your personal life, and I confess that I am more than slightly disturbed about my professional contributions to society.

The Alaskan economy is based on the extraction of scarce resources, oil currently, in a previous boom it was gold, and originally the attraction was furs. The challenge for this economy is how to formulate a long term plan for sustainable development which is based less on the resource of the moment and more on the long term comparative advantages of Alaska. With no state income tax, and with no state sales tax, Alaska may have the potential to attract wealthy individuals who may wish to declare the state as their residence and actually reside up here for only a few months each year. It may also offer a favorable environment for long term trusts, if only our banks would focus on that option. In the interim, the political types are totally focused on additional exploration for oil and the possibility of a natural gas pipeline. At this time the state has the financial ability to waive tuition for all students at the main campus of the University of Alaska in Fairbanks and turn it into a world-class institution. The attraction of international talent could bring the ideas necessary to build a sustainable economy not solely based on natural resources. Instead, the wisdom of the state is to use scarce resources to buy down the interest rates on all new Alaskan residential mortgages to 10 percent, so that our small population does not feel the impact of those absurdly high mortgage rates you all are suffering in the Lower Forty-Eight. While this provides us with wonderful housing, no one addresses the issue of where the money will come from to maintain these homes when the current extraction resource, oil, is depleted.

The mountains, the ocean, the eternal snow makes Alaska a beautiful mistress of youth one never wants to leave. Looking around, one notices how few persons over the age of forty-five actually live here, and it causes questions. Is this just a place to gain traction for a career outside, and will this great city of Anchorage someday suffer the same fate as Nome has after the gold was extracted? The only really stable employer in town is the federal government, through the air force base and other activities. Eventually tourism will add jobs to the economy, but those are the lower paying types of jobs which have not brought prosperity to such places as the Caribbean.

So, you see I am at last facing the choice of departing Alaska to get back closer to larger population bases where opportunities for contributions to the system are likely to be of longer duration. There is still the contemplation that somehow there must be a way to produce a living from that old family farm. You are correct in that I need to be more forgiving of our uncle, for it was he who allowed me to invest my first $1,000 in the stock market (from the sale of cows), and the leader of Iran who was interested in Pan Am World Airways drove the value of the investment to $1,600 within three months. There was no better way to become a capitalist at age twelve in the hills.

Chapter XXIII

Dear younger cousin,

I regret hearing of your professional difficulties; for I know the drive to contribute something is not simply confined to the private sector. Have you considered thoughts in the area of disaster economics? As you know, empires do not generally fall so much from the superior forces of the barbarians than they do from the rot of the internal structure. Originally, most cultures call on the general male population to serve in the military, but as empires grow it seems that most move to a professional army. Does this sequence of events remind you of a country considerably closer to home? All of your profession, economists, focuses on the actions of the so-called "rational" man in a given set of circumstances. A much more interesting set of questions is how the "rational" economic man would behave if he is confronted with a consistent and sustained chain of actions by an "irrational" (at least from an economic perspective) individual or individuals. Certainly not the normal course of thought in your profession, but one where you might strike such an independent and original thought as to tether your career for some time to come.

When I was younger and in Alaska, I confronted an economically irrational individual who was acting in a perfectly rational manner given his set of circumstances. I was responsible for the safety deposit box area of the Mall Branch on Northern Lights Boulevard, when a gentleman asked to retrieve something from his safety deposit box. After I had unlocked the banks lock and was waiting for him to obtain whatever he was searching for, he suddenly stated, "I do not want to alarm you, but I am getting a pistol out of my lockbox." Well, obviously he was successful in alarming me, and we had a discussion in the vault about exactly what the bank did *not* permit to be stored in safety deposit boxes. It turned out that his spouse refused to allow him to have a pistol in their home, but he enjoyed target practice with a pistol. For him, the rational decision was to store the sidearm in a secure location outside of his home, and the bank's lockbox facility appeared to be an excellent choice. I explained to him that no amount of money in payment would make the bank believe it was rational to allow weapons to be stored in a vault where substantial money was stored. He agreed to move his prized sidearm to another location, but it was a case of a rational personal decision (from the perspective of his marriage) being totally irrational within the context of our economic system.

I was glad to hear of your trip to Pittsburg, and although not the typical tourist destination, at least it was outside and fully paid for by the bank. It was a coup to successfully combine a dating experience with a job interview, and the young lady will probably never appreciate the extent of coordination I imagine it took to time the event sequence. You have a good point about the limitations of the Alaskan environment on the social situation. I am increasingly convinced that the inordinate amount of time which I spent working as a youth would have been better spent dating members of the opposite gender. If getting along with the opposite gender is an art, and most certainly not a science of exactness, it is the relentless practice of the art which most probably brings the greatest success. As such, I entered into wedlock with only the basest knowledge of how to successfully engage in long-term communication with the opposite gender. In retrospect, the acquisition of such knowledge would have been far more valuable on a present value basis than the acquired cash flow from the relentless work. Yes, I can hear you now, reminding me that our family focused on work and that interpersonal relationships were not deemed horribly important even within the clan. But I believe our family is most unusual and that most families are much more involved with their personal relationships. If leaving Alaska is necessary to engage in a more lively social life, as well as to provide more professional opportunities for independent thought, it would seem to be the most rational avenue of choice.

My span of authority has expanded again, and now executive management has entrusted me with providing guidance for agriculture loans through something that I refer to as BAR (Base Agricultural Rate). The entire idea behind BAR is that the vast majority of our agricultural loans are seasonal crop loans of short duration (paid off with crop proceeds). Instead of thinking of these loans in relation to the prime rate for commercial loans, which tend to be of longer duration, I am planning to capture much more market share through aggressive pricing based on the short-term duration of the loans. By replacing short-term investment securities with additional agricultural loans for nine months of each year, the annualized net interest margin of the bank can be significantly increased. The traditional bankers will most likely cede us the field of play (yes, pun intended), and shift to longer term investment securities which carry far more interest rate risk. The math seems to indicate that victory is all but assured, as the only uncontrolled variable is the human nature of the competitors and traditional resistance to change in thinking is on my side.

As is customary, we should speak of math somewhat obliquely, but please ponder these circumstances and relate your opinion. As a balloon expands, with its mass spread over an ever-greater area, the surface density of this particular balloon varies greatly due to small variations in the initial force which caused it to expand. The surface density variations cause infinitely small sections of the balloon to collapse back toward the center. Once the balloon has inflated beyond one thousandth millionth of the pre-inflation volume, it is impossible to concentrate sufficient mass at any particular point to allow a well caused by the mass concentration to penetrate all the way to the center of the inflation phenomenon. For purposes of thought, consider there is no external pressure on the balloon, which allows portions of its mass to be spread infinitely thin and still retain the fabric of existence. What might have occurred at the bottom of that gravity well when the mass was sufficiently concentrated to allow connection to the center? The shear mass of the cascade of matter down an infinitely narrow well could not be duplicated today, due to the size of the balloon and the thinness of the matter that comprises it. Today, any such wells would be doomed to dissipate as the fabric of the balloon would eventually overwhelm the mass contained within them. My thoughts are drawn to the conclusion that such a well, when the balloon was very small caused the inflation phenomenon to occur. I will not speak of how, for if the beauty of your math matches my thoughts it will be apparent. The resulting pressure on the external fabric of the balloon would continually accelerate the expansion of the balloon due to the confluence of events within. The mere sequence of such thoughts disturbs me, as the apparent result could be misused only once, and in fact our current circumstances might well be the result of such an action.

No one in our family has suffered the failure of a divorce since our arrival on this continent in 1698, but I fear that I will be remembered as being the first who has broken this chain of success in domestic bliss. My ability to successfully interact with the opposite gender is apparently somewhat limited, and I do not know how to repair the feelings when the spouse has lost their long term commitment to a relationship. Perhaps I just have an insufferable drive to repair all things, and I just must admit that broken personal relationships can not be repaired. I am constantly reminded of that nursery ditty about the inability of vast resources to reassemble a shattered egg. It is perversely sad to be able to comprehend a problem and not have the foggiest thought on how to resolve it. Abstract, rational thought can be such a refuge from the infinite variables of complex human interactions.

Your thoughts on the long run consequences of the leverage asset tendencies of our generation are most disturbing. Yes, I agree the prosperity of these years has to some extent been based on the relentless expansion of the labor force through increased female participation, along with the use of credit by a wide swath of the population (perhaps imprudently) and a general rise in productivity. You are correct that the federal government will most likely promote further personal use of credit as it serves their immediate purpose of reducing the unemployment rate through the economic activity it creates. If our national economy is increasingly based on thought (services), rather than product and if the value of thought is increasingly fleeting due to ever better communication and education among other countries, are we increasing the welfare of the world through our largess? Traditional economics would decry such heresy by saying that comparative advantage would always leave us with a superior position in something to trade. However, such reasoning is based on the behavior of "rational" men in which individuals in other nations recognize it is in their long-term economic advantage to allow free trade and to allow comparative advantage to flourish to enhance their standard of living. What if these trading partners are more interested in something such as religion or politics than the general economic welfare of their populations? In such circumstances, might not they purposely drag their feet in allowing such services as we might provide to be available to their populations until the knowledge has been so dispersed as to allow the services to be produced within their own borders? To defeat a free-trade nation over the long run, it would appear that a strategy of trading products for knowledge will ultimately equalize the level of knowledge, while leaving one trading partner with far more ability to produce products. It is the ability to produce products which ultimately makes a nation a military power of some significance. The nation of ideas is left with the last defense of mutually assured destruction. Not exactly a pleasant scenario to contemplate for our golden years.

I have taken a mini vacation to the Oregon coast, but the weather was dreadful and not much pleasure in the moments. The winter trip to Arizona went reasonably well, with all seeming to enjoy themselves, including our uncle and aunt. The orange trees in the cities of southern Arizona are a great pleasure to see as a respite from even our mild Idaho winters. Thank you for having a few kind thoughts about our kin and do try to remember that at least up to this point they have done nothing disloyal to the long term interest of the family.

Consideration is being given to the purchase of another theatre in a community further up the Snake River Valley. It is an older single-screen theatre, but it is in much better shape than the first one I acquired (it actually has a functional heating system). The balcony in this one resembles an opera house in that it wraps around the side of the second floor. An older couple owns the theatre, and they are looking to retire. Unfortunately, a fellow from Twin Falls is also interested, and he already owns several others throughout the area. If he is really serious, his pockets are most certainly deeper than mine. The fact that the current owners may be simply using me as a stalking horse in this matter is not a pleasant thought, but I am inclined to continue the pursuit. It would at least provide me with an exit from banking into a business over which I could have some control. It appears that three theatres in this area would be necessary to provide sufficient cash flow for a decent standard of living, if I was working full time in them. The life of a corporate migrant laborer is growing tedious, and it is difficult to ponder growing old working to make the shareholders ever richer. As to your thoughts on the family farm, I am certainly open to suggestions as to how to wring a living out of that worn out land. The best hope was that old oil well, but when it did not produce commercial quantities, I am afraid any hopes of sustained cash flow from the land were lost. The rock is not even granite, which might have been used to produce gravel. We are left with a multilayered combination of sandstone and shale, which does not easily produce anything salable.

Even the timber on the farm was cut over to produce firewood, until modern heating was introduced after WWII. Our great-grandfather cleared the fields of timber to be traded to the owner of the wood boiler powered cotton gin in exchange for the right to gin his cotton at no charge. Unfortunately, the hardwood will need another century before it has any value due to the rocky soil. All we have to offer the world is open space and water. In closing, remember Plato stating that a city (nation) built on materialism is but a community of "happy pigs." The trick is how to live in such a society, prosper, and still have time for the purity of abstract thought. Enjoy Alaska, but seek alternatives for happiness.

Chapter XXIV

Dear elder cousin,

Your letter dwelled at length on such a wide range of topics that from whence point to respond is not easily considered. Your objective to leave the banking profession appears based not upon any lack of success but in spite of it. The practical application of theoretical knowledge to that particular business has served you well, and carved a niche not many will dare to crowd into at the present time. It is in your reference to the classics that you show more of your thoughts than is customary. I also fear the loss of the true liberal arts education, where reference to the classical greats of first logical thought are best addressed. If we have truly created the society which Plato feared, I confess that you know one of the many happy pigs up here in Alaska. Or is it that you fear you have become one yourself? Being somewhat late to consider the monastery, might I suggest an academic life might be more suitable to your disposition. Yes, this runs counter to your training in the most advantageous methods to make money, but it fits your world viewpoint much more closely. Please do not take offense; the thought is only intended to provoke your thoughts and not any such temper, as I doubt any still exists.

At the other extreme, I am considering entering your profession (banking) somewhat belatedly for the sole pursuit of money. I have accepted another job interview with a commercial bank, this one in Dallas, which I will begin next week. Again, the premise is the application of mathematics to the business, but in this case they are inclined to see the logic of risk management. It is a large Texas institution, and I am most interested in what they may have to offer. The only initial hesitation is that if a position is offered, and if I accept, I will be trading one natural resource-oriented state for another only slightly less so. Even worse, the same raw material (petroleum) is the basis for wealth in both locales. I will let you know how the process goes. Besides, I have never been to Dallas.

Remember the thought that happiness is at best a fleeting instant to be savored in the moment, with little expectation of significant duration outside of the ordinary daily routine of life. I have now had an epiphany to add to my initial observation. Walking along a downtown Anchorage street during lunchtime, a truck pulled up alongside me, honked its horn, and a delightful young lady with blond hair waived and invited me to call her. We had only met once before at some social function, and I knew we were not well suited. She is at least five feet ten inches, thin, blond, and not the least engaging on an intellectual level. However, the moment she unexpectedly curved over to the side of the street, I experienced one of those moments of happiness. So, perhaps not only are those moments of extremely short duration, they may also be associated with the unexpected show of interest or appreciation in our existence or activities. Again, to be happy in the moment does not exclude the possibility of creating a chain of such moments with one particular individual; it only indicates that each moment may exist as a singularity. We have seen each other several times and I doubt that her interest in a short nerd may be sustained for any extended period. At best, I expect that I am a short excursion beyond the realm of more typical tall, dark and handsome individuals that better complement her appearance. I am in her debt for helping me contemplate and better understand happiness from a personal perspective.

On the matter of movie theatres, have you thought of the long-term prospects for such entertainment? Even if the medium survives television as an escape from the routine of household confinement that is such a bore, what is to say technology will not gradually shove it aside incrementally? In such an event sequence, you would be left owning considerable real estate, designed for one specific purpose, and not easily converted to another. Does this new facility offer the potential of converting it to another Spanish-language house, or will you have to make the jump to an English-speaking operation? Have you noticed that you tend to live a significant distance from your work and that you have even admitted it is to lessen the contact with your bosses? I know that dealing with normal individuals may be extremely stressful at times, but they really are most engaging if you will try to understand the routines of normal families and the lifecycle we are all engaged in completing. This distance you place between yourself and the world is not altogether healthy. The interaction with others is most helpful in better understanding yourself, at least from my experience. If you are intent on the pursuit of an independent business, might a recurring service that has less chance of being replaced quickly through technology be a better choice.

I have considered your thoughts on free trade from a non-traditional perspective, and combined with my own viewpoint of the leverage asset tendencies of our generation, the overall result may not be as bad as you seem to expect. While I agree that the result of a free-trade country such as ours would like to become, doing business with countries that are actually after intellectual capital is most realistic; I disagree with the possible consequences. The key is whether we are capable of producing new ideas and processes faster than they are capable of absorbing the same. If we are not up to this task, then free trade will benefit the traders and indirectly the political types accepting their donations. Conversely, if we can continue to attract the best and the brightest engineers in the world to our open social system and produce ideas and processes at a sustained heady pace, more jobs will be created in our country than are transferred out of it. The more likely problem will be the labor force. Up until this time in the progress of our so-called civilization, an individual who learned a particular skill was likely to be able to use it throughout his working life. There were of course continual exceptions to this generality, but your father is a fair example of an individual who worked forty-plus years for the same company, with only a break for WWII. We appear to have reached a confluence where the pace of change is rapidly depreciating the duration of value of any particular skill, while at the same time we have been successful in lengthening the potential useful life of employees through a superb healthcare system.

If this scenario is correct, there will be more than adequate employment for the young, as they learn the new skills necessary for the new jobs. It is the older segment of the workforce that will be forced to shoulder the burden for the transfer of ideas and processes overseas, for they will be forced to adapt in order to survive at a time in their lives where retirement should be the greatest concern. At the very point in their work lives, when previous generations had their peak earning years, our generation will face the changing demands of the workplace. We will have many options, either confronting a set of lessened expectations or trying new alternative forms of income producing activities. For those who have capital, the transition will be less jarring, but it is likely to have political consequences, for those without capital are likely to be far more numerous. Remember our grandmother, who never learned how to drive? In her youth, a horse and buggy would suffice, and she was comfortable with these. Yet she always depended on Grandfather for motorized transportation and never felt truly comfortable with the changes. The question is which part of the population will prevail at that advanced age, probably over fifty, the component capable of learning new techniques to produce cash flow, or the component waiting for someone else to drive? I believe most will resist simply being pushed out the door of commerce and will relentlessly try other pursuits than they were originally trained for.

I understand your discomfort with the sharing of ideas in commerce. It is one thing to sell another country an airplane but an entirely different matter to teach them how to build an airplane. Remember that over the long term, ideas simply can not be contained. It was the Chinese who acquired a Boeing 707 and completely disassembled it in order to learn how to duplicate the vehicle. The best that can be hoped for is to slow the transfer of ideas to the extent that our labor force is able to cope with the pace of change.

Your personal situation does not sound promising. Obviously, the replacement of a spouse, even to go so far as dating again, is a large emotional step after suffering emotional distress. Have you noticed how easy it is to inadvertently offend the other individual, or to be offended yourself by their actions. As we age I seem to be more willing to accept the fallibility of myself and our fellow travelers, expecting the imperfections with which I have more than my share. Perhaps in a truly intimate relationship, the unconditional acceptance and love of those imperfections is an actual basis of understanding and appreciating the human experience. Someone, and for the life of me, I can not remember who, once stated that most men are not worth much until after they are at least forty years of age. So perhaps we will both improve to a sufficient extent that the other gender can manage to be around us for sustained periods.

The strange world of Alaska continues to prove that the abnormal is not that unusual. The state continues to behave as if the cash flow associated with the North Slope oil will be a permanent fixture in our economy. For a state which has no income tax to continue to spend money on infrastructure at such an astounding rate shows either an unshakeable faith in the future, or financial imprudence. That the infrastructure may not be needed once the oil is depleted does not seem to occur to the political types. All they seem to notice is that they have the money now and are intent on spending it on something. The best that may be said is that at least those of us currently residing in this land of unusual beauty are also getting to enjoy its financial bounty at the same time.

The government is in the process of making the highway north out of Anchorage to Palmer (to the point where it splits to form the Parks Highway north to Fairbanks and the Glenn Highway east to Valdez) a four lane, divided highway. That Palmer has fewer than five thousand residents does not seem to have dissuaded the process, and many folks in Anchorage are considering obtaining weekend cabins on the lakes around Wasilla. When you were up here, Wasilla was simply a wide spot in the two-lane Parks Highway, but now strip shopping centers are springing up, and it is becoming increasingly residential. Although I support private ownership of almost all property, the type of development (no zoning), which is occurring makes one less unhappy with the prevalent government ownership of the vast open spaces in this state.

Going southeast from Anchorage, the government is going to develop a visitor's center at the outflow point of Portage Lake, so that the tourists may stand inside and enjoy the ice moving down the lake from Portage Glacier during the summer. The fact that the glacier is receding and no one knows when it will withdraw from the lake, which will reduce the tourist appeal, does not seem to be a consideration in the process. They are even talking about the possibility of a tour boat on this three-mile lake. The one enduring process the government is going to highlight is in the same area. They are building a walkway out to see one of the spots on the stream between Portage Lake and Turnagain Arm of Cook Inlet, where the salmon spawn. Did you ever have an opportunity to see the tidal bore come up Turnagain Arm? To see that six-foot wall of water pushing up the fjord is certainly a sight. The glacial silt gives the water such a milky tone. Take care, and remember the probable opportunities that the future holds for us both.

Chapter XXV

Dear younger cousin,

No offense was taken concerning your remarks about my dissatisfaction with my connection to the banking profession. It is most certainly true that it is a love/hate relationship, with the associated cash flow being most difficult to contemplate disappearing. You are also correct in that perhaps I am afraid that Plato would say that I have also become one of the pigs at the materialist trough, through the application of pure knowledge to pursuits that are perhaps not worthy of the time or distraction. We are most assuredly aware that happiness does not reside in the acquisition of any particular thing or experience, for can one say that they are happier in any moment when surrounded with the trappings of wealth than they are at such a moment as you described in your letter. The unexpected show of interest or appreciation is such a rarity that it simply grasps your very breath and provokes that unique moment of lasting remembrance. One simply cannot obtain such an experience through the solace of a bank account, regardless of the quantity of digits involved! I also offer my congratulations for your opportunity to provide companionship to such an attractive sounding female individual; may it last longer than you anticipate and bring even more of those rare moments.

We have one fellow at work, who outranks me in our hierarchy, who is so focused on furthering his career that I am sure he does not realize how absurd his actions appear. One of the members of our executive management team has a heart condition. The fellow I referenced keeps a bottle of oxygen behind his desk and is fully trained in resuscitation techniques should his services be needed quickly by our boss. Clearly the dictionary meaning of "obsess" would not do this poor fellow justice, who in all other respects appears to be a normal employee. In corporate business, it seems just performing a stellar job is no longer adequate in his thoughts and yet anticipating the macabre seems a bit beyond.

The chairman of our board of directors and I happened to be on the elevator alone one morning recently, and I remarked that he appeared unusually cheerful for so early in the morning. We actually commenced a personal conversation for the first time, and he confided that he had just arranged to have a sprinkler system installed in his lawn. For the first time in his life in our Treasure Valley of the Boise River, he was contemplating not having to drag the water hose around his lawn during our dry summers. This was from a man who earns a substantial six-figure income, and yet has denied himself such a simple convenience that probably most of his middle managers already have in their lawns. He is even past sixty years of age, compared to the youth of his management team. To answer your thought, no, I do not have a sprinkler system in my lawn. The one thing I am beginning to notice about the truly wealthy is that they have abhorrence for needless expenditures of capital in which they might otherwise invest. This of course does not apply to the newly wealthy, who appear initially to have an uncontrollable desire to acquire and display material aspects of their success. What would the luxury-goods sector do without the endless replenishment of new medical types, as the older retire?

I have given two speeches on the economy during the last month. Both were for meetings of the chamber of commerce, one in Boise and another far up the Snake River Valley beyond Twin Falls. Of course for the one in Boise, I spoke on the excellent diversity of our economy, for that is what they want to hear. Have you noticed that no one actually hires a speaker to say exactly what is on his mind? You may be assured that if I had actually mentioned that while diversified, the local economy is far too dependent on a relatively few large employers, my message would have not been so well received, and I expect the bank would have received a number of phone calls the next day from local business leaders. Once again, the devil is in the audience, and it is easy to understand the content of political speeches in that context. The other speech was far up river in an agricultural community, and it was during their annual chamber of commerce dinner. Once again I spoke of the bounty of their local economy and the hard won efforts of both they and their ancestors to bring forth produce from the rocky desert through irrigation. The reality is that I might have spoken about how they owe their prosperity to Castro and the trade policy of the US government! If they would realize that the internal price of sugar in the United States (from their sugar beets) is as high relative to the world price as to be almost obscene, they might question the basis of their own prosperity. We have no comparative advantage in the production of sugar! It is only that we refuse to allow imports of cheap Cuban sugar, from sugar cane, because of the communist nature of the Cuban government. I would have much enjoyed explaining that this conservative corner of our rural economy was much in debt to a leftist, elderly communist who is willing to keep his population in penury rather than change his type of government. Again, such honesty is not what folks want or even expect from public speakers at events such as chamber of commerce annual banquets. So, is the devil truly in the audience or in the speaker who realizes that he will only speak once if he dares to broach the truth in such a venue? A retort might be that this illusion of prosperity is maintained to keep the

United States from becoming dependent on foreign sugar, but I doubt that even federal economists could say that one with a straight face.

Your thoughts have been well considered in relation to the movie theatre business. Yes, it may well be that I am so consumed with departing the banking portion of commerce that the long term consequences of large commitments to fixed assets (real estate) specifically designed for one purpose have not been fully considered up to now. As it turns out, fortune has favored the gentleman from Twin Falls, and his bid for the theatre was accepted, and I was politely excused from the proceedings. It seems that he plans to turn that beautiful building from a single screen operation into a twin screen by throwing a wall down the center of the auditorium. From an architectural perspective, it is most disturbing to see such a fine structure torn asunder, and to make it worse, I believe the entire affair is being financed by one of my competitors in the banking business. I have a great desire to preserve things of beauty, both manmade and natural, but it seems that commerce rules most decisions in our country.

Consider another option for use of some of the farm land; a cemetery! There is no reason a cemetery should not be as handsome a location as a golf course, with walkways of remembrance rather than rows of depression. The idea would be to shift the focus to the joy of the individual's life above the inevitable sadness of the death and its affects on those who are always left behind. A cemetery with an upward vision seems more in keeping with the traditional beliefs of the rewards hereafter. I believe this idea would serve both of our purposes; something we can sell with a clear conscious and provide an upgrade to a traditional service.

Several issues spring to my thoughts on the practical side of this matter. First, what are the legal barriers to entry into the cemetery business? This will need to be discretely researched in such a manner that minimal attention is attracted to the potential endeavor. Secondly, an architectural rendering of the potential facility will need to be commissioned as a selling point. Next we will need to determine to what extent we might persuade funeral homes within a fifty-mile radius to participate and what, if any, restrictions on their participation may exist from a legal basis. The upfront costs of beginning the facility will need to be borne by us and we should expect costs similar to any startup enterprise. Cousin, you have both my attention and interest in this matter, proceed as you see fit. Remember that this topic of interest should remain between ourselves, as our older generation would probably not see any reasonable possibility of divorcing a cemetery from a church. We may need to wait until we have more control of the land, rather than a partial interest, to begin the endeavor but I see no reason why we can not go forward on a pro forma basis at this time.

One other thought on this matter: exactly where on the farm would we place such an endeavor? Would fifteen acres suffice, or do you believe more land would be necessary?

Should it be located some distance from the main road to ensure privacy, or adjacent to the road to lower the initial expense of development? Would it be too expensive to include a small lake (a practical use for our water)? Your thoughts on these matters would be appreciated.

As to the present situation of my personal life, I have resolved to take one day at a time and simply avoid being irritated at the developments. To believe in the inherent goodness of all individuals is to understand that we are all humans and by definition most likely make horrible mistakes from time to time. The mistakes do not make the individual any less desirable; in fact if they serve to further educate the individual about the process of life the mistakes may even have value. Goodness knows, I have made far more serious mistakes in both my professional and personal life than I care to remember, but each mistake persuades me to not choose a similar route again and I trust that even this old dog is capable of learning.

We enjoyed your comments on Highway 1, north out of Anchorage; it seems that the motto might be "build a four-lane divided highway, and they will come"! If you have the time, take the train up to Mt. McKinley, stay at the lodge, and ride the school bus back into the park. The mountain and the entire Alaskan Range are much more impressive when viewed from the north than looking north from Anchorage. You have mentioned "frost heaves"; let me add: avoid routes that say "Closed in winter." Take care, and keep thinking about the future.

Chapter XXVI

Dear elder cousin,

Your enthusiasm for the cemetery idea was much appreciated. It seems to indicate that we may be able to work together to better produce income from what appears to be a fairly worthless asset. As you requested, I have done some preliminary checking and there is a State cemetery board which oversees these types of facilities. Such a facility by itself does not seem to have much of a history of making money, according to industry sources. The cost of perpetual care is a substantial upfront burden taken off the initial sales price. Combining the upscale rural cemetery, with a chapel might be a superior combination. What do you think about the idea of having families sponsor a time of remembrance for loved ones located in the facility? This would provide a reason to use the chapel on a regular basis, perhaps every five years for each individual, so that previous generations are better remembered. In addition, if the chapel was located at the entrance area to the facility, it might also be used for weddings and provide an additional source of revenue. I do not believe it would be possible to go too upscale in the area of the cemetery, or "garden of remembrance." Your idea of landscaped walking trails is seemly, but I might add that a security fence and internal security system would place the facility far above current burial areas, which mostly are open to vandals. The matter is simply one of timing, with our acquisition of the land probably fifteen years hence. It would be better to proceed at this time, but the eldest generation would not support the endeavor. Yes, fifteen acres would be adequate, plus parking and a chapel area. The more secluded the better, as privacy adds to the atmosphere and assists in the contemplation of those visiting their loved ones.

As to the unending challenge of the female gender, I regret to mention that the acquaintance with the charming young blond ended far sooner than one would prefer. She met a fellow who works up on the North Slope, making far more money than I, and pretty much gave me my walking papers. Your faith in the inherent goodness of human nature is somewhat opposite to my belief that our culture has simply replaced the sword with the dollar bill in the competition for mates. I truly hope that it is you and not I who holds the correct perspective. Back in the hills, I was biased at an early age by a single telephone call to a young lady to whom I shall forever be in debt. At the naïve age of sixteen, one does not fully understand the culture. I had recently acquired a driver's license, although not a car, and telephoned a bright young lady to ask for a date. Remember that although I did not have a vehicle, I had access to our family car, so transportation seemed to not be an issue. We exchanged the customary pleasantries, and I inquired if she might be available Saturday night, for a movie and pizza. In my financial condition, it was really a grand offer beyond what I could sustain on an ongoing basis. She was a young lady who was truly wise beyond her years, for she told me rather bluntly that while we might be friends, she did not "go out with people like *you*"! The point is, I was of the wrong social class. Not only did my family not belong to the country club, we did not even play golf; nor did we maintain a boat over at the lake. The fact that I did not even have my own personal vehicle seemed to seal my social class. Even now I marvel at how such a seemingly pleasant member of the female gender could be so casually insulting without seeming to worry about any potential consequences.

The young lady is probably most responsible for my successful college education and what limited financial success I enjoy. It was as if someone turned on a blinding light and said, "Social equality, get real!" From that point onward in my high school days, I never even inquired if a young lady would enjoy an evening out before it was determined that she did *not* come from an affluent family. I became convinced, and remain to this day, that young ladies understand the ways of the world far sooner than naïve young men who are merely infatuated with the youth of the female gender. To that end, I am never surprised to be replaced by a fellow of higher social standing, or having a better paying job, as it is in the long-term financial interests of the female to make such choices in an objective manner and not be encumbered with the weight of emotions. Perhaps it would have been better for classical economics to focus on the "rational woman," instead of the better accepted "rational man." Yes, I can hear those thoughts now, and I am not so senile to not remember that the Greek perspective of "mankind" encompassed both genders, and it was the Romans who insisted on making the term not gender neutral. The point is my experience indicates that ladies pursue a much more purposeful course through life than most of us fellows.

A mental note has been made that if such time arrives as my financial standing is significantly above average, it will be best if I continue to appear below average when courting the opposite gender. How else to more clearly determine if the lady is truly interested in me as a person, instead of me as a provider of cash flow? Perhaps the view of a cynic, or an overly cautious individual, but it seems the most practical way to enter into a long term relationship in which both parties focus less on the material aspects of life.

Once again, I imagine you are belittling my lack of patience with our fellow man. Your perspective is that God does not make mistakes and the mere presence of such individuals as I have encountered drives home the point that they are placed among us to serve as warnings of what the world might become unless we persevere in a more righteous path. All I ask is if it is really necessary for this deity of yours to place so many signs along the path we tread. Marx was most certainly wrong about religion; it is not an opiate but simply a refuge from a world of relentless harshness. Once I thought that the tendency of the old to find solace in religion was closely correlated with their age, but now I tend to believe that it is more likely due to their longer term exposure to the remainder of humanity. Ponder a design for a chapel, something open to all faiths, for a "garden of remembrance" should have many paths. I have a tendency to enjoy the thirteenth century designs for places of Christian worship, yet I must remember that it is likely that changing demographics will bring other faiths into positions of more prominence in the decades ahead.

I have decided not to accept the position in Dallas, but I am more inclined to move out of the public sector and seek a position in the very banking industry which you are seeking to exit. If the world is bent on this materialism focus above all else, the least I might do is help it along to its most probable conclusion. The trip should be most interesting and financially rewarding to such an extent that I might be able to attract a long term interest from a member of the fairer sex. The plan is to find a financial institution of such size that a place may exist for an individual, such as me, to use math to manage interest rate risk in a neutral manner. The local bank which you worked for is still very profitable and locally owned, but I doubt that they would deem it a worthwhile financial expenditure to hire an individual for something that is not commonly done in their industry. It will probably need to be a far larger institution in a major city, which is willing to have a new small cog in their large mechanism. So, you may see that I am planning to eventually leave this Alaska which I love so much for the horrible congestion of the Lower Forty-Eight at some point. The timing will simply be a matter of when the most desirable opportunity arrives.

Looking at other potential monetary ventures when our turn finally arrives to manage the family farm, I have been thinking about such resources as we do have to use in the endeavor. First, the cattle make no economic profit when the cost of land and capital (fencing, corrals, tractors, and buildings) are included. They are only a public service to feed a nation that is more than likely to import an ever greater quantity of foreign food, if the government ever allows cheaper imports greater market access. The opportunity may lie, weirdly enough, in what we have to feed the cattle. Instead of thinking of the hay as only a factor of the production process, I envision hay as producing actual cash flow before it is fed to the cattle. Remember the old, classical British gardens, which sometimes had a maze to amuse guests? If the first cutting of hay is removed from the fields as usual and the second cutting completed by mid-September, why not use the second cutting to produce a maze. Those new four feet by five feet round hay bales which our Uncle is using to feed the cattle could be configured into a rather complicated and rational maze, perhaps even using a little math for entertainment. Our cousin up the valley has one of the round hay balers, and I believe our uncle is having him bale the hay at this time.

The neat feature about using such large hay bales is that the size is sufficient to build a large maze with only the second hay cutting. Another attractive feature is that one person on a tractor with a hay fork could rearrange the maze weekly for a fall season of perhaps, eight weeks, so that the maze is never exactly the same. Highway frontage is again the issue, for it should be close enough to the highway to be clearly visible and create an attraction in and of itself. Suitable games could be organized, with prizes for the fastest daily time either for individuals or teams. I believe they would not violate state law, for they would be games of skill, not chance. For the sake of safety and to ease the frustration of those who are geometrically challenged, we could acquire one of those tall, about fifteen feet, dear hunting towers they use down in the flats and place it on a hill above the maze. Actually, it would be best to acquire two identical towers so they could not easily be used as points of reference for those inside the maze. Individuals seeking assistance could wave a small flag and some of our family might be positioned on the towers to give assistance as necessary. This is probably not the retirement career you had envisioned, but it might be a chance to provide cash flow in a future that I am increasingly uneasy about. After the completion of the maze season, the tractor would be used to dismantle the maze and still feed the hay to the cattle. We might even be able to provide some seasonal employment for the upper valley if the games caught on with the public.

The future price of oil that the econometric models show is not promising, but my friends over in the petroleum revenue division are at least applying suitable probabilities to it so that the political types will not lose either their footing or their jobs. The problem is that as we transfer production of material aspects of our culture to other nations, they will become increasing consumers of oil. The result will most probably be increasing demand worldwide, which strangely enough, we the nation which started the process, will be least able to insulate ourselves against. The extraordinary low wages of countries we are most likely to transfer our pollution generating factories to, such as Latin America and India, mean those countries will still be able to compete effectively with high petroleum prices.

Unfortunately, it is the custom in America to raise the minimum wage at semi-regular intervals. If the wage level is not flexible downward at the bottom of the scale, a great leveling of the entire scale is most likely. The caveat to this is that only those jobs which may be readily transferred abroad will be affected initially, but the process may be best visualized as a small leak in a large dike. Wage levels for easily transferred processes will seek their own level, with only the cost of transportation and logistics management being a differential. If the minimum wage is too high to sustain those jobs within the nation, they will simply be transferred overseas. As wage levels are lowered for the base of the labor force, the old axiom that a rising tide lifts all boats will become apparent in reverse.

Even though an outflow of base-level jobs will occur, we will retain those jobs and processes in which we have a comparative advantage to other countries. These are most likely to be extremely high tech processes that require the unique type of academic freedom and economic rewards that are combined in America. In addition, I believe that we will find it in our economic self-interest to not share high tech military technology, so these jobs and the associated production processes will remain secure. Other areas which will cling to prosperity will be those which have significant structural barriers to entry, such as the medical profession due to the limited number of spaces in medical schools for potential doctors. Eventually, they will also become stressed as the lower levels of the wage scale will not be able to sustain the insurance system, choosing to risk going uninsured in order to enjoy some remaining aspects of their lifestyles.

The problem is that our domestic supplies of petroleum will have peaked prior to the transfer of a great amount of our manufacturing capacity abroad. We will be forced to compete in the world markets for an increasingly scarce resource, of which we will continue to be a major (if not the dominant) consumer. This chain of events will lead to ever-larger trade deficits, with the eventual realization that our credit rating as a nation will be at risk, due to an unsustainable cycle of increasing debt and consumption. The end result will be a declining value of the dollar relative to the nations to which we have transferred the manufacturing capacity and higher interest rates as required to fund the legacy deficit caused by our promise of social security payments to our generation and defense protection promised to wide areas of the world (such as South Korea and Japan). It is not a pleasant scenario but one that will result in a higher standard of living for much of the world outside the United States. It drives my desire to lay out a plan for relative family prosperity based on such resources as we may acquire over the next several decades.

If you believe even a small probability of my perspective exists, I recommend we both become net savers (compared with the general population). Whenever you believe it is feasible, family generational restraints permitting, we should start to acquire additional land around the traditional family farm. My preference is for those areas which are in timber, as it will most likely remain a viable resource with value. The combination of timber with paved road frontage is the most desirable, for it would give a window to market such services as a cemetery and the maze to the general public.

Your indulgence is requested, for I realize this letter has grown overly long, but such are the long evenings in Alaska. Back on the topic of the young lady, of whom I will no longer have the pleasure of her company. Have you ever noticed that when you open your personal life to someone, he or she seem to feel as if that person is permitted to speak to you in any manner? No one would dream of speaking to total strangers in such tones that supposedly intimate individuals speak within the privacy of their homes. Does civility end at the front door in our culture, and is there no recourse if one is insulted within the home other than the drastic measures of resigning from the relationship? I continue to be amazed at the wide variations in the American culture, which is undoubtedly due to a combination of the great melting pot with the insidious desire for individualism to prevail above the family. Back in the hills, the most serious offenses within the family resulted in the silence of those offended and one knew a significant line had been crossed and that backpedaling was required to maintain family harmony. Today, the individual offended seems to react instantly and harshly in an overt and loud verbal style that leaves the poor soul (perhaps me) with little recourse to redress the situation with any dignity. The result is that both parties seem to not know how to retrieve the serenity of the family setting that has been lost. I simply shall never engage in loud or vociferous conduct within my own home, even if the other party believes it is a sign of weakness not to, for I firmly believe such behavior is a rotting of the very basis of the intimate family unit.

Chapter XXVII

Dear younger cousin,

It seems we have the beginning of a family business plan combining various revenue producing streams to provide diversity within the available assets. One small problem is my health, which seems to be of an unstable nature. Although the doctors cannot determine the cause, I have experienced what a doctor called "discomfort" (since it has not happened to him) and what I call an episode of severe pain. For no apparent rhyme or reason, it happened with such intensity that I ended up on the floor, unable to get up until the event was over. To date, I have been fortunate that the event has occurred while I was home, and I made it to the bathroom in time to close the door behind me and simply slide to the floor. At the same time, the medical profession can find no apparent cause for the "discomfort." It is somewhat troubling, but I remind myself that the years are passing by and my health and appearance are of closer resemblance to my departed mother's than to the remainder of the apparent "immortals" in the clan. It always bothered me as a child that when I was taken ill, it was seen as a sign of weakness, even a systemic flaw, rather than simply something that was a relatively normal part of the human experience. Anyway, I trust that we will be of such health that we will have the opportunity to engage in these types of endeavors when our time finally arrives. Within the next five years, I intend to start accumulating land around the sides of the family farm when it becomes available.

At work, executive management gave me the assignment of writing the annual statement from the chairman of the board to the shareholders. It is to be included in the annual report and signed by the chairman. This is now our second chairman I have worked for in this institution, as the first one has retired. The new fellow seems as if he will be about the same to work with, and he does appreciate my limited writing ability. One does wonder how many shareholders really believe the so-called personal messages they receive from the leaders of corporations are actually written by the individual signing the message.

Our leader does at least read the document placed before him, although I have not been requested to revise anything going to the public up to this date.

We were most disheartened to hear that the Canadians are considering paving the remainder of the Alaskan Highway. Somehow I think that if I had to drive up hundreds of miles of what was loosely called "gravel" road to reach my goal, those which follow should have at least some of the same experience. Even in the short time I was in Alaska, they paved the route from the ferry terminal at Haines up to the Alcan and then all the way to the Alaskan border. I believe the Alaskan state government helped pay for that endeavor to provide better access for the tourist crowd who wished to combine the ferry with the inland route to Fairbanks.

I regret to hear you are so probably going to depart Alaska, for I know that even though it is a harsh mistress from a climate perspective, the shear beauty of her vastness is something to treasure always. Unfortunately the market is small and will probably remain so, due to the combination of the climate and resistance to development by the federal government. When I was in Alaska, there were only twelve commercial banks in the entire state, compared to nearly three hundred in the state from which we originated. Some of those twelve were even in such remote areas, the First National Bank of Ketchikan being a prime example; they were destined to remain small by a combination of location and purposeful ownership decisions. For those of us without equity to invest, I agree that Alaska is best considered a wonderful stopping off point in a career that at least will make colleagues wonder about us at other employers throughout our careers. It is always interesting when individuals ask why I started so far away from my home, and I have to tell them that there were simply no opportunities in our original locale and it was necessary to pursue the best jobs possible to meet financial commitments. One of the better things about the west of this United States is that a great number of individuals are new to the area, relative to back east, where family backgrounds may easily go back a couple of hundred years in the same general area. In the west, it certainly appears that ability and the pursuit of opportunity counts as least as much as family background, and I trust that it will remain that way for some time yet to come.

So you wish to become a banker! Well, you will most likely be a very good one, but I suggest you study your own thoughts on the probable economic scenario that awaits this country. If you are correct about the effect of free trade on the industrial base, which I agree has been totally skewed by the northern union demands for uneconomic wages, how will this process affect commercial banks? The one relentless process I see is "consolidation," not only in the industrial sector but in the service sector. The national sprawl of motel chains that has occurred since our youth will undoubtedly spread to most service sectors. This is likely to include commercial banking. So while banking will assuredly produce more income for you in the short and intermediate future, I believe that we both need to be aware that over the long term consolidation is inevitable. To that end think of your career choice as a game of musical chairs, where there will be less and less need for higher levels of managers due to the decreasing number of organizations. A flattening of the typical organizational chart will occur, with banks appearing much more like large national retail chains. Such organizations have the need for many store managers, a noble profession, but not a very well paid one with all the attendant headaches of running a separate organization without the compensation of a higher manager. Due to this process, banking would appear to be but a way stop along a career and not a destination. If we are going to do this family corporation venture, we might both be aware that the stops along the way are best enjoyed for the entertainment and cash flow and not thought of as any final stop where sufficient duration of employment will provide for retirement.

Your comments on the unfortunate process of communication within the typical American home were well put. No, I do not know how to address the issue, but what you encountered outside the bounds of matrimony most assuredly exists within them (at least in my experience). The problem appears associated with the consumption factor, for there is never sufficient resources to provide the lifestyle presented by the media and at the same time accumulate adequate capital for a business or retirement. I fear that the future of our generation will include a great many individuals who are disappointed with their lot in retirement. As I age, I give great latitude to our fellow man, as long as their activities cause no harm to others. Think back on your classical culture, and I believe the similarities between the "circuses," the excessive banquets, and the intrigue of the Senate compared to our modern equivalent shows that we have merely laid a thin veneer of technology on top of what is still basically a savage competition for scare resources. Inheritance is still the means through which most capital is acquired, along with well-planned marriages, although we insist on selling to the masses the American dream of wealth through work. They have about the same probability of being struck by lightning as becoming truly wealthy through traditional work, if they are forced to maintain a family and all it demands. The occasional individual who overcomes all adversity and truly achieves boundless financial success is so rare that our culture celebrates him in much the same manner as a triumph given to a conquering Roman general upon his return to the city.

Okay, I like your idea of a seasonal venture into mazes and it might even be viewed as an educational activity structured for entertainment. I have also had an idea of my own, which although not as creative, might well use some of that wide open space called the family farm. How about a driving range for golfers? Most ranges are such crowded affairs, with so little space between each individual that the experience is akin to being at a crowded fishing hole. What if we acquired land on both sides of the northern valley at its narrowest point and developed a driving range with targets on the opposing side of the valley? With appropriate landscaping, golf balls striking outside the targets might simply roll back down to the valley floor and reduce the time and expense of gathering the balls for the next day. While a golf course requires extensive maintenance of the greens and fairways, the grounds work on a driving range with targets would be far less. Given the amount of ground which we have to work with, we might go so far as to rent out the entire range for specific time periods to families or groups for outings. I realize this is not as creative as your seasonal maze, but it could be a pretty much year-round venture and provide an additional stream of revenue. Your thoughts would be appreciated on this matter. I shall try to do some basic research on golf driving ranges.

If you agree on the suitability of a chapel as another revenue channel, some thought needs to be given to the appearance and dimensions of the facility. In addition, it appears necessary for at least one of us to become ordained by some organized faith in order to perform the necessary rituals associated with marriage. In the matter of dimensions, I would prefer that it incorporate the "eternal ratio" of approximately 1.617 to 1. In this matter I am most resolved, for in addition to pleasing Iktinos, some few educated individuals might even notice the proportions. I still keep a framed print of the Parthenon on my office wall, and the architecture is still flawless some twenty-five hundred years later. Remember that the Parthenon was actually used as a Christian church after Constantine degreed the new religion to be that of the Empire. Using this framework, a small chapel of approximately thirty-five feet by fifty-six feet and one half should be adequate for most small gatherings. The windows would be approximately three feet wide by four feet, ten inches tall. The type of the exterior and interior appearance I leave to you, with the exception that the steeple should reach a height of approximately fifty-seven feet to conform to the historical guidelines.

Redressing your thoughts on the future economic clime we will confront, with my ideas of the flattening of the organizational structure, the development of a more leveled compensation scale for the masses seems inevitable. A greater disparity will develop between the wealthy elite and the masses and only the illusion of the American dream will preserve social harmony. Add to these thoughts the relentless leveraging of the national wealth through debt and I do not believe that most individuals will lower their standards of consumption simply due to stagnant real wages or sharply higher petroleum prices. Instead, it is more likely that the typical family will indulge themselves to the very limit of their financial resources. When considered on a national scale, this will result in an ever greater trade imbalance as we import the manufactured goods and increased petroleum required from abroad. Our success in generating revenue from services abroad will be touted but will total far less than our imports of products. Eventually, the developing nations will require investment in their own locales greater than we can provide, and a gradual withdrawal from our financial instruments will occur. The best scenario is a gradual leveling out of foreign investment in federal securities. In this case the internal level of interest rates will need to rise slowly, but relentlessly, to entice domestic investors to switch from consumption to investments. The process may be bumpy.

We might expect the government to delay the inevitable through deficit spending, of which a certain British economist would be proud, but it will be like fighting the very tides themselves. The bumpy upward trend of interest rates will first slow the rise in housing prices and ultimately cause their very reversal in most markets. At such point the all-American process of small down payment to gain from appreciation, will start to work in reverse. There should be no calamity, if the changes are incremental, instead just slowing the investment in the non-earning asset of housing as an investment and its true value as shelter will come to the fore. Let us know how the job search goes and I may be thinking about an alternative to the very banking industry you seek.

Chapter XXVIII

Dear elder cousin,

I must share another typically Alaskan occurrence in which I was recently involved. One of my friends submitted his resignation to a corporation with offices up here, in order to relocate to the outside. A mutual friend of ours asked him to stop by a local bar for final drink after work. This is not an uncommon gesture up here, and quaffing is so socially acceptable there seems a total disconnect with our backgrounds. I believe I was twelve before I even knew what a "package store" actually sold. As my friends entered the facility, they walked all the way to the back, and rounding a corner, discovered we had reserved the entire back room for about thirty of his closest friends. Entering into the festivities is all too easy at moments such as these, while remaining above the fray is by far the more respected approach, but I expect not nearly as much fun as the crowd seemed to be enjoying. For my soon-to-be-relocated friend, the combination of the late hour and the broad gesture of friendship were too great a temptation.

As the sixth Black Russian arrived at the head table for my friend, he apparently made the decision that he was not capable of driving across the frozen tundra to his home in Palmer (okay, it is not exactly tundra, but a hazardous drive in winter nonetheless). He then made what I believe were the first in a series of unfortunate choices. He requested that someone should call his wife and provide notification that he intended to spend the night in Anchorage rather than risk driving home in such a condition of intoxication. At first glance this seems like such a thoughtful and considerate gesture, one could hardly imagine it causing personal problems, but as I have not been wed, the subtleties of long-term relationships escape me. A learning experience was had by all, for it was discovered that in these moments of consideration, one should focus not only on having the appropriate call home made but on exactly whom one asks to make a call from a crowded bar. My friend made a definite mistake when he requested that one of the ladies at the gathering be the one to call his wife. I believe he finished the evening with approximately ten Black Russians.

Later on, a small group of us helped him acquire a hotel room and literally dropped him inside it. When he awoke the next day, he said he had no recollection of how he had gotten to that particular location, exactly what hotel he was in, or when the party had broken up. I believe he also made reference to feeling as if his head was about to explode. It was only upon arriving at his residence the next day that his wife felt obliged to clearly explain to him the gravity of the error in judgment he had made by having a lady call the previous night. I daresay the poor fellow could have hardly been in more trouble if he had not arranged a call at all; such are the pathways of good intentions.

As to the plan for your golf target driving range, do not disparage such an idea for the normality of it, for I support it wholeheartedly. Such customary activities are recurring ones and good potential sources of long term revenue. The idea of using the north valley at the narrowest point is very sound, along with the using of the natural incline of the opposing side to help collect the driven golf balls. The greater the number of such relatively small ventures which we may arrange around the family farm, the greater the probability of producing sufficient cash flow to support the family.

Our uncle is now focused on his idea of arranging through his political connections to have city water piped out to the area of the farm. It does not seem to matter to him that it is more than twenty miles from town; it is simply something he wants done. The water will need to be pumped uphill, for the area around the farm is about five hundred feet higher in elevation than the town along the edge of the delta where the water will originate. His plan is to have the area declared a pocket of rural poverty and obtain a combination of federal government grants and some long term loans to build the facilities. We are talking about millions of dollars of taxpayers' money to be spent on a very small number of individuals currently residing in the area. However, his hook is that the vast majority of the individuals have incomes far below the federally determined level of poverty, and that will assist him in being successful. It would actually be far cheaper to have the government drill each household a deep well, sufficiently so that it would not go dry in August. He has his heart set on city water though, and that is what he will undoubtedly obtain.

I oppose his plan for city water on several counts, not the least of which is the potential effect on land prices. Presently, folks are barely able to etch out a living on the worn out soil. The water is hard from the shallow wells, so water softeners must be installed in order for laundry to be done in a manner which will not harm clothes. The water table has been dropping as folks have literally been mining the underground water supply for over a century. Our springs in the east valley still flow, but that is simply because of the sudden drop in elevation plus the fact that there are no homes within a half-mile radius. The original dug well at the farm was thirty feet deep, three feet wide, and held sufficient water to provide for the family. It even provided annual employment for the fellow who came by each year and climbed down into the well during the dry season to scrub off such algae which might be growing on the stone walls of the well. By the time our grandfather got electricity, after WWII, he had a well drilled which was 160 feet deep, in order to get the bare minimum of a water supply. I believe new wells would need to be about five hundred feet deep to provide for a modern home.

The point is that lack of the water availability has effectively restrained development, due to the ever-increasing cost of drilling ever deeper wells. While his intentions are to help the remaining seventy-five or so families in and around the community, he simply cannot see the long-term consequences of what his actions will cause in the way of development. Today, the typical family farm in the area is about four hundred acres, with some more than twelve hundred acres. The properties usually remain within families, for there is no other apparent use for the land. With city water, our uncle will open the floodgates to the owners being able to subdivide their land into ten or even five acre lots. Remember, there is no rural zoning, so any such development does not have to be stick built homes but may include or even be made up entirely of mobile or modular houses. With each home will come the associated children, dogs, and horses, and the population density will change very quickly. While I have no hope of stopping his process, especially from this distance, arrangements have been made that will effectively put a cap on the disaster he is going to leave in his wake. The water development will have an effective cap of seven hundred fifty homes due to the size of the pipes, storage towers, and pumping stations necessary to bring the water up to altitude. Do not despair that all seven hundred fifty homes will be in the general vicinity of the farm, as the number includes all those which may sign on along the route out from town. In the immediate area of the farm this should contain the cancer of rural development to those land owners who develop their property first, while leaving a substantial portion of the upper valley in open land. It is the best which may be arranged given the circumstances. The sad fact is that he actually believes the primary purpose of this venture will be to raise the standard of living with better water for those already residing in the upper valley. The actual result will be a rise in their standard of living through monthly payments received from those ten and twenty acre lots that will be sold to new arrivals.

On the topic of these lots we can expect to see develop, not only will they diminish the scenic nature of the area; they will not really be fair to the purchasers. The probable buyers will be individuals wanting more home than they can afford in any of the small towns which surround the farm within a twenty-five mile radius. They will most probably not have white collar jobs, but exactly the type of jobs which we have been discussing that are most likely to be transferred overseas in the years ahead. Given that our state has one of the highest divorce rates in the nation, I believe many purchasers will fall victim to one of the three Ds: divorce, disability, or death prior to paying off their lots, which will probably be purchased on long term contracts (notes held by seller). A great deal for the seller, who most probably will obtain the land back when the buyer eventually defaults.

Yes, I can hear you now, but I simply will not be involved in such an overt confiscation of poor folks' hard-earned dollars. The only caveat would be a situation where it truly is our last recourse to manage our financial affairs. The poor souls also do not comprehend what is likely to happen to petroleum prices and the associated price of gasoline in the years ahead. Not only will they be saddled with monthly payments on their land, vehicles, and modular housing, the rising price of gasoline will steadily eat into their disposable income. I have considered making noise about the need for county-wide zoning, but such is the value of private property rights that no one will support the retention of open spaces over development as it is not in their short term financial best interest. To add insult to the process, the sellers who do repossess their land prior to it being paid off will actually receive improved property back. The initial buyers will have added a septic system and brought in electricity to their home sites. Currently, no perk test is even required for a septic system, but that problem may be addressed within the political process without overt opposition arising.

Your thoughts on starting the process of acquiring land within the next five years are well timed. Given the likely effect of the water system on land prices, I expect we will end up paying far more for the additional acreage than we otherwise would have without the intervention of our uncle. Although I try to focus on your suggestions of the inherent good in everyone, our grandfather's comments to me on the topic of his eldest son are always in the back of my thoughts. Who would know an individual much better than his father, as related to his basic motivations? Be cautious of what is said to our uncle on the matter of the water system, and certainly do not share the plan to acquire an additional 188 acres to complete the goal.

I will most certainly acquiesce to your ideas on the dimensions for the chapel and thank you for your support of the basic thesis. Even I can see that your desire to create something of lasting beauty is at least as important as the need to address the cash flow issue. Your trust on the exterior and my taste is most gratifying. Using your length of fifty-six and one half feet, visualize seven pairs of steel trusses set at intervals of approximately eight feet. Each pair of trusses will intersect at a height of forty-five feet, creating the necessary height within the chapel to draw the eye upward. The upward portion of each truss will continue for a distance of eleven and one-half feet beyond the intersection of each truss. The key to the optical illusion will be that the exterior wall will be made of glass from the top of each truss down to its horizontal intersection with the angle of each primary truss. The inward side of the angle of each truss would have a mirrored finish down the remainder of the distance. The objective will be to flood the interior with light from above, drawing the eyes upward in contemplation. The front of the chapel should have an entrance that utilizes again your eternal ratio, with stained glass windows offsetting each side of the entrance and being of the same proportion of 1.617 to 1. It is suggested that the back of the chapel be composed of three vertical portions, each of equal width. The two portions on each side would again be of a gilded nature, with the third and central portion being a wall of clear glass starting about the floor and being seventeen and one-half feet to the top of the glass (your eternal ratio again). If the same proportions are used for a garden, using our agreed upon approximate acreage, it would be nearly 734.5 feet wide and 1,186.4 feet in length to encompass slightly more than 871,200 square feet, or twenty acres. We will need an area with a small knoll to better site the chapel within the overall context. This will also reduce the landscaping expense.

Your approach seems to currently be taking a day-to-day approach to life, somewhat lacking in long term appeal, but very much within my belief that life is best lived in the very moment as the future is but a plan and a belief in the unknown. I'd best stop, as I sound increasingly like one of you religious types.

Yes, I agree with the probability of banking going the way of national motel chains, but let's not tell that to the bankers until long after I have successfully charted a course into your profession. While the future path of economic change is most assured, the timing is not so certain. I am banking (yes, pun intended) that the change will be so gradual that there will be sufficient time for a banking career of between one and two decades without having to work in either New York or Chicago. After such time we best have the family enterprises past the planning stage for banking consolidation will probably run rampant. Along the vein of economic thought that we have been discussing, your thesis of the probable long term rise in "real" interest rates (nominal rates less the rate of inflation) is most probable. On the proverbial other hand, I do not believe in linear probability of the event sequence. After using the fiscal stimulus of deficit spending, the Federal Reserve will at first try negative "real" interest rates to sustain economic expansion and entice the general population to keep borrowing. It will only be when their hand is forced by externalities, such as a sudden and sustained spike of a scarce commodity such as oil, that they will begin the inevitable rate hike sequence.

The creation of jobs within this country will not be sufficient to reduce the unemployment rate, so an odd occurrence will commence for which they will not be prepared. Inflation will be driven by commodity prices, not direct labor costs, and the real inflation adjusted incomes of the general population will begin the long decline. Given the prime duty to contain inflation, the Federal Reserve will raise interest rates as assuredly as a Broadway script. The higher level of interest rates will not initially contain the inflation, as it will be caused by the externality of commodity prices beyond our borders. As the international price of petroleum is pegged to the US dollar as the currency of the international realm, the higher interest rates will simply sustain the value of the dollar at an unreasonable level relative to other currencies. This will place a further damper on our exports as they will be expensive compared to our international competitors due to the strong value of the dollar relative to their currencies. The Fed will then be between a rock and a hard place, for to lower interest rates will simply result in inflation being generated from within the domestic economy (adding to the imported commodity inflation), but to not lower them will cause a continued drag on our ability to export products. Whoever is the unfortunate soul destined to be president during this chain of events will not even know what hit him, I suspect. Take care; if Socrates was right, only the grasp of math enables the grasp of ethics, and I believe the understanding of the future. Enjoy the moment, but grasp the inevitability of the future course!

What would you think of this scenario as an option for the future federal government when the probable event sequence occurs? If the Fed may be persuaded that the inflationary impact is solely of an external commodity origin, and that it will likely be offset by a continued decline in the price of imports as more manufacturing is shipped overseas to ever lower cost countries, why not allow the real interest rate to continue to be negative (below the rate of inflation)? Yes, I realize this will cause the actual holders of capital who are unwilling to take risk (the traditional widows and orphans example) to effectively gradually lose the real inflation adjusted value of their wealth. However, it will provide even greater incentive and ability for those with imagination to borrow funds for investment in the latest technology that has not yet been transferred abroad. The caveat is that the government would need to rein in the seemingly limitless use of funds for the unproductive housing sector, perhaps through a limit on the level of loans that could qualify for a federal tax deduction.

The other problem will be how to cure the federal government deficit, which otherwise will continually increase the amount of funds we must acquire from our trading partners to fund the continuing rise in our total public debt. While I have always had a somewhat of an Alexander Hamilton attitude toward public debt, as it is necessary to maintain and assure future access to funds if the country surely needs them, we will be far beyond that level when the crisis that I fear strikes. Raising taxes will not cure the problem, for such actions simply reduce the drive to produce additional marginal income (e.g., why work two jobs if the government takes a substantial portion of the extra effort for its own purpose?). It would seem likely that we will fall back on the Roman alternative of selectively deciding which parts of our empire to withdraw from in a subtle manner. Roman Britain was not left undefended because it was suddenly unsuitable, merely that the troops were needed for defensive purposes closer to Rome. A gradual reduction of our foreign military commitments will appear ever more rational, as folks notice that the countries taking our manufacturing jobs will probably have relatively few troops stationed outside of their borders. The geo-economic chess game is unfortunately real, and empires inevitably lose as they tend to overextend themselves. The trick is to assure that the final capitulation occurs after we are gone. Share your thoughts and tell me if I am being totally illogical.

Chapter XXIX

Dear younger cousin,

Prior to commenting on your frank portrayal of the probable future path of our nation from an economic perspective, let me share additional words from home. Yes, I am now thoroughly aware of our uncle's venture to provide city water to our rural countryside, and I completely concur with your perspective of the probable development it will bring upon its completion. Another factor you are apparently unaware of is that the State Game and Fish Commission have decided to build a dam five miles downstream from the east end of the farm. The purpose of this structure is not to generate power, flood control, or some worthwhile economic creation of wealth for the betterment of the society. It is designed for recreational purposes, specifically fishing. Due to the narrow nature of the valley, the lake will never be more than about a quarter of a mile wide, and the dam itself is only planned to be somewhat more than fifty feet high. The dam will be of the earthen variety, instead of the more expensive concrete. Due to the gradual slope of the stream after it leaves the end of our farm, great portions of the lake will never be more than ten feet deep, even during the wet season. They plan to leave the tree stumps in the lake to better provide habitat for fishes, which combined with the narrow nature of the lake will at least preempt the use of the facility for water skiing.

Just as the water system being advocated by our uncle will bring in additional residents through the lower costs associated with obtaining domestic water, the lake will bring in weekend fishing residents and one can easily foresee weekend cabins and retirement homes being developed along the wooded shoreline of the lake. It is a continual amazement to me that one of the poorest states in the union can expend scarce resources on providing more recreational activities for the general population and at the same time tell them (with a straight face) that ever higher tuition is required to send their children to college. It is again the American dream to have it all and the government's desire to acquiesce to their ever-larger wants that hastens the inevitable consequences written about in your last letter. In all cases the intentions are good, but it is the pathway being paved toward the economic edge I find extremely disturbing. On a personal note, it is of course not in our best interests to see such a development occur before we acquire the necessary land, as it is surely going to raise the costs of land acquisition. The State Game and Fish Commission notified our uncle that the lowest five acres of the farm will now be in a one hundred year floodplain, which of course means that this particular small portion of the place will now be worthless from an economic perspective, as no mortgage can be obtained to build any structure on such a floodplain. The next neighbor downstream was informed that about fifty acres of his property would be in such a floodplain, and he managed to obtain a hefty financial payment from the state, what I view as the taking of his land for the so-called "public" purpose of recreation. Our uncle simply signed away the easement (without our signatures), as he did not think the monetary loss was significant. No, of course he did not consult me on the matter, but I heard about it from a reliable source.

On a lighter note, I must relay an event that occurred in one of our branches that has provided some enjoyment. We have a young trainee, Debbie, an MBA no less (when I received my MBA, there were only about five thousand per year being earned in the entire nation! Now it seems more and more schools are offering the degree, and there is little in the way of clear-cut standards, so you need to really ask some questions about the programs they have completed when you hire these new graduates). She is learning the ropes of banking by serving first as a teller and then higher positions in a branch. The operations officer in the branch where he is working is one of the most pleasant individuals I have met (no, she is not available for you to date, as she is married). The branch is located inside a small shopping mall and has a walk-up facility on the main mall corridor. The idea was that individuals simply wishing to conduct a brief transaction would not even have to enter the lobby; instead they could simply use the teller window in the mall corridor. As these are the easier transactions, the operations officer had stationed the young MBA at this location to minimize the risk to her daily operation from mistakes. The branch itself is accessed by the employees through a back door, instead of the lobby door that opens to the mall.

When Debbie found out the young fellow was having a birthday, she and her employees decided to help him celebrate the occasion without telling him. This was accomplished by coming into the branch early and decorating the mall side of his teller window, which he could not see from inside the branch. Along with the customary "Happy Birthday" signs, Debbie had signs made up that stated in large letters, "Wave to me, it's my birthday." The poor young fellow stood in the teller station all morning and could not understand why everyone was so friendly to him that morning. It was only when he left the branch for lunch in the mall that he saw the signs and realized what had been done. Debbie said he professed to be embarrassed by what she had done, but I believe it was in fact one of those rare moments of happiness we have discussed. An unexpected show of friendliness by his fellow employees, with public acceptance, could not but have helped the young fellow feel fortunate.

We had an earthquake! It was not an overly large one, so I don't know whether you heard about it on the news. On the commonly used scale it measured about a five, but it occurred during business hours on a weekday. After having experienced all the usual shakes in Alaska, it really sort of reminded me of those enjoyable days up north, but the employees were asked to evacuate the building. Frankly, I considered just ignoring the request, for I was aware that if the building was going to collapse, it would likely do so before most of us were outside. But at times such as these, I always try to be the good corporate citizen, so I joined the masses going down the staircases. The building was swaying slightly and the plaster in the stairwell cracked in one place as we were descending, and it made an interesting sound as it shifted. After we all made it outside, we simply stood around for a while until it was deemed safe to go back into the building (as if anyone actually knew whether the initial quake was simply a forerunner to a larger one, or a singular event by itself). Earthquakes are something of a rarity down here, but I always have to remind myself that on the west side of the Rockies, they really can happen almost anywhere. Everyone seems to have forgotten that a seven-plus event happened in the Yellowstone area in the 1950s before there were many people in the area. When I was in Alaska, it always seemed that the quakes were almost seasonal, with more during the spring, but perhaps the feeling was because the big one that destroyed Anchorage in the early 1960s occurred during the spring. In our little state capital, there was no significant damage from this little shake, but it did seem to affect folks' nerves as they are not sufficiently comfortable with mild quakes.

Your presentation of the external features of the proposed farm chapel is most suitable and will make it distinctive, while incorporating the familiar proportions I most enjoy. While most individuals back in the hills will not notice the ratio borrowed from the Parthenon, I would like to stress that the Greeks borrowed it themselves. Have you ever noticed that the ratio of the length of the base of the pyramids at Giza to the height of the structures is approximately the same ratio of 1.617 to 1? The problem with getting an exact proportion is that the marble cap stones that covered the sides of the structures have been removed over the eons by architectural thieves, but the basic ratio cannot be hidden. It would seem that the "eternal ratio" has been around for a long time, so I see no reason why we should not borrow it. With your high windows running along side each side of the chapel, and the large window at the end focusing attention, combining to bring the focal point both upward and forward, I see no reason to even have lower windows on each side. I did catch the symbolism with the eight steel trusses on each side; the space between each truss effectively creates seven spaces along the exterior wall of each side for a total of fourteen spaces. Did you think you could just slide that bit of folklore by me? This incorporation of the fourteen Stations of the Cross into the very structure of the building is something that I do not object to, but for a non-religious individual you have an odd way of incorporating the supposed historical facets of the religion into the physical structure.

We have not resolved the matter of the material to use for the exterior of the sides below the point where the glass joins the extremity of the high point of the trusses to the lower point. I like the way the slope of the building sides effectively minimizes the roof, but it leaves open the question of the material for the sides. I would of course prefer marble, but it is such a soft stone and so porous that it presents many challenges in maintenance. Somehow, stone siding seems so much more permanent than the customary white wood siding of rural churches. The exact selection of the stone I leave up to you, but please be reasonable. On the matter of the interior features, the mirrors to reflect the light from above sound great, but I am afraid we will never be able to afford your gilded features. I hope that you will be able to live with polished brass. They have developed features that help it retain the gleam of a new metal for a lengthy period and it is so much more reasonable than anything gilded. Also remember we will be constructing this in the hills, using local contractors, and anything significantly beyond what they are accustomed to will simply invite problems with the construction. It is just a minor distraction, but I notice that your exterior design omits my steeple in order to fully incorporate the proper ratio in the dimensions. Could you please come up with something that will allow external placement of at least one cross in a somewhat prominent location?

In my corporate life, I have reached a number of management decisions. It is obvious that the only thing that really matters is the recognition of the value of your contribution to the enterprise. The production of routine reports, the regular analysis, and the expected performance appears to be the most assured way into that corporate "box" that everyone is striving to avoid. I am now delegating all routine functions, regardless of the purported high value to the organization. I believe that in reality, such matters are of little career value, for my superiors simply expect the routine to be performed well, and you are definitely not compensated well for just doing what is expected! I have a bit of a conflict with another individual in the organization, which is new to me. He is a friend of executive management, which complicates the situation. An interesting individual to watch, his strategy seems to be that loud vocalizations in meetings connotes thought and appears to sway the consensus through the sheer force of his personality rather than reason. I believe that in our society, such individuals with overbearing personalities and strong personal bonds with those in leadership positions will generally prevail over logic and thought. My immediate superior will be retiring in less than two years, so I should probably be contemplating change, if not in location, at least in organization. The problem of course is that when you are working in a city of only about one hundred thousand residents, thoughts of change force you to consider geographical relocation and the nearest city of any size close to Boise is Salt Lake City and that is more than three hundred miles away.

I also need to consider selling my movie theatre, although it is something I really do not want to do. It was originally intended as an external distraction to take my thoughts away from the banking industry for even a short period of time, but I have found great enjoyment in the little enterprise.

Living in a sparsely populated area, such as Alaska or Idaho, has the wonderful advantage of the wide-open spaces, but it forces such sudden and drastic changes when a career shift becomes necessary. As an example, there are more people residing in the two-county area of Dallas/Fort Worth than there are in Alaska and Idaho combined. While those folks definitely do not have any scenery to lift their spirits, they have many more options to change employers without having to relocate across state lines and mountain ranges. I never considered these things when I was younger and headed out west. On another positive note, I have finally finished paying off my student loans, so monthly cash flow is again improved. Actually, they could have been paid off sooner, but their low interest rates made it more advantageous to place the funds in other ventures. If you have time, take the road to Hope on the way to Seward, and only the last ten miles are not paved. May your economic thoughts be focused on personal profits.

Chapter XXX

Dear eldest cousin (E),

So in a very short time period, the family farm has gone from being located in a totally undeveloped rural area to an area where city water and recreational fishing are soon to be available! We either need to make a commitment to acquire land before too long, or we will be surrounded by development. I am definitely leaving the field of public service, as the short hours and long vacations simply do not compensate for the extent of the shortfall in monetary reward. Just to let you know, I have had my first interview with a banking organization in Columbus, Ohio. It is the large type of commercial enterprise that is likely to endure for some number of years, even if we are correct about consolidation. The corporate headquarters is in a far larger city than any in our home state, but sufficiently smaller than Chicago or New York so that it is relatively easy to get around in on a commuting basis. Now the catch is waiting until they call for a second interview, without calling them and appearing anxious.

Up here, the banking culture appears to be getting ever more brutal as banks cut back on their staffing due to the soft nature of our local economy. Two stories are circulating around town. One bank seems to have waited until a lady vice president (a vice president with twenty-plus years of experience) took a vacation down to Seattle, and then the bank sent a senior vice president down to meet with her at the hotel in Seattle to tell her she should also use the trip for job hunting. In the public sector in Alaska, such actions simply would never be taken. Another local commercial bank actually replaced a financial officer while he was on vacation, which he discovered when he returned and another individual was sitting behind his desk. I may eventually regret entering into this field, for there seem to be little regarding rules of behavior to govern the affair. The monetary factor—and certainly not personal happiness—is the driving force in this endeavor. It continues to amaze me when I hear people speak of finding fulfillment in their work. It would not be called work if it was not inherently unpleasant and something that we must be paid to do in order to obtain our services. I have requested that if the Ohio bank wishes my services, they will need to pay a signing bonus of at least $5,000 and compensate me for all my moving expenses to the Lower Forty-Eight. Even at that, I do not anticipate making a financial gain from the move until after the first few months in the new job.

Your advice was very good concerning Hope. It is such a small, out-of-the-way community that I had completely missed it in my explorations of the Alaskan countryside (the part that can be reached by road). Although not much more than a wide spot in the road, the location on Turnagain Arm's south shore gives you a splendid view of the Chugach Mountains plunging down to the sea on the north shore. Again, I will miss living in the majesty of Alaska (if they come through with the job offer), and if I could determine a reasonable way to forge a career up here that provides some semblance of such combination of stability and monetary reward I would never even consider leaving. I always remember that your father worked for the same company for more than forty-five years, with only a brief break for time spent in the Pacific during WWII, and retired never having had to prepare a résumé for a new job interview. There are simply too many of our generation competing for the scarce resources of employment to expect such stability during the remaining years of our careers.

Thank you for your kind words concerning the basic structure of the proposed farm chapel. Of course I shall bend to reason in reference to the interior gilding, but would it not look grand! On the exterior, you are correct about the marble—too soft and porous, with maintenance required to retain the correct appearance over time. As an alternative, I would propose granite, a much more durable stone that also has a distinguished appearance. Besides, the heathens stripped the marble exterior from the pyramids not long after the collapse of the First Dynasty, leaving us with the unsightly stepped appearance everyone seems to believe is what was intended. On the subject of the steeple, or lack thereof, for budgetary reasons, why not place the steeple beyond the structure in the "Garden of Remembrance"? It could be located beyond the large window at the end of the chapel so the congregation could view it throughout the service. On the question of the podium and small choir section, I would prefer the old New England model of having the podium located offset to the side of the end of the chapel, somewhat elevated over the congregation. Instead of placing the choir behind the pulpit, putting them on the opposing side of the chapel would provide better balance and take up less space. For music, a piano would suffice, as proficient organ players are increasingly difficult to procure. We might even be able to arrange the availability of musicians through some of the surrounding colleges. I think I remember an appropriate knoll to situate the chapel upon, but unfortunately, it is just beyond our current borders, so land acquisition is definitely required.

It is apparent you are not pleased with your current employer, so perhaps relocation would also be best for you to seriously consider. I understand the distance factor those of us living in the sparsely populated areas of this country have to consider when changing jobs, which of course I also did not contemplate as a new college graduate. So wherever you choose to head, it will most likely be a substantial jump from your present location. The migrant labor title does seem increasingly suitable.

News from our old college in Illinois has reached me in Alaska. Remember how the sports teams, such as they were without athletic scholarships to speak of, were always referred to as the "Siwash"? This was a corruption of the original French "sauvage," meaning savage. The current student body is deeming such a term politically incorrect, as they take the reference to be offensive toward Native Americans. I fear both the lack of understanding of the current group of students and the willingness of the faculty and administration to cave in to their demands. Perhaps if the English department required reading the novels by a certain 1857 alumni of our institution, the students would understand that he coined the word "Siwash" not to refer to the Native Americans but as a reference to the collegians he remembered were acting like savages. Certainly every culture has savages within it, and the phrase seemed most fitting to describe the athletic component of our institution. Enrollment is somewhat diminished from the peak years of the baby-boom generation, but this is to be expected as the generation following us has far fewer individuals from which to draw students. Yes, I can hear you now, reminding me that the exact use of the word Siwash was by the Chinook Indians who were not pronouncing the French word correctly. It is my belief that they were not using the word to refer to themselves but instead to reference the newcomers from the East. In either case, the word is not and never has been intended to be demeaning toward Native Americans, and I believe the students are simply sifting for issues since such weighty matters as the draft no longer exist to focus their attention. I have no idea what new name they may develop to change the name of the Silver Turkey trophy awarded to the annual winner of the game with the neighboring college (Monmouth College). Frankly, I find the Silver Turkey phrase to be much more demeaning to the regal wild turkey than the Siwash nickname ever could be to those athletes of our generation.

Your earthquake seemed to have brought back your memories of the recurring ones we have up here, which we never mention to potential tourists or investors. They certainly are part of the landscape, along with the volcanoes. Do you remember seeing the huge white hulk of the Redoubt Volcano across lower Cool Inlet from Clam Gulch, or the even larger Illiamna from further down the Kenai Peninsula, located over on the Alaskan Peninsula across Cook Inlet? Such sights simply cannot be easily seen in the Lower Forty-Eight, and I will, in fact, miss the *place* of Alaska even more than the people I have met up here.

Back on my future economic scenario, which might be referred to as "why you should never sell the family farm," I believe I last was thinking of an ugly situation in which a commodity crisis was driving domestic inflation while freedom of trade was causing the stagnation in the level of employment and wages. At the same time, the minimum wage will prevent the base level of wages from adjusting downward, although there will be a great flattening of the wage scale. Our foreign competitors, assuming they understand the game better than we do, should attempt to artificially maintain a subsidized price of oil, to the extent they are net exporters of the product, through government intervention. As petroleum plays a much smaller domestic role in those economies—although they are not and probably never will be as energy efficient in producing gross domestic product from a barrel of oil as we are—but they will become more efficient in the years ahead. The net result should be that the impact of a sustained period of high petroleum prices would be expected to have a lesser impact on their economies than ours. At some critical point, their domestic economies will become their driving force for demand, as their banking systems develop and such things as credit cards become readily available to their populations. Even if our demand for their products stabilizes instead of growing, the increasing demand from within their own countries should suffice to continue to raise the standard of living of what we now call the "developing" countries. The only caveat is that such positive events are only probable in those industrializing countries with stable internal political structures. This would likely apply to India and China in the future. China, in particular, has a history of several millennium of autocratic rule of some type, which generally provides prolonged periods of social stability between the inevitable upheavals. I am still unsure what probable oil reserves they will find in the South China Sea or elsewhere off their coast.

Where will that development leave the good old US of A? As the wage curve flattens, there will be demands that the sacrifices of a lower standard of living be shared among greater segments of the population. I would imagine that one of the first groups to be attacked will be those receiving pensions from companies in dire financial straits because of the sustained high price of oil. Through bankruptcy, companies will unload those pension commitments, and employees will begin to comprehend that those relentless Madison Avenue sirens are more than a little akin to their ancient Greek counterparts who lured sailors to their destructions. As those presently employed see their retired parents and other relatives having substantial portions of their retirement incomes diminished, is it not likely that they will begin to curb their addiction to debt and attempt (vainly I fear) to belatedly plan for their own retirements with their own work (not a corporation's promises).

If such a point is reached, I can only foresee a cascade effect. The political types will have a federal budget that will simply refuse to remain balanced. The level of pension debt owed to our generation, the baby boomers, simply will not be payable, and all will come home to roost. The logical step will be to increase the retirement age, but since the employment market will be stagnant, the government will essentially be telling folks that they best be able to fend for themselves during the awkward gap between the time that corporations eliminate them for being too expensive and when they will eventually qualify for social security. If the "wrong" political types gain hold, movement may even be made to limit recipients of social security to only those of the middle class and below (effectively turning it into a pure tax on higher income earners). This would nationalize the contributions of those unfortunate to have made more money during their working years, in the name of the greater good. Through such a combination of leveling of the wage levels of those still working, a reduction in private pension burdens on corporations, and finally a reduction in the national burden of social security, the country will attempt to maintain sufficient competitiveness to secure those jobs that will be left. It is not a pleasant scenario, and certainly not one that will get anyone elected if he or she dare mention the possibility; but I wonder if I am alone in these thoughts.

As for the Federal Reserve, I suspect that too late they will realize the wrong war is being fought and allow inflation to gain the upper hand in a belated attempt to save jobs through the decline in the value of the dollar (a weak dollar policy). As more and more of the national debt will be owned by foreigners, the burden of a weakening dollar will be pushed partially back abroad along with our declining standard of living. Okay, I am convinced; the land acquisition should begin if we intend to remain in this country.

If the Columbus bank comes through with the job offer, I will attempt to purchase the forty acres to the northwest border of the farm. This is the same forty acres that our uncle was given by our grandfather at the end of WWII and then turned around and sold in order to make the down payment on that gasoline bulk plant in town. He will not be pleased when I repurchase it, so I will attempt to keep a low profile. While the interim years of his planned onslaught on our serenity will doubtless result in the development we both fear, any sustained period of high gasoline prices that might develop in the long term is likely to delay the tide. The initial development in such a rural location will probably be individuals seeking a piece of the countryside they cannot afford in a more urban setting. They will most likely acquire the maximum amount of land they can afford, along with the price of modular housing and vehicle payments. We might think of these individuals as akin to being the first wave on the beaches: gallant but destined to face a difficult struggle. The economic scenario would indicate that they are likely to have a period of fewer than two decades before the sustained rise in gasoline prices makes daily commutes of more than fifty miles round trip uneconomical for the typical wage earner back in the hills. If the location was in a more prosperous state, we might expect the first wave to sustain itself, but in one of the poorest states in the union, these folks are probably not destined to be so fortunate.

The reason I am proposing starting with this particular piece of property is that a county road borders it on two sides. As it is a square forty acres, this arrangement results in nearly half a mile of road frontage (more than the entire family farm). The road curves away from it during the last three hundred feet. It borders the family farm for a full quarter mile and has slightly more than a quarter mile of Clifty Creek running through it. The road is currently graveled, but we both know the historical trend toward paving. The area closest to the road is reasonably level, but the back side has bluffs more than fifty feet above the creek. It would be simply too easy to develop by running a road parallel to the bluffs, but set back about three hundred feet, and creating lots overlooking the valley below. Share your thoughts; I am being irrational or too sentimental? I plan to stop the development process nearest the farm!

Chapter XXXI

Dear younger cousin(Y),

You definitely have a plan of action, and it has my wholehearted support. Being unmarried gives us both far greater freedom of action with regard to real estate investments than I believe most married individuals have due to the need to reach a consensus. The bank in the Midwest sounds great, and although based in Ohio, it would put you scarcely a day's drive from the hills. Compared to our mutual locations over these too many years, it would be practically next door to home.

On the matter of your economic scenario, I would wish to temper it somewhat. Remember that most of the leading OPEC economists were educated in this country, and it is almost as if we are engaged in a chess game with ourselves. They are fully aware, after the gasoline shocks of the 1970s, that too rapid an increase in the price of petroleum will produce a recession along with a significant downward movement in the international price of their resource. It will be in their best interest to maintain a price range in the moderate area until the developing countries are fully hooked on oil. Just like fishing in the Des Arc, they will only fully support a sustained increase in the price of petroleum after the hook is completely set in the mouth of the unsuspecting developing countries. At that point, they should be pretty unconcerned about further growth in our demand, as our declining domestic production will result in ever greater imports of their product even if our demand remains constant. Just so we are both clear in this matter, I believe in your basic scenario, but I believe that it will unfold over a period of decades and not be fully appreciated until the third decade of the twenty-first century. At that point, the developed countries will not have the financial ability to rapidly change energy sources due to the burden of supporting their aging populations and their perceived necessity to maintain control of their global commercial empires through a far-flung military. The developing nations will not fully appreciate their dilemma due to their focus on their upward trending standards of living and the need to maintain social stability. The core oil producing Middle East nations have sufficient petroleum reserves to produce through the entire 21st century.

I suspect they will also come to remember some past perceived territorial wrongs. India is most likely to address the Pakistan border question, while China would remember the territory Russia wrested from them in the North and Japan in the Southeast (Taiwan). Until the burden of our generation is fully lifted by our demise, and the military empire is largely drawn back toward our borders, the Middle East portion of OPEC will enjoy a considerable period of sustained prosperity. I imagine that for the Muslim faith (the newest of the great religions), the twenty-first century will most resemble the thirteenth century of Christianity, with great focus on religion and the prosperity to make their equivalent of the great European cathedrals a reality wherever they choose. *Se non è vero, è ben trovato*! ("If it's not true, it's a good story." Or, according to Merriam-Webster: "Even if it is not true, it is well conceived.")

I believe the overall plan we have for the family assets is sound, but it will truly take two of us working to achieve it. Presuming you snare that job in Ohio, perhaps you can get in on some of those stock options the eastern banks are offering and accelerate your financial success far beyond that of myself.

In other news from the farm, a fellow from down in the flats has purchased the waterfalls on Clifty Creek. This is the small (six-feet-tall), thirty-feet-wide falls you probably remember from our childhood. He acquired about six acres of land (word is he paid more than $5,000 per acre), which gave him about a hundred feet of road frontage on that same county road you are considering acquiring land on and the half of the waterfall that is on his side of the stream. When I was a boy, the land on the family farm side of the falls sold for sixty dollars per acre and Grandfather felt sorry for the poor family who purchased twenty-three acres of the hillside, which was covered with rocks. Remember the old swimming hole below the falls? It is only about forty feet long and never deeper than five feet. Anyway, the gentleman intends to develop the acreage and build a walkway down to the falls. Obviously he has not encountered all the snakes those of us locals tend to focus on in swimming areas. I believe the intent is to rent out the facility for weddings. Does this begin to sound familiar? Your desire to start the land acquisition process is well timed. The only negatives he faces are a matter of timing and location. I believe he is perhaps a decade or so too early in the development process and he is located a quarter mile off the main road. The county road that runs up by the entrance he has acquired first passes the old—and closed—general store before winding past the foundation of the old cotton gin. It is not exactly a grand entrance for a wedding party to pass through. His very actions do seem to mirror our thoughts that development is inevitable, unless we acquire sufficient land to control the process.

If he has adequate financial resources to purchase the old general store building and demolish it, with a finishing touch of paving the road from the highway to his entrance, he may stand a chance of becoming successful. I do not know any of the background of the gentleman, or anything of his financial resources, so about all we can do is hope that he is as limited as we are in our current ability to take action. It does seem that nondenominational locations are increasingly being chosen for wedding sites.

Yes, you are correct; I am growing ever more dissatisfied with the daily grind of producing insightful results for stockholder wealth enhancement while working for a salary without any long-term benefit from the ideas I contribute daily. The company does have a retirement plan, but it requires ten years of continuous employment to become vested, and there seems little possibility of that occurring. The workplace has become even drearier, if that is possible. A transfer of power to a third chairman has occurred. This is now the third chairman I have worked for within a five-year period. It does not enhance one's feeling of job security to see executive management change so often. The abilities of the new leader appear well focused—perhaps too well focused. Having relocated to Boise from the West Coast, the staff does seem to have questions about what his long-term plan may be for the institution. I don't know whether I have mentioned it or not, but most of our employees are long-term residents of the Treasure Valley, and I am one of the few from outside the area. A close associate of mine in the Trust department has even put it rather bluntly "For what purpose but to build a bank if not to sell it?"

It seems that we are surrounded by the developer, a dealmaker type, both in business and back on the family homestead. The new chairman does appear too young, too good at banking, and too polished to imagine being stranded in the outback of Idaho for a lengthy period of time. My immediate boss, the vice chairman, has been passed over for the position of chairman again and is now within a year of his anticipated retirement. He has already chosen his likely successor (not me), and although a fine individual, he has little use for my perspectives on continuous change as a management perspective. Fortunately, he is not burdened with having as much banking experience as me, so he brings a fresher viewpoint and a closer personal relationship with my boss. Persistent, gradual change is just not the fashion, with everyone instead choosing to swing for the far walls and looking for those home runs.

Instead of looking for another banking position—for I seem destined to always be in the background serving some executive officer either in the capacity of math orientation, creative orientation, or written focus—I have decided to pursue the college teaching career. You questioned whether I could support the change in cash flow, and I truly do not know the answer. The problem in college teaching is not experience, for I have years of that in various institutions both in Alaska and Idaho, but a problem in qualifications. While in the business community, my master's degree from Vanderbilt seems to make me overqualified and even makes some individuals uncomfortable around me; in the academic community, a doctorate is almost like a union card. Without such a degree it is almost impossible to obtain tenure, which resigns one to a period of employment of generally not more than seven years at any one institution before having to move on to another school. The alternative is seeking to teach in the community college system of some large public university, where a master's degree would suffice but where the compensation would never amount to a great deal.

The real problem of course is that I am at a very awkward age. It seems that I am too young to resign myself to an unhappy few decades of working in an industry that does not exactly seem enamored with me, yet I have too much age to easily start over again. Although I could go back after a doctorate, I still can remember guys in the doctorate program (when I was earning my master's) who had been in the program for years. Unlike a master's program, the pursuit of a doctorate really has no definite end (although some programs limit it to seven years). In a doctorate program, not only are you expected to teach—similar to the indentured servant program of days gone by—but you are expected to create something truly original in your dissertation. While the teaching is easily understood, as it provides the university with a low-cost alternative for teaching entry-level undergraduate courses, the satisfaction of the independent research requirement is the ultimate challenge. Your faculty committee must first approve the basic idea behind your work and then generally approve of an abstract that is required prior to even beginning the work. Finally, there is not just a final approval of the dissertation, but "guidance" provided by the faculty committee along the path to enlightenment. I have seen fellows near breakdowns because they had no idea how long the process might drag on. So if you pursue the doctorate, you are consigned to more than half a decade of poverty while you work on it. Conversely, if you go directly to teaching with the master's degree, you have immediate cash flow, but it will never amount to a great deal. While spending seven years or so on the process is not unreasonable for someone in his twenties, I am somewhat beyond the age at which a commitment of such length to secure a career change would be reasonable. Further, as a full-time graduate student pursuing a doctorate, my standard of living would be reduced to about that of a typical graduate student, and I have become somewhat accustomed to decent furniture and housing. There are no easy choices.

Here are just a few suggestions on your hopeful pending relocation, based on my experience in changing jobs. You need to ask for temporary living expenses to span a sufficient period to ensure that you are never in a position of having to make two house payments. I believe that the employer should commit to a maximum of six months, which will provide you with motivation to sell your Alaskan place but ample time so that you do not have to part with it at fire-sale prices. The signing bonus you have asked for seems adequate, but I have always found that it is best to provoke some slight indignation from the prospective employer by asking for more than I expect to receive. Respect is won through hard bargaining in business, not capitulation. In my experience, when I and the employer were somewhat dissatisfied with the ultimate signing bonus, this was the time that what was probably the best bargain was struck. I would interject a word of warning on going-away parties, but your earlier description of that poor soul who got far more than he bargained for through his Alaskan going-away party should be sufficient.

In the banking profession, you have missed the earlier debacle of asset based lending, in which loans were made on the basis of the value of the underlying asset. This was very similar to pawnshop lending, but the bankers did not perceive it as such. The banking industry then stumbled onto the reality that without cash flow to support the payments, the market value of collateral was often less than an appraiser would suppose. Then if the banker repossessed the collateral, it often had to be sold at a substantial loss. We are all now turning to the new idea of cash flow lending in which it is not the value of the underlying asset (for what banker who has sold a repossessed asset once would ever want to do it again?), but the foundation of the cash flow is what really matters in lending. When interest rates rose significantly on home mortgages, it turned out that what mattered most was not the so-called value of the homes but whether folks could make the necessary payments to purchase the homes. Although we have learned a lesson, it may well have a negative impact on my ability to sell my own home in Idaho. Remember people saying that real estate is such a great investment?

Chapter XXXII

Dear E,

They asked me back for a second interview in Columbus, Ohio, at Banc One's corporate headquarters, and I believe I have successfully arranged a change in my career path. An offer was made and has been accepted, which incorporated some of your good advice. They are going to cover my living expenses for the first six months, limited to housing, while I rid myself of the Alaskan residence. The signing bonus was agreed upon, along with the coverage of all moving expenses. Do you sometimes feel as if we are but tourists in this great land, with the corporations paying our way from one locale to another? I know it is the value of our ideas that opens these doors for us, but it is so unlike the customary stable positions many others seem to enjoy.

I made one last report in Alaska prior to going for the final interview and decided to do the presentation slightly differently. In state government, customary reports are endless pages of verbiage. For this report, I decided to include black and white photos, due to the clarity of black and white compared to color. The report was initially arranged with blank spots on each page. After it was proofed, I simply used two-sided tape to affix each photo in the desired location. Then using the original document, I copied the report on a high quality commercial copier. The result was a report that looked reasonably well, and the recipients of the report seemed more amazed at the presentation than they were with the contents. The entire process was both amusing and sad, for it drove home the point to me **that the general population is often more taken in by the novelty of a new experience than the content of the experience.**. The original thoughts within the report were of far greater importance for the long-term stability of Alaska, but it seems folks are much more interested in the façade than understanding the more difficult contents behind the pretty pictures. I have made a mental note of the cultural anomaly and will strive to make use of it in my business career. If someone could develop a way to make this process of combining reports and photos a bit simpler to accomplish, I would think it might become widespread in the business community.

After the business interview in Columbus, I rented a car and headed back to those southern hills for a few days of remembrance. The siding you have put on the family home looks very nice, and I appreciate the expenditure of scarce resources to preserve our past. Several issues need to be addressed, some of which I have already taken action on, and I most certainly hope you approve. The roofing on the house was literally falling off. Remember how Grandfather always demanded that cedar shingles be used and insisted that the home looks best that way? When I inquired what the cost of sixty-four squares (ten by ten feet per square) of cedar shingles was, including installation, it was astronomical. For that reason, I have arranged for the home to have new asphalt shingles, and the process has been cleared with our uncle. It seems that as long as we spend our money on the preservation process, he does not object. Since he was born in the home in 1914, and raised there as well, it amazes me how unconcerned he is about the upkeep of the place. The windows are also going to need to be repaired or replaced as the old double hung wooden ones are literally rotting out. The house has neither heat nor cooling, so the humidity is taking a dreadful toll. The furniture is being degraded by the environment. The dining room table, around which all those old family gatherings occurred, was of most immediate concern. I just have too many memories of the thoughts expressed around that table, the wonderful food prepared by our grandmother, and the feeling that the family was something of substance to allow the table to fall apart. Yes, sentiment rears its head!

To preserve the dining set I have had it taken to an antique furniture restoration service, and I am going to spend a four digit amount to restore it and the chairs. The leather on each of the chairs is going to have to be replaced and the whole affair refinished. What bothers me is that none of this would have been necessary had our uncle chosen to maintain the place correctly. His priorities are simply beyond my grasp, as he has arranged to have a phone installed in the barn so he can be reached when he is on the farm (which seems to be daily). A homestead with a barn phone but no maintenance of the home beyond what you and I are capable of providing seems strange. Do you remember that the dining table was given to our grandmother by her brother Jimmie? He did not have any children, but I believe he also treasured our grandmother as the best of family. I do not know where he obtained it, or how long he might have had it prior to giving it to Grandmother.

On the matter of the land, I went down to the county courthouse and determined who the current owner of those forty acres is on the northwest corner of the family farm. It turns out he lives in Arizona, so I would suppose that he either inherited the land, or has purchased it for retirement purposes. I intend to contact him when I get settled in Ohio. I took some photos of the family farm and the land which I will try to purchase, these are enclosed. Hope you are not too shocked by the deteriorating appearance of the place. Our grandfather would not be amused.

Notice in the photos that the original cedar posts that Grandfather put in when he switched to cattle after WWII are still being used by our uncle. I had hoped he might have installed some of those new metal fence posts, but he is not inclined to spend the money on upkeep. It is interesting to watch him give money away, such as to the church, in such quantities that he could replace every fencepost on the farm in a year if the funds were just redirected. His concern is much more focused on his appearance in his community than on family matters.

Proving that generosity has its rewards, the community where our uncle was mayor for a couple of decades has decided to name a civic center type of building after him. Perhaps it is just a cry for immortality and attention by an older man who has no children. He does not seem to realize that a decade after he is gone, few will remember him and fewer will care about his donations. Instead, they will be searching for the next old fellow whose pockets may be plundered in the name of the betterment of the community. Even though I have no children as of this time, I do understand the harsh realities of our society and do not care to be remembered specifically after my demise. Instead, I hope to have had just the slightest opportunity to nudge the general course of affairs in such a way as to lengthen the period of enlightenment over the inevitable intermittent periods of darkness suffered by our fellow man. I believe that true faith is best expressed privately and not through dispersion of money in a public manner.

Consolidation is all around us. Remember the two churches down by the cemetery? Well, the dwindling population of the rural area has been insufficient to support both, when combined with a general withdrawal from church attendance. The Methodist church not only closed, it was torn down, and the Church of Christ is the surviving entity of the Christian faith in the upper valley. Competition and consolidation seem likely to continue among the Christian faith, for the gap between the general level of education and the general level of faith seems to be inversely related. It has been brought to my attention that only two of the apostles actually referenced the virgin birth in the Bible. The modern ability to pick apart the pieces of the biblical presentation completely overlooks the great need to adhere to the general principles of the Christian doctrine. Although your faith and understanding of the details involved is certainly better than my own, I still remember earning that God and Country medal as an Eagle Scout. I firmly believe that it almost requires the belief by the general population in the concepts of heaven, hell, and well-intentioned government for a society to flourish. In each of these three key areas, I believe dry rot, which will not easily be removed, has set in.

Back to our discussion of the future economy: yes, of course I do not believe in a linear future and realize that the many twists will blur the trend. Nevertheless, I firmly believe that the trend is set and is unlikely to be deferred indefinitely. Yes, the trick for OPEC will be a sustained period of high prices, but not so high as to lead to over investment in other energy sources by the consuming countries. I believe that most individuals completely miss the connection between oil and religion. The vast majority of OPEC reserves are in the Arab Middle East, with the inclusion of the non-Arab Iran. In the areas where the greatest amounts of petroleum reserves are located, the governments not only support the Muslim faith but prohibit the open and sometimes even cloistered practice of the Christian faith. Conversely, in Western countries, our very ideal of freedom demands that we allow the practice of the Muslim faith and the spread of it through our general population. Never has a war of cultures been waged so adeptly. If the communists had simply been insightful enough to declare their world vision a religion, our principles would have openly allowed their establishment of cells, or should I say churches, throughout the land. As the Muslim faith has not suffered the severe schism between government and faith that the Christian faith has been fortunate to withstand, it is impossible to support the Arab governments by purchasing their oil and not be supporting the spread of the most intolerant of world religions. We are talking about the convert-or-die type of mentality that allowed them to destroy the Christian faith and native languages from Egypt across North Africa and to the very doorsteps of central Europe. We will validate their very worldview by allowing them open access to our knowledge and universities while not requiring them to allow the open practice of all faiths within their borders. This is not free trade in religion. As their petroleum reserves will outlast ours by more than a century, it will be a bit dicey if the Christian faith can hang on until the economic disparity of resources is ultimately more even through the depletion of the same. On these occasions I confess there are some favorable aspects of having no linear descendents who will be troubled by the developments of which we speak. I remain strongly committed to free trade in all product and ideas, including religion, as in diversity there is greater understanding by all.

However, I am developing a strong admiration for the Muslim faith, its leaders, and those who adhere to it; for they combine the attributes of the righteous with the intelligence and strategy of Constantine. Truly a remarkable culture; in which the faith pervades all aspects of society and demands obedience on a scale not seen in our culture for centuries. I fear they are the better for it and our culture the lesser, as the Western focus on individual self-fulfillment (the pursuit of happiness); lessens the ties of family identity and responsibility.

The mere fact that the nations having the key resource reserves will be holding sway over the most intolerant religious activists should bear watching closely. Only fools would not be aware that while the American empire is not likely to be destroyed from without, there are other approaches to economic and religious domination. The communists refused to allow large numbers of their youth to be educated in our nation, and that failure has presented them with a serious handicap in the understanding of our culture.

Even now, the largest component of foreign students at my old school in the Midwest is from the petroleum bearing regions of the Middle East. This ability to learn from within how the American culture operates, and yet maintain their own distinct identity in their home lands will make the Muslim economic block a much more formidable competitor. If economic stagnation can be guided along by the maintenance of high oil prices by OPEC, the American stupidity of investment in the wasteful asset of housing, and the freedom to steal our intellectual advantage through open access to our educational system the Muslim faith may well be the long-term winner. I only hope America is not destined to be another Athens, but a brief moment of intellectual freedom in a prolonged period of religious and political darkness. There can be no moderate economists in this debate. Forgive these thoughts, for I am aware that even mentioning the possibility that our framework of freedom will not triumph over all opponents is at odds with the traditional American perspective. But I believe in planning for the worst and hoping for the best.

I went up to the restaurant on top of a downtown Anchorage hotel—remember the one with the health club in the basement?—and had a beautiful dinner. Looking out over the town, remembering all the great experiences it has given me, I can only hope that I have contributed something to help it endure for decades to come. Knowing it was built on top of this horrible clay and silt that turns to slush in a major earthquake does not encourage long-term plans. Education is both a blessing and a curse, for if one does not understand the geological risks involved in this setting, it is probably far more enjoyable. This term I have been teaching at Anchorage Community College, freshman introduction to business, and that is yet another pleasure this venture into business will preclude. I believe, based on my observations of the business community, that once I am engaged in the commercial sector, little time will be left for any academic pursuits. I shall not copy your pattern of day and night work. You seem to dedicate most of every day and night to work for monetary gain, while I enjoy contemplation.

Our grandfather's nephew has passed away, and his farm up the valley will be divided amongst his four children. We are blessed to have such good cousins residing in close proximity to the farm. I believe that instead of continuing their farm as a unit, as we have, they are choosing to split it into four sections (one for each offspring). The positive benefit to this is that they will not have to reach a continual consensus with each other in order to get things done, as we must. The negative aspect is that the land which grandfather's nephew acquired over a lifetime of hard physical labor will be split up. As some of his offspring have more than one child, I imagine that the four parts will be split up again during our lifetimes. The son who continues to live in the upper valley is helping our uncle with the farm in connection with the annual hay crop. I only hope that our uncle pays him sufficiently for his contribution. If we can continue to get along and not focus on the value of the land, perhaps our family farm will endure for yet another generation or two. Eventually, folks will not care to remember that it was in the 1850s that a group from Kentucky came by way of riverboat and wagon into the wilderness of the hills and settled in a place that reminded them of where they had departed from. The school teacher was the individual who actually named the area, for he thought that it was a "romantic" setting and thus Romance was born. They spent that first winter down in the lower valley along the Des Arc before establishing the community in the upper valley. I truly never think of us as owners of the land, merely caretakers.

Grandfather was a wonder in his time when it came to making land deals. When he agreed to sell that ten acres down by the cemetery to the community to build a school on, he insisted that the clause be included that if and when the community decided to not use it as a school, he would receive it back. In return, he gained a place for himself and Grandmother to teach school while they lived for forty years only a half mile from where they taught. I believe Grandmother's father, the Gettysburg veteran, would have enjoyed Grandfather if he had lived long enough to meet him. That he survived the Civil War only to be killed by lightning while plowing a field was something Grandmother would not discuss.

Take care, and ponder whether we really are just "caretakers." Can anyone really ever own anything? As a side-bar, I would close this letter with an old story told of Alexander the Great by St. Augustine of Hippo. When I pirate was brought before him for sentencing Alexander questioned why the scoundrel was taking of what he wanted from travelers on the sea. The pirate answered Alexander that he had noticed was doing much of the same; except that the Emperor had a fleet of ships and he, being a poor pirate, only had one. While the poor fellow soon learned to not engage in mental jousting with Emperors; he clearly made a final point before his demise. So, in matters of my new corporate life, when asked why actions were taken, honest answers, but tempered with humility will be the course of any discourse with those senior managers making inquiries.

Chapter XXXIII

Dear Y,

You are to be greatly applauded for making a transition from the public to private sector and a move across the continent simultaneously! We would most enjoy if you could arrange to stop in Idaho on your way across the country.

One of my colleagues at work has a young child who is simply one of the best behaved little people you will ever meet. He was given a play tent, which was put up in their great room (the Western equivalent of a living room and den combined) and you would have thought he had acquired a castle of his own. Yes, I know it does not really fit any vision of interior décor, but the enjoyment the little fellow seems to get from the experience is more than sufficient to compensate his parents for their unique living arrangements. When visiting him I have taken to reading to him from the *Wall Street Journal*. As long as one puts the correct inflections into the reading, so that it sounds interesting, he really does not seem to care that the exact nuances of the material have no meaning to him. Small children may be one of the few great rewards we are blessed with in this life.

One of my work colleagues has developed a possible escape route for himself to become self-employed. Commercial banks are forever calling around to the branch offices of other commercial banks and pretending to be prospective customers, while asking what the competitor is paying in interest rates on various maturity certificates of deposit. It is a horrible waste of time for all the banks involved in each market. They simply refuse to view money as a commodity (yes, I know requiring economics courses for bankers would be radical) and seem to believe that it actually has significantly different values in different markets.

In my own pricing models, I tend to view each state as a separate market (which is also wrong), but my management judges part of my performance on the levels of deposits (volume and average cost) in each state we operate in. Anyway, the fellow at work has determined that bankers would pay for someone else to provide them with a weekly report on what other banks in their markets are paying in the way of interest rates on deposits. In some respects this is a great service, as it will eliminate an endless series of phone calls and replace them with a series of faxes and phone calls from his service. He will then compile the data by bank for each market and forward the data to those subscribers of his service in the various markets. I believe he will be successful, for he will be fulfilling a perceived need, even if the bankers do not understand the commodity basis of money. *Corporations may be incubators of entrepreneurs in some respects, for they drive people to be insightful and creative in order to derive some hope of escaping their confines.* It would be best for the economy and the corporations if there was some way to adequately reward rank and file individuals for developing and implementing ideas within corporations. Folks seem to learn, after their first few contributions to corporate profitability, that the rewards are not commensurate with the contributions.

When I first relocated to Idaho, I waited for nearly six months prior to making any contributions of ideas to avoid the anti-newcomer bias. My boss even had requested that I limit my discussions with fellow employees and run all ideas through him. Finally, I decided to send out a memo on a small issue that simply needed some fine tuning. It was a great pleasure when executive management notified me that the idea was being implemented. At the next quarterly management meeting, I was sitting on the back row (okay, no back–row-Baptist jokes, I know my faults are legion), when an executive officer called out my name. He asked that I come down to the front and proceeded to tell the crowd of about one hundred about this idea I had forwarded to him. He explained that it was so simple that anyone in the room should have already thought of it. I was not sure at this point whether I was being insulted or commended. In order to support this type of intellectual contribution, he announced that the corporation was going to reward my efforts, and he bent over to take something out of a sack. When he presented me with a ham, I simply said that the gift was totally unexpected. The remarkable thing about the entire incident was that he was serious and very sincere; it was not intended as a joke or an insult but an actual commendation for my efforts. At the cocktail hour after the meeting, I made a point of carrying the ham under my arm to show my sincere appreciation for the corporation's generosity. When I came home that evening, I could not resist calling back to the hills to mention that my employer provided food as a fringe benefit upon occasion. The suggestion only saved the company about $10,000 per year, so it was not really very important, but the point here is about the difference between the perception of value between the originator of ideas within the corporation and the recognition of value by the corporation. It is the magnitude of that gap that seems to drive so many to become entrepreneurs. I would not even remember the incident today if the company had not given me any reward; it is only the fact that the reward they chose to give was unusual that keeps it in my thoughts.

I have now completed my fifth year with the company, and it will surely be my last. For my five-year award for service, the bank had the word processing department print up a certificate of appreciation on a plain piece of paper. Again, they were completely sincere in their efforts but are also apparently somewhat oblivious to the effect such actions have on the typical employee. Rather than a "form" certificate, a form letter of appreciation sent to the employee's home with a personal signature by an executive officer would have a much more positive impact. It is of course best not to mention such ideas for improvement in employee relations at the time of receiving the certificates, but I believe there are ways to highlight the strangeness of corporate life without offending anyone. I took the certificate to a local frame shop and spent a hundred dollars to have a five cent certificate framed in a glided frame (yes, your idea for the chapel occurred to me). The certificate is hanging in my office on the wall directly behind my desk. You would be amused at the number of individuals who come into my office and ask exactly how such a handsome award was earned. I always relish sharing the fact that it is a five year "survival award" that is given to every employee who successfully completes five years of service in the organization.

Cynics are not born but are carefully nurtured within the corporate environment, where they seem to prey on each other. I pray that you will fare better than I, and I imagine that you will, for you have a far greater capacity to engage humanity on a day-to-day basis than I have ever enjoyed. Now that you have committed to come over to the other side, I believe I can share these events with you as a way to better prepare you for what may lie ahead.

Back when I first arrived in this warm valley, I did not think to question the matter of annual bonuses. At the end of the first year, between Christmas and New Year's, my boss walked into my office and handed me an envelope. I placed it on my desk and asked how I might help him. He said that I should open the envelope now, and I complied. Contained within the envelope was fifty dollars. I asked what the money was for, and he replied that it was my annual bonus. He proceeded to explain that it would have been more, but since I had not started at the beginning of the year, it had been prorated. Again, I told him it was totally unexpected and expressed my appreciation as expected. The truth is, if a corporation cannot afford to give an annual bonus to an officer that will more than provide for that employee to have dinner out with a date, probably no bonus should be given at all. We all internalize the value of our annual raises, so even several months after we have received them; everyone is convinced they are worth every penny of the raise. The "annual" bonus should not necessarily be annual, for it too becomes internalized and expected regardless of performance if it is just another commonplace occurrence. For employee morale, it would be best to only reward employees who have been promoted or otherwise singled out for significant contributions than to reward everyone simply for the "attendance" factor. In that way, bonuses would never be expected or anticipated for the normal performance of an employee's duties. Today, it seems that the annual bonus in our company is as much a part of the holiday season as Christmas.

The fact that your signing bonus was one hundred times greater than my first annual bonus speaks loudly for your probable corporate success. Perhaps it also makes you understand why I am continuing to search for another alternative to fill my days than this particular corporate environment. *Remember, in all things concerning business in a corporation; always ask yourself what the other individual's true motives are, for they rarely ever are what the presenter would have you believe.* In business, there are few, if any, real friends and consist mainly of individuals interested in how you may contribute to their betterment. Test this in your public organization by seeing how many of those you believe to be friends even bother to send a Christmas card after you have left Alaska. I believe you will discover that "out of sight" is truly "out of mind," and once you no longer have any impact on their daily business, you will be casually brushed aside as so much clutter that must be taken out of the house. This is the culture we live in—the façade of friendliness, carefully covering the harshness of the necessity to maintain only those relationships that provide either a direct or indirect economic benefit. It is only the truly wealthy, or the unfortunate poor, who have either the money or time to indulge themselves with true friendships.

Thank you for taking care of the shingles on the family home. You are absolutely correct about the pictures; it would appear as if we come from abject poverty given the condition of the estate. I know that Grandfather would be concerned and we must correct the situation when we can, but I believe it must be deferred until after our uncle has departed. He has his own personal challenges, as our aunt is also not known for her patience. She greatly enjoyed the social events connected with being the mayor's wife for the past two decades, and it filled a void of their not having children, but now our uncle is almost her sole focus outside of church. On that basis, I am not surprised that he retreats to the farm on an almost daily basis (per your description). It is not such a distance to travel if it is necessary to achieve a peaceful state of mind. Although you have not yet been married, I assure you that I have the utmost respect for retired men who have no interests outside the home and somehow manage to coexist with their spouses of so many years on a daily basis within a confined space. I believe it is the rare marriage that allows both partners prolonged enjoyment of mutual companionship, and it is the resistance to change that better explains the vast majority of long-term marriages. Yes, you are correct; the cynic in me seems to have few bounds this year. Perhaps the American tendency to build homes of ever-increasing size is really a cry for more personal space within the family unit.

In case anything ever happens to me, look in the back bedroom of the family home (the one off the porch behind the kitchen). Under the bed you will find two framed portraits. The young lady is Laura, who died in 1918 at age twenty. The other portrait of the young baby is of Rocs Ann, Laura's only child. Laura was our grandfather's young sister, and he was never able to bear looking at her portrait while he was alive. The problem was that it reminded him of her marriage at a young age to a close neighbor, a Champlee, who moved her down out of the hills into the delta where she and the child did not last a year. They are both buried down at the end of the lane in the cemetery. I do not know whatever happened to the Champlee fellow, but Grandfather held him personally responsible for having taken Laura and the child into such an unhealthy environment in search of richer land. There are no Champlees in the valley today. Grandfather not only purchased their home and incorporated the land into our family farm; he burned down their old home after he acquired it and completely removed all traces that it ever existed. You will see from the portrait that Laura had auburn hair, like my mother's. Again, if anything happens to me, Grandfather would desire that Laura's tombstone and her child's be maintained even more than his own. You will find that the portrait of her has an uncanny resemblance to our great-grandmother in her youth, which was done on glass plate sometime between 1841 and 1851. To this day I do not know what happened to all that jewelry great-grandmother is wearing in her portrait, but remember that before the War of Northern Aggression, her family had been planters in South Carolina. Their last name was Rice. I suspect the jewelry went to help finance the war effort. The result of that effort fully supports the argument for investment across national boundaries as a final bulwark against another worst-case scenario such as what resulted for the family after that war.

Cousin, while I agree with much about your view of the probable course of economic events, we disagree on several important details. I have no doubt that the course of world economic development will eventually lead to the price increases in the key petroleum resources rising far faster than inflation. It is the likely *duration* of the process on which we disagree. Just as a drug dealer knows fully well that to maximize revenue from his clientele he must keep prices high, he also knows that he must avoid killing off his customer base by keeping them alive and producing sufficient revenue to purchase his product. Price volatility is also his friend, for it keeps the possible competitor drugs unsure of how much they can expend to enter into his market. Our friends in the Middle East most certainly have dual objectives of spreading their faith and increasing their revenue skimmed off the profitable capitalistic economies of the world. But you also must consider that their governments are based more on an almost family force, far distant from the republics of most developed nations. That structure will lengthen the inevitable conflict of your concerns. The hierarchy in those countries cannot feel overly secure in their positions, for what happened to the Shah of Iran is not so remote as to be forgotten. In order to ensure that the financial positions of the ruling class are secure, it will be necessary for them to invest abroad, and our country is the most stable long-term investment locale for principle one wishes to preserve for indefinite periods. So a significant portion of that obscene price for petroleum will likely be recycled back into investments in none other than US government securities. In this matter we are most fortunate, for the other nations which will likely be the fastest growing consumers of petroleum, the developing nations, are definitely not the type of places that conservative investors would be willing to place long term investments which must carry a low risk of default. So while our country will consume between 20 and 30 percent of the annual world petroleum production for a long period of time, we will only be importing about half of that amount due to our declining but still material domestic supplies. From this fortuitous relationship, I expect that the countries of the Middle East will want our domestic stability to continue for a long time. Besides, they are aware if they push the price too far, even the tar sands up near the Yukon Territory will become economical. The extraction of oil from the Yukon tar sands requires a significant amount of energy from natural gas, as well as the use of material amounts of water in order to produce a more traditional petroleum product.

Where we agree is the probability that it will not be in the Muslim religion's best interest to have the American commercial empire continue to dominate world commerce. To aid the spread of their religion, from a military perspective it would be best if America was not so dominate in the world. Knowing that the Soviet Union is a hollow shell, even more paranoid than the survivors of the Confederacy, the Muslim faith will most likely first be successful in reclaiming those portions of the southern Soviet Union that were captured by first the czars and then the communists. The territory is adjacent to countries which already have been subdued by the Muslims, and extension of control is most easily accomplished in such geographical situations. The far western portion of China is another possible target for expansion of their faith, as historically it was Muslim before the current communist regime. Their challenge with China is that it has a tendency to simply absorb minor cultures and endure through sheer force of numbers. Meanwhile, in the Middle East, the governments will need to provide a suitable standard of living for an ever-larger privileged class who are not accustomed to working. Remember, large components of their population went from being nomads (if inland) and fisherman (if coastal), to living in urban environments in fewer than two generations. In this respect they are not much different than our forbearers prior to the full implementation of the Industrial Revolution.

On the matter of your concern of the spread of their religion within our country, I place my faith in education. Their religion is largely based on unquestioning obedience to a small literati religious group. Remember, this is much the same basis as developed in the Christian faith during the first thousand years of its existence. Constantine also swept across North Africa after concerning to the Christian faith. What has been done before, will generally be done again, such is the nature of mankind. They limit highly advanced education to only a portion of their population (outside of learning their book of worship) due to their belief that women should not contribute to economies outside the home in most respects. As to folks with different sexual perspectives, they do not condone their very existence, whereas we provide at least the appearance of equal opportunity for all. Education is somewhat like water: it tends to seep into places it is not always desired. In the Christian faith, it was the printing press and the conversion of the Bible into local languages which not only spread the faith; but also created the culture of learning through questions that opened many doors beyond religion. With increased freedom of movement and more open access to knowledge, ever-greater sections of the population of the Middle East will catch glimpses of enlightenment and question the basis for their society.

Chapter XXXIV

Dear E,

Thank you for boarding me on my way through the Pacific Northwest to my new position in the Midwest. On the matter of your ex-wife, I fear you expected too much, for marriage is a job of great patience and little immediate reward. She came from the northern cultural background. Please remember that their culture actually won the war, and we reside somewhat as relics of a different tradition of family interaction. You purposely chose to marry outside our culture, and as such, you were responsible for aligning the differences between both cultures within a single family unit, a task I would never consider approaching after our discussions of your efforts. Remember that our uncle specifically told you that the family did not really care about what you did when you chose to reside in the north as long as you did not marry one of them. Even I believe that the provincial attitudes of some of our family members have more than a kernel of truth in them. Your home is certainly one you would not likely see back in the hills, but it is pleasant in an unusual way. I still would rather reside in the country, but I clearly understand your choice of that small town outside Boise, rather than living in the city proper. The mountains were also a pleasure, although somewhat smaller than those in Alaska, and they still are large compared to the hills of our youth. I shall always remember that the original name of your community of residence was Rattlesnake Gulch (a wise marketing move by the early settlers to change the name to bring in more settlers, and Mountain View is so much more appropriate).

I also enjoyed the sightseeing in southern Idaho. Specifically, I have the photo I took of the sign on that dirt road to Bruneau Canyon that clearly states to watch for falling objects as you are now entering a US Air Force bomb testing range. I still believe you about the fact that they only drop dummy bombs on targets, but frankly, I would have turned around at that point if I had been driving. The canyon, though, was definitely worth the trip! I liked it much more than the Grand Canyon due to its dramatic plunge into the abyss and its narrow nature.

The other attraction was that we were the only folks there, and when I visited the Grand Canyon, I felt like I was in the midst of throngs of people visiting some religious shrine. Perhaps it will be a while before the multitude discovers the wonder of Bruneau Canyon. I believe that guardrails would take away so much from the eight hundred-or-so-foot cliffs and the visual nearness of the opposing side of the canyon. The other place I enjoyed was the Thousand Springs, which come out of the lava wall of the Snake River Canyon down stream from Twin Falls. They also seem sufficiently off the interstate highway to remain mostly unspoiled. The only thing that was slightly disappointing was the Bruneau Sand Dunes. Yes, I realize they are the tallest sand dunes in North America, but looking at a four hundred-plus foot tall pile of sand is just not really exciting, and I would recommend deleting it from your tour list. I guess I will always look at tourist attractions with the perspective of that young cave guide back in the hills, before education opened so many doors for me.

I also enjoyed seeing your movie theatre, and I am so pleased that you have it up for sale. That seems to be the clearest indication that you are serious about seeking other opportunities, even if they require relocation. You have certainly added to the value of the building with your improvements, and having it listed on the National Historical Registrar cannot hurt the sale prospects. The life of an entrepreneur seems so desirable compared to the bureaucracies within organizations we both endure, but it just does not have the required stability for someone looking to be married early in life. Yes, I can hear you now, saying that stability in any job is only an illusion and that we really are not so far removed from our hunter ancestors as we are constantly seeking a new opportunity over the next hill. From time to time, I choose to live the illusion, for it at least allows the individual the dignity to believe he is actually important in some way and not just the factor of production we both recognize as the reality of the world. Perhaps when we eventually take control of the family farm, our finances will enable us to better enjoy the ventures of an entrepreneur without undue risk to our personal financial well-being.

On the family farm situation, I contacted that gentleman in Arizona about the forty acres on the northwest corner. At first he did not believe I was talking about the same forty acres he owns, as he described it as a fenced pasture. I sent him photos I took when I was down there last time, and he called back and was astounded at how it had grown up in brush. Even worse, apparently, someone has stolen not only the barbed wire of his fence line but the fence posts themselves. In a poor rural setting, it is simply not possible to be an absentee landowner, unless you have a relative or trusted friend close to the property. He even told me that there was a well house and a pump in a well on the property the last time he had seen it (more than several years ago). I unfortunately had to tell him, which he could see from the photos anyway, that there does not appear to be any trace of a well house, which I suppose some group of thieves stole, but they seem to have pulled the very pump out of the well. As a result of the revelation of the actual condition of his property, he agreed to sell it to me. I will use the signing bonus for the down payment, and he has agreed to hold the note while I make payments over a seven-year period. Upon occasion I wonder what it would be like to actually pay cash for something, rather than pay for it over time. At any rate, the 812 acres of the family farm has now been expanded by nearly 5 percent, and we have gained close to a half mile of county road frontage and a quarter mile or so of both sides of Clifty Creek starting directly below the waterfall. The forty acres joins the family farm for a quarter of a mile, so that only leaves about five miles of border that needs to be taken out to either a creek or a road to assure a stable boundary. I have already told our uncle what I have done and still do not actually know whether he approves or disapproves. There is an odd similarity between the way we do not display our emotions within the family and the culture of the Far East. At least we have begun the acquisition process, and perhaps the other 145 or so acres will not be postponed until we are old fellows.

A couple of small incidents occurred on the trip back across the country after leaving your place. Going north out of Yellowstone (was not overly impressed) into Montana, it was evening and the alternator went out on my car. This mechanical problem had never happened to me before, but as the lights gradually dimmed and died as I drove, it appeared to be a serious problem. I got behind a large truck and followed him closely in the dark for a number of miles. My engine literally stopped as we were approaching a small community, and I coasted into the town. Without the alternator, the battery had been completely drained. The closest business was a small café, which was in the process of closing, but they were so kind as to call a local fellow who repaired autos in a garage behind his home. After towing my vehicle to his place, he found that he had, by chance of fate, an alternator that would fit the vehicle. He said that if he had not had that part, he would have had to order one the next day from Bozeman. The repairs were completed before midnight, and I continued east. The hospitality and willingness of folks to help a stranger in difficulty is something truly remarkable in the West, which I believe is lacking in most of the East. I took the northern route across the country and came down the Upper Peninsula of Michigan across the only bridge to get to Mackinaw City. The bridge is one I would not recommend, as it resembles the arc of a bow in the air, to allow sufficient space for large ships to pass beneath, and the floor of the bridge in the middle section is a metal grate. This clearly allows one to see the cold waters of the lake far below as you drive across this two lane wonder. Given that there was no other alternative I proceeded, but I am more comfortable on bridges I cannot see through. They even have drivers to take those reluctant souls across who would rather not drive it themselves; leave it to the Yankees to provide expensive public services. The remainder of the trip was without incident and I am safely entrenched in the Midwest.

The bank has put me up in an extended-stay efficiency motel, with daily maid service and a small kitchen. They will pay for this lifestyle for up to six months, while my Alaska home sells. The city traffic is not a pleasant experience, and I work directly in the downtown area. Parking is somewhat expensive, and you must hike a pretty good distance to the office from the nearest affordable parking garage. I have a number of employees, and one of them has already let me know he would like my job. It seems I do not have to worry about any of that backstabbing behavior in this office, as the culture seems to have progressed to the use of frontal thrusts with a short sword. My experience to date appears to indicate that most business individuals are type A personalities, with little regard for the overall corporate welfare, as long as they walk out of the building each day feeling that they have enhanced their personal careers to the maximum amount possible. The culture is both far different from my experience in the public sector and my youth in the hills. It is somewhat similar to that which I experienced going to college in the Midwest. You can almost see the hostility in the eyes of individuals who have spent years surviving the corporate wars.

Initially I am focusing on transfer pricing, a system whereby branch offices with more deposits than loans are paid a fair price for their excess deposits by branch offices with the opposite problem (more loans than deposits). The idea is to fairly reward everyone for their contribution to the organization. During the first week, my boss gave me the assignment of selling an extra $100 million in auto loans from the main bank to our affiliated banks around the state. That assignment took two days, but it helped change my image from a government employee type to a sales employee type. The next step is to focus on a bit of the math to see if we can add value other than through the actions of a salesman (a noble profession, but not the one for which I was trained).

I already saw my first example of Yankee interaction when passing by some other department down the hall. The department manager came out of his office and literally threw a report across a crowded room of analysts and loudly indicated that, in his opinion, the work basically was viewed as cow throughput. Actually, he used somewhat more direct language, as an older fellow might have used out behind the barn in the country, but I trust my interpretation serves to convey the intensity of the moment. In our hill culture, we spend time talking around the issues, to preserve interpersonal relationships we value due to the lasting nature of family residences. In this urban jungle, they have no time to even care about interpersonal relationships, so the interaction in the office is direct and even brutal if one fails to meet expectations.

The corporate culture back east is a wonder to observe. The executive management of our institution has decreed that no snack foods will be permitted in the corporate headquarters. Given my habit of enjoying a candy bar on occasion, I find myself resulting to subterfuge to enjoy an illicit sugar fix. Word in the halls is that one executive even has been known to drop into an office after hours and search desk drawers for candy an employee might have sneaked into the office, but I truly hope such talk is just corporate legend.

Soon after my arrival, my boss took me up to the executive suite, where the vice chairman welcomed me to the organization and handed me the "corporate tie." At this point I was beginning to wonder whether I had joined a fraternity or a commercial banking enterprise. I am afraid I stand out both physically and in attitude from the vast multitude of these individuals, for I have seen only one other individual with red hair and few if any smiles. This is probably what you have been enduring for a good many years in Idaho and Alaskan banking, but it is a bit of an adjustment for me. Your analysis of friendship in the business and public sectors has proved correct, for since I departed Alaska, there has been no contact from any of those I believed to be friends (even though my phone numbers were provided to them).

Your fine tuning of my insight into the future probable economic developments was most helpful. I do buy into your thesis of the probable reinvestment of petroleum proceeds obtained by the Middle-Eastern countries back into the US economy. There is still the question of exactly how much leakage will exist in this circle of dependence, as their ruling class will need to balance the pretense of concern for their subjects with a personal need to have significant assets beyond their borders to sustain their extended families after any dislocation due to political instability. As you say, a good number of the ruling class have been educated in the United States or Britain, and one would believe that the poor end that the Romanoff dynasty suffered was probably of interest in their historical studies. Your focus on the more recent dismissal of the Iranian leader by his people is an even more closely associated event with their region. From the Romanoff experience, they will have learned that one must modernize and still retain control by preventing the foundation of any potent opposition. The Romanoff's did not take opposition leaders seriously if they were out of country, and the Iranian leader made the same error. I suspect that the Middle-Eastern despots will keep a much closer watch on their subjects. I also agree it will be in their interest to maintain our position of dominance for stability, with a reduced military ability due to our financial constraints.

Do you remember the last great Roman conquest, north of the Danube along the coast of the Black Sea? After that last great conquest, the usual tonnage of gold from new domains ceased, and eventually the coinage of the realm was reduced from pure silver to only a 40 percent content. The debasing of the coinage was said to not be of importance, as the power of Rome stood behind the money. Does this sound oddly familiar to you? Remember in our youth that the coinage was made of silver, and even the paper money was backed by silver and proudly proclaimed so with the phrase "Silver Certificate" on each and every piece of currency. Now we have eliminated the silver from all coinage and replaced it with junk metal, and proudly proclaim that our citizens have become of such sophistication that they realize that the currency is fiat money (backed by the full faith and credit of the federal government). So, your future of reinvestment back into US government securities works well as long as the entire world monetary system keeps the faith, so to speak, in the eternity of existence for the US federal government. As long as other countries are willing to hold the dollar as part of their reserves, in place of gold or silver, the continuation of the system of international credit will prevail. Does it strike you that what we may have done is to establish a new religion? If there is any sudden or even prolonged gradual decline of faith in the dollar, and those foreign entities no longer wish to hold them as a reserve currency, the dollars must come home with such a rush that a transformation from a wealthy to a poor country could be at such a pace that few could avoid the consequences. This is a worst-case scenario in which your educated Muslim elite lose control of their dominions to their religious masses that care more about their eternal belief system than the immediate life style of their countries. If that development should occur, the recycling of dollars from the purchase of Middle East oil back into US government debt would cease, as the conservative religious types over there would not condone capitalistic infidels' investments. So it would seem that the long-term survival of the circular flow of capital that you have envisioned is strongly correlated with the continued survival of the very despotic system of government in the Middle East, which is so objectionable to our sensibilities. While I support the logic, such faith on the continuation of governments whose oppression of their populations is so counter to the enlightenment of Western thought appears to require a more devout economist than my training has produced.

A counter argument would be that the concentration of such massive remaining supplies of petroleum within a small geographical area, having a modest population, will present a target that eventually some developed nation or group of developed nations will attempt to seize. A final crusade would not focus on Palestine—leave that to the Muslims—but instead upon the Persian Gulf oil fields. It is not a pleasant argument, but Western governments seem to always present the façade of enlightenment until their economies are threatened. The odd thing about this potential development is that as long as the United States remains a creditor nation, it would appear to be in our self interest to ensure that the ownership of the petroleum reserves remains with governments willing to continue to invest in US government securities. This would preclude us from intervening in their monarchy, unless we were willing to take the ultimate step and annex the petroleum bearing reserves directly as our territory. I simply do not see that occurring and believe that any direct intervention would be out of stupidity, or vanity; but I always remember that those individuals leading governments do not often discourse about long-term economic developments relative to history.

The best scenario for our country is for a free nation with a stable or slightly falling standard of living over a series of decades, as we transition from being the ultimate world leader to a country with influence more closely in tune with our proportion of world population. I truly hope that the stagnation does not occur until after our working lives, for so much of the American personality is based on the belief in an ever better material future for us and our descendents. Just as Rome existed for centuries after that last great "triumph" of military might, our commercial empire may succeed in maintaining the façade of control for many decades yet to come. Take care and seek employment a little closer to home if you can, for I believe the transition to our time of control is not so far away as one might believe.

On family matters, thank you for the information on Laura and the portraits of her and the child. In the event of your unwelcome demise (it better not happen), the portraits will be displayed in a place of honor in the family home. I believe we may have started the process of property acquisition about ten years too late, as the cost will definitely be substantial given the impact of the impending water system and the nearby lake. The plan is sound but may be more costly than we had imagined. The nondenominational chapel may even be more popular with a larger population base in the area. Do you remember that the Parthenon was not only a Christian church after the end of the Pagan era but served time as a mosque before it was rescued? It is regrettable that we have not been able to restore the great Eastern Church building in Constantinople which now serves as a museum back into a proper religious monument. However, I always remember that everyone believes their own religion to be Orthodox, the one true way, and the reality is that it is likely that Providence would have many roads leading to enlightenment. It is merely our vanity, mine own included, which places one faith above another. The truth is that it is the "faith" in the divine which matters most and that most human religious arguments are akin to the fruitless task of arguing how many angels could sit on the head of a pin.

On your geographical dispersion pattern you anticipate for the Muslim faith, I find no fault in your logic. To take it steps further, incursions into Europe and the Far East may also occur. The Europeans have brought the Muslim faith home with them after their folly in North Africa, and they will learn this is not the normal immigrant group. The Muslims are not likely to assimilate into the Western culture of openness and mutual respect. The simple thought of a French Muslim is of and by itself an oxymoron and somewhat humorous. That the only truly secular Muslim nation, Turkey, has not been entirely successful in suppressing the religious fanatics within its confines after so many decades portends a rough road for the French.

Your analogy of water and education both seeping into places they are not wanted is sound, but remember, it took fully eight hundred years before knowledge began to overcome the stranglehold of the Catholic church on logic and reason after the fall of Rome. If the Muslims are truly six hundred or more years along the similar theological path which Christianity has tread, based on the date of the creation of their religion plus the lack of a historical reformation in their faith such as Christianity endured, and the failure to embrace science unless required in a military sense argues that the seepage of enlightenment will be a slow process. Remember, even we suffered through such individuals as Oliver Cromwell well into the period in which enlightenment had begun to take hold. Isaac Newton was sixteen when Cromwell, the lord protector of England, died. May we be so fortunate to have logic surpass fanatics in the Middle East. My respect for those adhering to the Muslim faith continues; as it is a challenging religion to adhere to on a daily basis. Their assimilation of the cultures they engulf, such as the defunct kingdoms of North Africa and Constantinople is so complete that entire languages and histories have disappeared. In their success they bring to my thoughts the Chinese process of expansion through assimilation; although the Muslim faith operates in a much faster time scheme. One religion, one language, one key resource; they are a people bound together and destined for continued success. Yes, I know that this overlooks the most populous Muslim nation of Indonesian, but that great experiment will test the scale as the expansion of China meets the expansion of the Muslim faith. At this point, I would weigh on the side of the Muslim culture for victory; as all faith tends to overcome material illusions and China has taken great steps to eliminate their faith within.

Chapter XXXV

Dear Y,

We enjoyed your brief stay during your trip across the country. I trust that now you better understand the inter-mountain West, an openness not approaching that which is Alaska, but still a feeling far better than the closed-in sense that pervades the eastern parts of this country. Thank you for the kind words concerning my ex-spouse, and you are correct, I should have thought better than to have entered into a contractual relationship if I could not make a success of it. Glad you enjoyed the Idaho scenery; perhaps you will have an opportunity to see northern Idaho in the future (it is the much greener part of the state).

On the home front, there have been a number of developments you should be aware of, if word has not already reached you. Our uncle has been diagnosed with prostate cancer. Instead of having the prostate removed, which would have been the most radical but probably the best course of treatment, he went down to Texas and had a new type of treatment. They actually implanted small radioactive pellets within the prostate gland. His is a slow-growing type of cancer, and this treatment option is supposed to slow the growth of the tumors. As he is already seventy-plus years of age, it is just as likely that something other than this particular type of cancer will kill him. Yes, I am having the same thoughts as you on this subject. Your mother, both of our grandparents, and now our uncle all having some type of cancer would appear to make it reasonably easy to foretell our eventual fate.

Partially due to these developments, I have decided to take action on the land situation around the family farm. The movie theatre has now sold, so some small semblance of liquidity has been restored. I really did not enjoy letting that little business go and will surely be glad when we have some control over sufficient assets to try other ventures back in the hills. I have contacted a real estate agent (not the best of ideas I know, as it will probably cost me more than your direct route of solicitation with a land owner), and requested that he look into whether a sixty acre parcel on the north side of the farm would be available. According to the ownership map of the county I have acquired, it abuts the farm for a quarter mile and runs back three eighths of a mile until it joins Romance Road. Contained within the parcel is another one quarter mile of Clifty Creek, plus the quarter mile of county road frontage. The property is located about a quarter mile downstream from the acreage you acquired. You actually will have the better piece of land, if I am successful in this acquisition, for this land rises by more than two hundred feet in elevation from the road frontage and then drops nearly the same distance to the creek in the valley bottom before rising a final one hundred feet in elevation to join the family farm. It is second- and third-growth forest, with one small field growing up, according to the real estate agent. I remember it from my youth, and it was a bit of a hike to get over, even when I was young. If we acquire it, together with the acreage you have purchased we will have effectively prevented development of a half mile of bottom land along the creek. Our total county road frontage will also begin to be respectable. If the fellow is reasonable on price, I will not hesitate to pursue.

In a total waste of money, I was forced to admit that I needed a new vehicle. No, I did not actually purchase a *new* vehicle, but the one I acquired is new to me. After parts of the old vehicle started falling off on the highway, I knew it was only a matter of time. Hated to part with the old car, it had taken me to Alaska and back. One of the nice things about living in Alaska was that I never left Anchorage too much in the winter after snow had set in for the duration, and as a result, few miles were put on the car up there. I have driven it for a decade, and perhaps it was time to part company. Guess I never really will be a style maven! Have you ever looked around and noticed all the folks driving new cars and wonder how they can ever expect to accumulate investment assets while indulging in needless capital expenditures? Once a decade or so should suffice for me in the exchanging of vehicles (my new one has fewer than twenty thousand miles on it).

On the subject of cars, I learned another corporate lesson at the bank. One of my colleagues in the trust department, a vice president, appeared to be walking home from work each evening. I offered to give him a lift, as he lives in Boise proper, and it would not be much out of my way as I leave town in the evening. At lunch he confided in me that he actually had purchased a new car, a *real* new car (not a pre-owned one), and he was parking it a number of blocks away from the bank in a parking garage so that other people at the bank would not know he had acquired such a vehicle.
It is a sports car, the totally irrational type that the emotional side of you begs for, but which you know is beyond reason. *His perception of corporate culture is that you should never be seen driving a vehicle newer or more expensive than the one driven by your direct boss.* He believes that to do so implies that either you do not know how to manage your assets prudently, or conversely, your boss may believe that you have become so successful in the management of your assets that he may try to get away with a thinner

salary raise than you deserve. This is a completely new avenue of personal interaction I have never considered, as I seem to drive vehicles until they fall apart. His reasoning appears to be logical, given the human process of always comparing material possessions to those around us. It also supports my thought that it is always better to remain visibly poor and place hard-earned funds in assets that are not always readily apparent to those around you.

The entire auto business has also reminded me of a somewhat similar situation in Alaska. Although it happened at another bank than the one I worked for, a friend of mine who worked for the other bank told me about it when I was up there. A young lady who worked at their bank had come into some money and placed it in certificates of deposit in the bank under her own name. It was a substantial six-digit amount, which back then was a fair sum even up in Alaska. I still remember him telling me that a member of management had mentioned the amount of funds the young lady had on deposit when they were budgeting annual raises. He felt that her perceived financial security had an adverse impact on her salary adjustment. After I heard about that incident, I always maintained another personal account in a different bank than the one in which I worked, so that my performance would be judged independently of my saving habits. There is even the odd possibility that driving an old classic vehicle like I have done may have had a positive impact on my salary adjustments over the years.

Our new chairman appointed a new president of our Idaho subsidiary bank, and to his credit he seems to have made a sound choice. I happened to be up on the nineteenth floor when the new president was coming down from the boardroom after his first monthly presentation to the board of directors. We were the only ones on the elevator, and he turned to me and asked if I noticed anything wrong with him. I actually did not and replied to the same effect. He just looked at me and said, "Look closely at my suit coat and my pants." It seems that he had gotten up early to get to work for this special day and had not turned on all the closet lights so as to not wake up his spouse; unfortunately, he had selected a coat from one suit and a pair of pants from another slightly different suit. He had not noticed the lapse in judgment until he had gotten up to speak in front of the board. Now he is concerned that the board will think he either has no taste in clothes or is colorblind. I did not think it was either the place or time to tell him that the new chairman really is colorblind. Instead, I told him that the content of his presentation was of much greater concern than the details of his wardrobe. Alas, I fear that I probably gave him too much assurance, for I am becoming increasingly convinced that the outward appearance is often misconstrued as being indicative of the inner content. We are very lucky that the "Prime E" was not judged on his outward appearance, or we might not still have a very clear understanding of the universe. I will always find it amusing that the Prime E never learned to drive a vehicle, as he did not deem it worth the time or effort. Next month our Bank president will undoubtedly get dressed with every light turned on prior to the board meeting.

I have decided to look outside banking and even beyond business for something to occupy both time and mind. Just as you suspect that the time for us to transition back to the hills is drawing nearer, the health of our uncle would seem to further point in that direction. Banking is truly a business that I enjoy and that I seem to be reasonably good at on a daily basis. It is the endless corporate politics that are beginning to wear on me and distract my thoughts from the more important task of steadily increasing shareholder wealth. On that topic, the few banks we have acquired in Oregon, Washington, and Utah have firmly convinced me that we do not need more than twelve thousand commercial banks in this country. The future is likely to be dominated by larger banks, such as the one you have started working for, and the idea of needing a local banker will eventually seem as quaint to most city folks as the old country store. I would imagine that smaller banks will persist in the semi-rural small towns, where folks will be better served by individual bankers who know them than by wonks of larger out-of-town institutions. The efficiencies that may be gained from mergers within urban areas are simply so great, with the elimination of duplicate back-room operational areas, that management sees it as an easy way to satisfy shareholder demands for the creation of additional wealth.

To weather the impending storm of mergers I have decided to seek a college teaching position. It is one of the small advantages of being overeducated and having a graduate degree that allows me to even indulge the consideration of this career change. I believe the social prospects will become slimmer, due to my downward salary adjustment, but I am resigned to that aspect. To pursue this course, I have subscribed to a national publication (The Journal of Higher Education) in which colleges advertise the teaching positions they have available. It is a wonder that someone does not produce a similar publication for the banking industry. I will let you know if anything positive comes of this search. You may find some amusement in it, considering the banking interviews I have had all over this great country. If I am successful in finding such a position, I believe I will need to work two jobs to produce sufficient cash flow. Since I already teach in the evenings, this possibility of duel employment does not deter me.

We have spoken previously of the probable increasingly fleeting value of knowledge due to the very ease with which it can now be acquired. When I first earned my Master's Degree, there were fewer than five thousand MBAs being granted in this country annually. The number of schools that had an accredited MBA program was pretty limited, and usually only top-school degrees were the ones considered to be of much value. Today more than forty thousand MBAs are being minted annually, with ever-more schools offering a program that is relatively inexpensive to offer (compared to the sciences). The point is that with corporate consolidation likely to become a national trend lasting decades, who is going to employ the mass of these students as managers? The consolidation will require fewer real managers, and the competition for those precious slots will be increasingly intense as the game of musical chairs progresses. Already we have some individuals working as tellers who have undergraduate degrees! The drive to ever more education is simply producing a greater supply than is needed in some fields, such as business, and the college graduates are displacing the poor high-school-only graduates who might have previously captured these low-level positions. The value of knowledge is truly fleeting, and it provides some incentive to maintain some insights close to the vest. If the knowledge provides some security of employment, and the employer truly does not require that you divulge all the details, there is merit in silence.

Your points on the Muslim view toward the advancement of knowledge are well taken, for they will never support any such pursuit that might even touch on their core beliefs. Again, remember this is similar and consistent with the actions of the Christian Popes in regard to early thought on the possibility that the Earth was not the center of the universe. Though they destroyed the great civilizations of North Africa and the Middle East, and even imposed their own language, we are indebted to them for acting as a vessel that held a vast reservoir of mathematical knowledge until the Western culture was again prepared to take up the torch. Not only did they hold the vessel of sacred math during the insanity of the Western dark ages, they added to the vessel developments in algebra and other complex thoughts. I will not completely condemn any faith that at least has a rudimentary respect for logic, and their culture has held the light of logic in centuries past and probably will again. Given the uncertainty in the world, we may even need them again and a better allied group would be difficult to find anywhere if our causes were aligned. Yes, Providence is all knowing and who can say that one road is truly better than another for all roads were created by Providence. Enjoy the greenery in the East!

Chapter XXXVI

Dear E,

I was so pleased to hear you are taking the necessary steps to take yourself out of a daily business position you no longer enjoy. As much as we both recognize the need to produce cash flow, this still must be viewed within the context of an innate personal need for some semblance of happiness. Even if happiness is the rarest element on this planet, we still need to place ourselves in those locations where we are most likely to experience the fleeting moments in which it unfolds. I have had much better luck tracking game during my youth in the hills than I have ever had in finding the trail into a woman's heart. Here in the Midwest I have somewhat grown accustomed to the daily maid service in this extended living facility where I reside while awaiting the sale of the Alaskan residence. Of course, life would be much more pleasant with a real live-in woman to speak to about the course of life's events and to share experiences with, but I have not been fortunate to find a suitable individual willing to stomach me on a daily basis. It is becoming more apparent with the passing of each week that I will probably incur some loss in capital from the sale of that home, as the Alaskan economy is going through one of its recurring weak periods.

Down here, I have been looking for housing in the outlying areas. It will be nowhere near as scenic as your small community, but I intend to at least get far enough over the horizon so that the downtown office buildings are not an overbearing presence. The probable commuting time will be between an hour and an hour and a half each way, but the transportation expense will be somewhat offset by the lower cost of housing in the outlying areas. This time I intend to purchase a home that is beneath my means (you see that I do take heed of some of your advice, which is posed only as commentary in your prose). By doing such, it is less likely I will suffer any future significant capital loss when the time comes to sell it and head back south into the hills. With perfect hindsight, I can now see that I should have just leased a place in Alaska. Anytime you are employed in a highly volatile resource-based local economy, and the duration of employment is expected to be five years or fewer, I would now recommend leasing over the purchase option. Such short durations of residence limit the possibility of capital gains while transferring the risk of the local resource economy to your own balance sheet. For someone in the business of determining risk management for commercial banks (my new field of endeavor), I should have known better!

They allow me access to the executive dining room suite at work, so it appears that my relative status is halfway respectable. I am allowed up to two uses of a small dining room, which seats up to six, each month. There is no restriction on my guests, within the parameters of customers or fellow employees. The setup threw me at first, for they placed a remote control beside my place at the table. It finally occurred to me that I was supposed to order the next course of the meal by using the remote. These are things you do not learn in school or back in the hills.

So far I have only made one social faux pas. Prior to a meeting, one of our executive officers had placed his feet up on the conference table as we waited for the head fellow to arrive. I noticed that the bottom of his shoes appeared to still have the price written on them. After the meeting, I thought I would just be helpful (yes, I can hear you: never try to be helpful on anything but business issues) and mentioned to him in private that he might want to clean off the instep of his shoes. He looked at me as if I had just gotten off the boat and coolly said that the numbers were not a price but his locker number at his club and that they are used by the shoeshine fellow to ensure they are returned to the proper locker. I believe I backed out of the situation as politely as I could, but until I am more familiar with such aspects of the local culture, I shall hold my tongue on personal matters.

I learned another corporate cultural bit of information, which again illustrates the differences between separate parts of this country. If we see another officer quaffing any spirituous beverage in any downtown restaurant during lunch, it is a personnel policy that we must report it to his superior and he will be sent home for the remainder of the day as a first warning. As I do not really drink anyway, this matter has no personal impact on me, but compare it to out west where even if we did not drink it seemed impolite to not order a beer if everyone else at the luncheon table had already done so. The Midwestern cultural values are a far reach from the sawdust floors at a number of Alaskan establishments we both have frequented in the past. They remind me more of the dry counties of our youth.

The immediate downtown is also different, with the state capital building located directly in the middle of what we would recognize as the town square. Large banks, hotels, and office buildings surround it, but beneath its grounds is a large parking garage, with underground connections to the buildings on the outside of the square. This allows us to go across the square for lunch or whatever by going beneath the streets, and it surely is a great idea given the winter climate. Yes, I know the climate of this state is practically tropical compared to Alaska, but they still have snow and cold rains.

On the matter of land, if you are successful in your acquisition, it will bring us more than halfway to our goal. The combination of your land and mine will add one hundred acres to the 812 acre base of the family farm, an increase of more than 12 percent. We are fortunate that development has not yet commenced in earnest in the area, for I cannot imagine what it might cost once the inevitable process begins around us. Have you ever noticed that everyone bemoans the deteriorating environment, but few take the necessary personal steps that would slow the process? I am increasingly weary of northern persons portraying themselves as friends of the environment because they are concerned about the degrading of it in some far-off land. If only a few hundred thousand individuals would do as we are—purchase a fair amount of acreage and just leave it in a natural state—the overall environment would be much improved. Yet it seems that it is much more fashionable to acquire the latest model car or ever-larger home and just vote for politicians who declare themselves environmentalists. Americans who do not even own a quarter section of land themselves will travel the world over, as if they are the squire of the manor and indulge themselves with vistas not too far removed from what is available in our own country. Perhaps someday a religion will preach that to honor nature by revering it, without treading on it, is a sound manner to pay homage to the deity. Do not worry; I have not converted to Shintoism. There are merely different avenues in which to admire creation. The public seems to think that creating national parks, where the masses may congregate each summer, is preservation. I believe they are simply deluding themselves, and the political class uses this as yet another format of providing circuses to the masses. Rome would be proud at the very scale of the attractions, but I am continually saddened by the profound lack of public understanding. A spot of nature is really not "nature" if it is trod upon by several million visitors each year. May your Bruneau Canyon be unfound by the multitudes for years into the future.

On the matter of whom should we leave the property to, I concur with you and will leave to you such real property as I may have an interest in back in the hills. I believe that the income from such financial assets as each of us should accumulate would need to be utilized by our survivors in the preservation of what we are creating. As you have indicated that I will be your heir in the event of your departure, I can think of no better way to reciprocate the gesture. We both seem to share the same perspective on development and developers (who are generally wonderful people, but not the type I would ever have in my home).

Should I pass before our project of land acquisition is completed, let me share a little secret. Remember that cave you always wanted to find? On the forty acres I acquired, there are two caves. The first is barely a cave, not more than ten feet across and twenty-five feet deep. You will find it in the west face of the bluff overlooking Clifty Creek, about six hundred feet downstream from the waterfall. If you are approaching it from the west, be careful, for it is easy to walk off the edge of the bluff, and it is some drop to the creek below. It is much more easily found by walking upstream and looking up to your right. The second cave is really a cavern of some significance, but much more dangerous. On the top of the precipice where the creek turns east, there is a hole about three feet across back some ten feet from the edge. Shine a light down it and you will understand why I did not dare descend it as a youth. While I always enjoyed crawling in the depths of the caves near where I worked, if there was any need for rope to descend, that was the point where I turned around. You were always better at rope climbing than I and perhaps you may decide to give it a try. Please be sure to have that final will notarized before you go into the depths, if you visit the hills, for I will bear no legal liability now that you have been warned of the danger.

Another new development in the hills: it seems the state government has discovered a new way to waste taxpayer's money. They have purchased a substantial number of black bears (for me, more than one bear is substantial) and have released them into the national forests around the state. While usually harmless, we both know from our Alaskan experiences that there is no such thing as a domesticated bear (either black or brown). These things will multiply, and the state will not step up to take responsibility for the damage they will do to property and perhaps even people. Such irresponsible acts by individuals would be met with prosecution, but our public servants call it "restoring the environment." As our ancestors were thoughtful enough to rid the hills of any bears by killing every single one in the entire state, I simply do not appreciate this governmental act. However, there is a certain perverse logic to it all, for if most of the ordinary jobs for the masses go offshore, they may need sufficient wildlife for a subsistence lifestyle. Allow me some warped humor, for the twists and turns of representative democracy are a wonder to behold.

I was thinking of Grandfather a few days ago. Did you also learn to drive in that old 1930-something Plymouth on the farm lane? He was so patient with me as I dealt with the manual transmission and the necessary coordination. Do you remember that the choke button was on the upper left dashboard and the vehicle even had running boards that were covered by the closed doors? The back doors opened with the hinges at the rear of the door, somewhat of a dangerous design, but oddly stylish. It is a car I would enjoy still owning today, but he sold it before he knew I wanted it. A lesson learned was that if you want something; never hesitate to make your wants known if there is even the remotest chance that you may be able to afford it. That vehicle even had the optional heater, which was a real luxury in the 1930s. I was always much better at driving the old Ford tractor, with the clutch clearly under the left foot and the throttle lever on the steering wheel.

In other farm news, a sad note to report: our uncle took some photos of the new roof to send to me (see enclosed), and look carefully at what he has done. Notice that the chimney from the living room has disappeared. It seems that the rock was not stable, but rather than contacting either of us to obtain additional funding for repairs, he simply had the portion of the chimney protruding above the roof taken off and roofed over it. We are now left with a fireplace in the living room, which does not have any roof outlet and will never be used as a fireplace again. He does try, but I wish he would not be nearly so thrifty with our money. It is obvious that he thinks us to be less than level headed to want to preserve the place.

I differ on your analysis of the obvious building excess of MBAs in the nation. While they may believe that obtaining a master's degree in business will surely provide them with better employment, your view of the supply and demand for such degrees would suggest otherwise in the long term. From my more positive perspective, I believe that additional education is never fully wasted, for a more educated population is usually a more rational one. Even if the largest portion of such graduates is ultimately disappointed in their attempts to become top corporate executives, and that the multitudes would suggest such disappointment is likely, they will have had the opportunity to be exposed to the brutal day-to-day confrontation that is capitalistic management. From my brief employment in one of the best corporations in the private sector, it most reminds me of a combat experience where the never-ending casualties are simply part of the process. To be a casualty is not a sin, but to have never dared venture into the morass of business life is to live unaware of the constant struggle that surrounds our existence. This may also be used as an alternate definition of a public servant, speaking as one who has now been on both sides of the economy. I would be more concerned if there was a rush toward degrees in public administration.

Your suggestion toward moderation in my views of our brethren the Muslims is well taken but not easily swallowed. It may well be that we need such examples of different cultures to prevent us from becoming too complacent about our liberties. One can never imagine a Muslim-based constitution including any phrase even remotely related to "the pursuit of happiness." Well, at least not for the half of their population where service outside the home is all but prohibited in the most conservative of regimes. As long as their petroleum lasts, they are likely to resist changes that might contribute to the worldwide accumulation of knowledge. Eventually they will again contribute great thoughts of logic to the world, perhaps in the very math precepts their ancestors bestowed upon humanity; but I fear any such time will be after I have passed.

The countryside in the Midwest is very green, and living in the far north for so long I had forgotten about all the agriculture stretching to the horizon (without irrigation). When you look at the older farm homes, it is apparent just how affluent these folks were during the nineteenth century. The older homes are all built of brick, usually two floors, with a central hall. They are simply beyond the imagination of any hill farmer, whether in the nineteenth century or today. Our homes were all built with wood façades, and a good many, such as ours, were built of wood cut on the farm itself. Brick was something that wealthy city folks indulged themselves with, but it was never seen in the hills. The topsoil is, of course, black as night and deeper than a tractor, so they just do not understand the challenge of farming in red clay with an abundant supply of rocks. It is little wonder they won the war, as this land must have produced wealth so easily that they quickly accumulated sufficient capital to invest in industry.

One of my young employees is proving a bit of a challenge, and he will probably not be satisfied until I have either found him a higher position elsewhere in the organization or he has won my job. I have resolved to help myself by gifting him to another manager. Even the Trojan horse persists today in the business environment. We are a large bank but are concentrated on providing credit to individuals. Executive management has stated that they would much rather loan relatively small amounts at very high rates to a large number of individuals than loan large amounts of money at low rates to a relatively few large businesses. The logic is sound, and the rate at which credit cards may be placed with the masses is truly astounding; but state law back in the hills would prohibit the interest rates we charge for the convenience of this credit. It is somewhat like being in the business of running a casino. In either case, you know that some of your patrons will likely suffer from your business activities, but you are also aware that if you do not provide the service, they are just as likely to go elsewhere to procure the same service.

From an economic perspective, the more rational approach would be to have a national usury law with an interest rate that would apply the brakes to the uncontrolled growth of unsecured credit in the form of credit cards. Simply using a spread of about 6 percent over the six month US Treasury bill interest rate as a limit would prevent bankers from appearing to provide a public service while really allowing poor folks to make themselves poorer. As I work in the banking industry, this would not be in my self-interest at the moment, so once again I find myself unable to speak publicly thoughts that might offer some public benefit.

Without the restraint of a national usury law, bankers are free to locate their credit card operations in those states that allow the highest interest rates for unsecured debt. The poor indentured servants (I mean debtors) are allowed to transfer as much of their wealth to the banks as they desire, as long as they keep up the minimum monthly payments. They are treated worse than the sharecroppers after the war, for they can truly end up with less than nothing. When some ultimately default, bankruptcy is their only option, and their credit records are spoiled for many years. Yet the banking industry is not held to blame, for all we did was provide the cash flow they so craved. By this standard, why should we hold a drug dealer responsible, for he is but catering to the wants of his customer (which will ultimately be the ruin of many such customers)? Yet I am able to predict within reason the probable default rate of a large number of small borrowers with such accuracy that the risk to my employer is well managed.

While this huge credit addiction is developing, the political types distract the voters with talk of pollution. I just wish that someone would have the nerve to point out that stricter pollution standards in one nation simply shifts the pollution to a poorer country with lower standards. This liberal arts graduate will need to keep a low profile in the business environment.

When we as bankers have "helped" everyone who wants to be an unsecured creditor achieve their limit in that regard, where else will we turn to further our feast? I would suggest that as inflation will likely persist at least around the minimum 3 percent level (for to go lower would risk a deflation event), there will appear to be the illusion of wealth in the housing stock of this country. Notice that I say illusion, for wealth implies the ability to create economic value independent of the object. Housing is only an investment as long as the greater fool arrives with sufficient funding to acquire the home. Our parents' generation has built up great equity in their homes, which bankers will find some way to tap.

Another odd thing about the business of financing American homes is that we finance them for up to thirty years, knowing full well that significant and expensive parts of these homes will need replacing or major maintenance prior to the end of the thirty-year period. This is just another trend—auto loans were once of short duration—for we knew as a country that autos required maintenance, and who would want to be saddled with a monthly payment and the required maintenance of an older car? Yes, I have just convinced myself to purchase some stock in commercial banks, for the very nature of the enterprise will probably produce a handsome return even if the remainder of the country suffers from the probable prolonged stagnation that I fear. Truly, education is both a blessing and a curse, for it would be far easier to believe this venture (banking) is truly a public service (akin to a utility) if I did not spend so much time thinking about where trends are likely to lead.

Just as employer-provided medical insurance after WWII has led to ever-more wealthy doctors, the lack of a national usury law has left the barn door open so that bankers may help themselves to the livestock under the pretense of just providing feed. There are many sound reasons our fellow hill folk have such a distrust of strangers who offer to provide help. It is much easier to work within a kinship framework where unworthy actions will be quickly addressed.

Send word when you find that teaching job; perhaps it will provide some years of respite before we take on the task of making the family farm some type of profitable venture, while preserving the area around it for decades to come. I have been most fortunate to find one of the best banks to work for, dedicated to shareholder wealth enhancement, and it is providing me valuable training in business behavior.

Chapter XXXVII

Dear Y,

It seems you are beginning to understand the reality of day-to-day corporate endeavors. Although you will enjoy the money and perks, you may find, as I have, an increasing lack of trust for anyone who even smiles at you in a business setting. It is always the question of what exactly is on their agenda. My best defense was to never develop any close relationships other than with either the chairman or vice chairman. The stress of maintaining the façade is simply not sustainable for me anymore, but I have found an exit door.

More news on my twisted career path later, but first an update on land acquisition developments back on the family farm. The realtor has assisted me in reaching an agreement to acquire the sixty acres we spoke about earlier. The present owner is an architect who was planning to build a retirement home for himself on the side of the hill overlooking the valley and the creek below. Unfortunately, he has suffered personal developments in his life that have made him open to the sale of the land. Although one hesitates to benefit from the misfortune of others, at this time it is to his advantage to sell and mine to buy. I intend to close the deal next month on a trip through the hills. The negative aspect of the matter is that the seller is a reasonably affluent individual, so there was little in the way of negotiation on price if I wanted to save the land from development. Given my plans to change career paths, it will be necessary to make a substantial down payment and then spread the remainder over an eleven-year period to make the monthly burden modest enough for my future circumstances. I thought of your comments on the need for a national usury rate during the discussions and certainly wish it was in effect now. However, we both know the distortions rent controls have on markets, so is it really worthwhile to protect the high-risk borrower?

The seller is a fine fellow, well educated, but does not seem to understand the long-term effects of filling the countryside with a home on every sixty acres (turning the countryside into a large-scale subdivision). I believe this will be my only land acquisition for the next eleven years (the term of the loan), unless something unexpectedly changes my financial condition.

I have been on a job interview with the University of Kentucky Community College System. They have offered me a position teaching marketing, general business, and accounting courses. These are all subjects I have taught before, during my part-time career as an adjunct instructor. The location of the campus I have been assigned to is not where I would have thought my career would take me, but such is fate. Although you have never heard of Cumberland, Kentucky (located in Harlan County), an atlas will convince you that I have surely lost all my senses. In the far eastern corner of Kentucky, near the Virginia state line, this little town is located in a deep valley at the headwaters of the Cumberland River. It is slightly ironic that this is the same stream that eventually passes though Nashville, Tennessee. I do not believe it was mentioned in my studies at Vanderbilt. The town is in the shadow of Black Mountain, the tallest mountain in Kentucky (more than four thousand feet), and you can feel the explosions from the coal mines while on the modest campus. I still do not have the slightest idea where I will live, but given the limited choices, that does not appear to be a major decision. The compensation will be approximately one quarter of my previous salary, but I am only expected to teach sixteen hours, four courses, during each week. I expect this will be about as close to retirement as I can get and still claim to be working.

My thoughts simply need a break from the corporate world, and my emotions need a break from involvement with members of the opposite gender. You may find it necessary to develop personal relationships with colleagues in the business world, and perhaps they will even benefit you, but always think into the future and contemplate how business developments will affect the friendships. As to dating relationships, this is probably as close to that monastery we joke about as an alternative career.

My work colleagues seem to believe I might as well have joined the Peace Corps. In fact, that is very close to the truth, for I am not at all happy with what I have had to do this past decade to enhance the efficiency of American business, as well as the cost so many lives have had to bear for my thoughts. Only as a detached observer does one realize that for each and every increased operational efficiency which is deployed, that I know is for the greater good of society, some individual has had to face the blunt end of my thoughts with a lower paying job, or a different job, or in some cases with no job at all. I believe it is time for someone else to be the sharp end of the sword, for I have grown weary of telling individuals that we must provide them with the opportunity to seek employment elsewhere. Do you sometimes think at length about the law of comparative advantage? I know the theory is correct, and that every nation should concentrate on those industries and processes in which it has a comparative advantage over other nations. What if the other nations know the theory but simply refuse to play the game fairly, by placing obtuse barriers to the very products and services that we have a comparative advantage in producing more efficiently? If we fail to recognize these barriers as attempts to weaken our economy, they will end up with jobs that should rightly remain here if we were on a level playing field.

Specifically, I think about the issues of pollution and minimum wages in respect to comparative advantage. As America seems to demand ever-increasing standards of cleanliness for our manufacturing jobs (even as we demand lower prices for the goods they produce), a shift will occur. Little pollution controls exist in developing countries, for hungry populations value work above cleaner environments. The result will be a shift of manufacturing jobs offshore. The only ones that may be expected to remain are those in which the transportation expense and technology transfer expense is sufficient to offset the cost of pollution controls within our nation. In effect, we will force the remainder of the world to become our garbage heap. The usual caveats remain on the cost of utilities, and other factors of production must also be considered, but I believe that the magnitude of pollution control expenses will be the driving force for many industries.

The other factor is our obscene minimum wage laws, which artificially hold up the standard of living for the lowest paying jobs. In the short run, this is nothing but another form of taxation upon the better paid individuals, as the middle and upper classes are forced to pay higher prices than the products or services from the lower wage segment are actually worth in the world marketplace. In the long run, these laws will force even more jobs offshore, as why would you choose to pay a southern textile worker even the minimum wage when a similar worker in India might be had for a tenth of the wage? It is not the laws I object to (for their intentions are good) but the lack of thorough reasoning behind their relation to the international trade aspects of our economy.

I fully support free trade with any nation that upholds the same standards of pollution control and labor laws as we have set as our minimum standard. Otherwise, it seems we are really saying that it is acceptable for other people to work in polluted environments that we would not stand for in our backyards, working with labor laws that would be totally unacceptable in this or any country. If we are no better than this, we should not be surprised when the massive manufacturing capacity of this nation is drained away and along with it the great portion of good paying jobs for those individuals with less than a college education. The political class simply makes me ill with their talk of raising the minimum wage, while failing to mention the competitive effects on labor. From their perverse logic, if raising the minimum wage to five dollars per hour is great, why not go ahead and raise it to twenty dollars per hour? Perhaps in their hearts they know the long-term damage they are inflicting not only on this country but on the entire world.

I believe I am not the only one who would benefit from some time in the mountains to fully contemplate what has been left in our wake. Do you think it ironic that a nation would outlaw slavery in one century and more than a century later think that it is completely moral for poor folks in developing nations to work in such filth that a slave owner would not have dreamed of keeping his property in such conditions? I do not believe we have progressed all that far if all that is necessary to smooth our sensibilities is to move the problem offshore and out of sight! One world, one standard of labor! Only in this manner may the pollution problem really be addressed before the world wakes up to what we have dumped in their yards.

Our uncle has been at it again. It seems he can always find some way to add complexity to our lives. He signed up one hundred acres of the farm for a ten-year government program. Of course he did not believe it was necessary to even consult either of us about the long-term impact of what he has done, as he views us as less than junior partners. The federal government has a program to take poor quality land out of production, and ours certainly qualifies in that regard. He has taken one hundred acres, which one of our cousins has been, growing wheat on, and leased it to the federal government for ten years for fifty dollars per acre per year. Yes, he did assure me that he would disburse the appropriate proportion to each of us, but that is not the point. In order to lease the land, he had to agree to plant it with pine trees! After a decade, the government will cease paying, but at his age he really does not care about the long-term effects. Those pine trees will need to be thinned at about twenty-five years; it would be twenty years if they were in good soil, and they are honest in telling you that almost nothing will be made from the thinning. It is only after the thinning and another twenty years of growth that they will make good saw logs and will really have any value. Care to add forty-five years to your age to see the perverse humor in all of this? I will never live to see the cutting that will make money, and if you do (due to your younger age), the funds might be useful for a nursing home facility.

Fifty acres of this was the rolling fields in the Northwest corner, up the hill from the creek, and the other fifty acres is located down under the hill at the far east end of the place above the Des Arc. In either case, I much preferred the fields surrounded by hardwoods. There is also the matter of rattlesnakes, which seem to prefer the setting of a pine plantation. The matter is done and there is no undoing it without resorting to legal action, and I will not tangle with the old man. Even if we were to cut every pine tree after the lease is over and after he passes, the cost of removing all of the stumps is beyond the possibility of considering. He may not be able to take the farm with him, but he has managed to arrange to have a lasting impact on it after he is gone. They have sold their large home in town and moved into a smaller townhouse. I always enjoyed their large home. As a child, the walk-in bathtub overlooking the high walled garden outside always looked so gentile. Of course the vaulted redwood ceilings and walls, with those two massive stone fireplaces just made it seem like a mansion compared to our more normal surroundings. Did I ever tell you that he purchased five city lots just so he could have a winding driveway to that home through some old growth cedar trees? I have never been able to fault the man for knowing how to live. It was during one of his trips on which I was allowed to tag along as a child that I first learned the proper use of a finger bowl at a meal. I really owe the man so much for showing me such a great amount of the world beyond the hills when I was young, but he can still be so irritating at times that I fully understand our grandfather's distrust of his actions. He was built for the modern business world, for he never let anything stand between him and whatever he wanted to accomplish. So, welcome to the pine plantation business, cousin!

I do not know what will result from the sale of my Idaho home, but I do not believe that any equity will come my way due to the local market conditions. You are correct, it is a quirky home, but it will always remind me of how pleasant surroundings can balance an unpleasant lifestyle.

Leaving Idaho for the coal fields of Kentucky also feels strange. I have taken a last stroll down the walking path beside the Boise River. It is so tranquil, with the trees shading the stream and the kids floating down the river on inner tubes. It is just a great community and one I would recommend to anyone with sufficient wealth as a great place to raise a family. Well, we started out in Virginia in 1698 and now I will only be about fifteen miles over the sate line into Kentucky, so perhaps something good will come out of this chain of events yet.

Chapter XXXVIII

Dear E,

It did take an atlas, but I located your new destination of Cumberland, Kentucky. You definitely should not have to worry about traffic congestion on the way to teach your classes! I am so glad you found something that hopefully will provide a little joy in your life, at least on the professional level. Perhaps this plan to take time in the mountains might be best seen as both a professional and personal choice.

Do not worry about the family land situation. Your contribution of sixty acres sends us well on our way when combined with the forty acres I have already acquired. Although the combined one hundred acres between the two of us is still far less than the family holdings of 812 acres, we have a total of three fourths of a mile of road frontage (far more than all previous generations have added). I have taken steps to add another two and one half acres along the southwest corner of the place. Remember that odd little triangle of land that was created when the state highway department moved Highway 31 when we were young? They straightened the road, but by doing so, they removed four hundred fifty feet of highway frontage that previously belonged to the family farm. The west end of the triangle comes to a point where the farm entrance leaves the highway beside the cemetery. This piece of property has about six hundred feet of paved road frontage and is about three hundred fifty feet wide at the east end of the triangle of land. An elderly gentleman owns it, and it will cost me an obscene amount of money when viewed on a per-acre basis. I prefer to think about the price in relation to the amount of road frontage relative to the forty acres of the family farm that lies directly behind it. He was prepared to sell it to another individual who was going to put at least two homes on it. If such a development had taken place, it would have done severe damage to the long-term value of the property. The family land would have ended up being situated so that the view would have been overlooking the back of two homes, and the back of homes is never the best maintained part.

The other party looking at the property was the local cemetery, which had considered acquiring it for expansion. This would have made the entrance to the family farm a lane with a cemetery on both sides—again, not exactly the best way to enhance the long-term value of the property over the next fifty years. I anticipate closing on the property within a month. So while it is only two and one half acres, I like to think it is a relatively important piece of the puzzle. It is a clear field, not fenced, and I will need to have someone mow it on a regular basis.

On the matter of usury laws, I sympathize with the burden of the interest rate you must bear on your land acquisition. At least you were not forced to sit across from some young banker of lesser experience, who would have perused your personal financial statements like some novel and pronounced judgment on your long-term ability to handle the loan. It is a constant amazement to me about the difference between unsecured and secured credit in this country. The financial institution I work for has discovered full well how much individuals dislike having to disclose intimate financial details to a stranger in a suit, in order to obtain credit. A good deal of the growth in unsecured credit card debt may be traced to this personal bias for privacy. The bank develops mailing lists of prospective credit card borrowers (unsecured debt) and approves them primarily on the basis of their credit scores. This is simply a measure of how timely they pay their debts and the total of their outstanding debt. The gap in this procedure is that it does not show such personal secured debt that you have incurred on the land, which is owed to another individual outside of the normal financial institution circles.

The reality is that it is a mere snapshot of the individual's personal financial condition, nowhere near as complete as the local banker would know from dealings in the community. Individuals would rather pay us 18 percent interest and retain their privacy than open their personal affairs to a local banker and only pay 12 percent. While we advertise credit cards on the ease and convenience factor, we are really selling privacy and dignity. From my perspective, the small downside to this is that we may inadvertently extend credit to a number of individuals who do not deserve it and will eventually cost us a loss on the loan. These higher levels of losses are basically paid for by the better disciplined individuals who are successful in their financial affairs and are willing to pay to retain their privacy. I sometimes find the smaller banks entertaining when their advertisements stress their local ownership. Our customers are exactly those individuals who do not want local individuals or local financial institutions to be intimately aware of the changes in their personal borrowings from year to year and are willing to pay us a premium to retain their anonymity. You are correct; a national usury law would distort the markets like rent control. It would prevent banks from charging sufficiently high interest rates to cover the potential losses from individuals with high risk loans. Without the ability to take risk, untold numbers of individuals would not have the ability to start new businesses and create jobs. It would become a national speed limit on personal risk management. From a business perspective, it would be a severe negative in banking. Financial institutions such as my employer have found a niche to reach a national clientele without building facilities everywhere, combining privacy with the convenience of the postal service. In our increasingly crowded country, privacy is something individuals will pay a hefty premium for without any complaints.

I have purchased a small house about forty miles outside the city center, which will definitely fulfill all my needs. It is an older home, more than one hundred years old, and made of brick. I do not mean the brick façade we are accustomed to in post-WWII homes in the South. This is a two-story brick home with a central staircase. The interior walls are made of brick three rows thick, and the exterior walls are even thicker. A front porch has a swing and a small, fenced-in backyard. The home does not have any garage, which is a definite negative in this Midwestern climate of significant winters. There are three bedrooms upstairs, along with a single bath serving all three bedrooms. The downstairs has only the living room, parlor, dining room, kitchen, den, and another full bath that was added onto the back of the home about fifty years ago. Due to its location, which is not the best, I was able to acquire the home for only $35,000. In this case, I am not making the same mistake of over investing in a home, as I did in Alaska. By the way, my Alaska residence sold, but at a substantial loss. Not only did my equity disappear, but at the closing I was forced to present a check for more than $12,000 to cover the difference between the lower selling price and the greater amount of the mortgage, plus the fee paid to the realtor.

If anyone ever tells me again of the great profit potential in residential real estate, I will simply listen and wish him the best of luck. The combination of the customary low down payment with the huge mortgage leaves the homeowner with all the risk of any potential downturn in the local economy. Residential real estate validates local economic conditions. Individuals buy into this program without realizing that there is no way to shield themselves from the risk of plummeting home values if the local economy goes bad. It only takes a sudden factory closure or other disruption to the local economy for folks to find themselves in the same situation I have suffered (having a mortgage that is greater than the value of the home).

After this experience, I will try to minimize my leverage in any real estate that I anticipate selling in my lifetime. This tactic will limit my ability to prosper from the insane herd mentality of ever-greater borrowing that drives home prices up even further in areas with stable and growing economies. I am much more comfortable with the long-term security of knowing that every financial bubble I am aware of has been tied either directly or indirectly to excessive borrowing in some manner. Is the tulip bubble of many centuries ago, when the Dutch drove up the price of tulip bulbs, any more odd than what our country is doing to housing prices? In both cases, each society chose to invest in non-earning assets that were acquired not for the potential cash flow they might produce but for the anticipated increase in the value of the asset itself. The process ended badly for the Dutch, and I fear a similar but lengthier pattern for our country will follow.

The demographics would seem to indicate that the country in general has another twenty to thirty years of significant housing appreciation, until our generation starts retiring and dying. The downside to this is that such a sustained period relies on the government maintaining the illusion of housing as an investment and not simply a place of shelter. One thing I do remember of our youthful training is to always be skeptical about governmental actions. For every government must always sell the idea that its actions are for the greater good, while at the same time take such actions that will ensure it sustains itself. The latter motive is usually dominant, and I believe that the people suffer by trying to live the illusion. A conservative life may be somewhat dull but perhaps more financially rewarding. Do you think I have developed a bias from having to write that $12,000 check, plus watching years of my equity evaporate?

I understand your dismay at our uncle's decision to place such beautiful fields into a long-term venture of short-leaf pine trees. He has not seen the timber growth rates in the Pacific Northwest, much less the coastal Canadian softwood forests, which have growth rates far out-stripping the slower growth of our southern forests. This is without even considering the poor soil on the family farm. It will also result in a higher concentration of rattlesnakes in the woods than we have had to deal with in the pastures. On the positive side, at least the government is paying him something for the first ten years of the venture. You are absolutely correct, if there is to be any positive outcome to his investment in softwood timber, it will occur when we are both older fellows. Trying to put a positive spin on this unplanned diversification, we may now add pine to our portion of the assets. Perhaps pine may even have a decent price trend as long as the country keeps a limit on how much cheap Canadian timber may be brought into America.

Yes, I agree about the shifting of our pollution offshore through the movement of the nation's factories. This is inevitable as long as we allow other nations to become our garbage dumps. Free trade is not really free if the externalities of pollution borne by the exporting country are not factored into the equation. I do not know how to slow the spread of technology that will allow the process to continue. Remember the poor Carthaginians. They were masters of their world until a single ship fell into Roman hands. The Romans had never even had a navy, so they simply took the Carthaginian vessel apart and studied it. Then they built an entire navy on the same basic design and attacked Carthage in their first conflict at sea. When Rome combined its army on board the new ships, the fate of Carthage was forever determined. The loss of a great civilization that had survived for seven centuries was brought about in great degree by the loss of that single combat ship. I always remember Cato arising in the Roman Senate, showing figs that were said to grow but three days sail from Rome, and simply stating, "Delenda est

Carthago" ("*Carthage* must be destroyed"). If the Romans had never learned how to fight at sea, the disaster would never have occurred.

Today, I believe the Chinese, who decades ago obtained and then dissembled an American Boeing 707 jet and then built copies of it are to some degree the modern equivalent of the Romans. They appear to simply want to acquire technology and will eventually want to trade, but few will notice that this so-called friendly nation will continue to maintain the largest standing army in the world. It is likely to end badly, but perhaps we will already be gone.

The other threat will be the literal interpretation of the Koran. I only wish the political types would take the time to read the 114 suras (chapters) of the Koran and notice that one specifically states that when one meets the infidel in battle, the infidel is to be relieved of his head. Our increasingly secular culture will appear as evil incarnate to the Muslim faithful. Just as we agree that our political types should be required to study economics, I would rest better if the public demanded at least some understanding of historical trends over the last few millenniums. We seem to elect creatures of appearance and do not demand much in substance for our senators. While one man, one vote is a most noble concept for the nation of farmers which Jefferson envisioned; the urban American culture which has developed is more akin to the rule of mob in ancient Rome. We too have the Senate to temper the wild swings of the multitudes; but any earnest body of thoughtful citizens can be taken apart by a single determined individual with wide popular support. I believe such was the demise of the Roman Republic after that fateful crossing of the Rubicon.

Let me know when you are settled down in the mountains and I shall come down to visit; on the map it does not appear to be more than about an eight- or nine-hour drive.

Chapter XXXIX

Dear Y,

Your thoughts should not be shared with the general population on the upcoming conflict that is probable between the three great cultures of the world. The masses and most of our politicians still think in terms of nation states and not on the larger scale of cultures. I believe that just as the city state of Greece eventually yielded to the nation state, a similar transition will occur to the three great cultures. To whatever extent we are blessed with a gift of foresight; it is counterbalanced by the consequences of sharing such thoughts with others. Privacy of thought allows freedom of planning for future events likely to occur.

On the matter of cultures, it is interesting to observe the differences I have found here in the mountains of far eastern Kentucky. The homes are packed closely together along the few streets that are possible in these narrow, deep valleys. I am renting a place near downtown Cumberland, a second-floor apartment over the home of an older couple. To say that I have made a change in lifestyle compared to my previous home is a massive understatement.

On the positive side, I do have a private office to prepare my lessons in, located in the main administration building on campus. The office is located on the second floor and overlooks a small atrium. Without any outside windows, it is easy to focus on the task at hand and not consider the location. There is the usual small-town, small-campus gossip, but I intend to stay reasonably to myself and not become involved in local affairs to such extent as is possible. The rest of the faculty and students do not seem to know quite what to make of me. Most of the faculty and all of the students are from Kentucky, and an outsider such as me evokes some curiosity. One faculty member told me that a student had asked him if I was in some type of witness protection program, so it seems that I am at least providing some entertainment.

I do not have a telephone in my apartment; it just seems an unnecessary expense given my reduced financial circumstances. For that matter, I also do not have a television. When I finish my lesson preparation for the next day in my office, I simply go down to the atrium and use the campus television to catch the evening news (really the only thing of much value to watch). They close the main building at 10:00 pm, after the cleaning crew has finished, and I retire to my apartment for the evening, so it seems a routine has already been established. Accounting is the first class I teach in the mornings, and there is no other class in the room prior. It is the customary tiered-seating classroom so the students have a clear view of the blackboards. Notice the plural? The room has a series of blackboards, three deep, in the front of the room. In the evening the night before class, I simply fill the blackboards with the problems and examples I plan to go over. In this manner, I never have to turn my back on the students to write on the board while the class is in session. It allows me to maintain their focus on the subject at hand and also to ascertain which faces appear confused or bored with the material. It seems the students were also taken aback with this method of instruction, for I believe that prior accounting instructors spent most of their time writing on the board during class and talking over their shoulders.

The composition of accounting classes has also greatly changed during the years since I was an accounting student. In those increasingly olden times, we only had one female accounting student in my entire graduating class. Everyone in the department knew her by name, simply because of the oddity of her being in the class and not just because she was a very attractive coed. My introductory accounting class is almost entirely female, with just a few token males. The vast majority of the students are of the non-traditional type, not fresh out of high school. These folks have families and are seeking a way to enter the workforce at some level above the minimum wage type of job that their high school education currently qualifies them for. One lady came up to the front of the classroom after a class and wanted to apologize to me beforehand. She told me that when winter closed in, she expected to have to miss some classes. I told her I would need to know exactly why and she replied that when the creek in front of their home froze over, her husband would not let her drive over it. While the creek freezing seems reasonably normal in these rustic settings, what struck me was her actually following her husband's wishes. In my experience to date, this is just not a normal occurrence in many modern American families I am familiar with. I have been told by other ladies that it is the local norm for the women to prepare a full breakfast—eggs, bacon, toast, and the works—for their husbands in these mountains before they leave for classes. Eventually, I imagine, the husbands in these mountains will have a rude cultural awakening, but for the present they seem to be living, if not in another century, at least in a regional culture that is far different from what I have seen as the norm elsewhere in this nation. Most of the husbands are coal miners, and most of the male students seem to have worked in the mines prior to coming back to school. They generally appear to have suffered some accident that has made mining work no longer physically feasible, or else they are willing to take a lesser paying job just to work above ground. The coal business pays their employees very well, but it is dangerous work even with the modern equipment and rules that are used today.

Of course I want you to come down and visit, for as you said, it is only about a day's drive from your Midwestern location. I would only request that you defer your visit until spring, so that I may become better established in my new job and community. At the moment I believe that outside visitors would simply add more questions as to why I am even here. While I have not quite joined a monastery, this location is close enough to that environment to give me ample time to contemplate the path of my life, both retrospectively and prospectively.

Speaking of the insecurity of American jobs, I believe that college instructors (at least on the undergraduate level) should be looking over their shoulders. While the rest of the economy adapted to mass production early in this century, dramatically raising the production per worker, the educational sector has simply added more workers to meet the greater demand. While this has provided ample employment for the academic types and those such as me who are simply seeking a respite from the rigors of business combat, it is more closely akin to the horse and buggy than to modern production processes. I teach a number of different business courses and must prepare daily for each different subject. If the academic sector allowed greater specialization, an instructor might teach only one single course, but teach it to a great many more students. In this way, the time spent in preparation could be greatly reduced. A simple closed circuit television system might be used to send the lectures into a great many classrooms simultaneously, with the students allowed to submit questions by means of long distance phone lines. This would eliminate the unnecessary student contact that occurs when one tries to win favor by dropping into your office for a discussion, when you know the real purpose is to try to bias you toward the student. I have pretty well let it be known that my office is open for classroom material discussions only, and I expect them to explain to me why the question could not be addressed in the classroom setting. If such a system was adopted, I believe that the productivity, measured by the number of students served per instructor, might easily be doubled. Initially, some of the cost savings might need to be offset by the hiring of low-paid proctors to ensure that remote classrooms remain focused on the course material. For that matter, I find it unnecessary that most A-level students even bother to attend class very often. That segment of the student body can generally absorb the material simply by reading the text; they usually desire no interaction with the instructor and should be excused except for test days and term papers.

Back to our discussion of the upcoming clash of cultures in the next century, which seems to be a continuing source of entertainment for both of us. Each of the cultures has some probability of becoming dominant. The increasingly secular Western culture has the advantage in continuing to be on the forefront of technology. The Middle Eastern culture has the advantage of an almost cult-like adherence to a single belief structure which places greater importance on an existence after death than in life itself (this is the type of belief that creates martyrs and zealots). The Far Eastern cultures have the advantage in the sheer numbers of individuals at their call, who will eventually demand more space as their standard of living rises. The probable sequence should be religious culture prevailing over secular, with the final clash between the religious culture and the Far Eastern cultures of central governance through power rather than mere popular mandate. To look the future firmly in the face and acknowledge that our side is most likely to be vanquished first is to embrace reality and perhaps nudge the outcome just a bit more to our liking. Given the choice of whether to be followed by the Middle-Eastern cultures or the cultures of the Far East, to me the choice is reasonably clear. The Middle Eastern culture and the Far Eastern cultures are both self-centered; as are most cultures, but the Middle Eastern culture ties together parts of the Greek, Egyptian, Roman, and Persian histories under one religion. It is most likely to survive the normal schisms and emerge even stronger in the centuries ahead. The eventual victory of logic will allow a rebirth of an enlightened belief in a deity who values life in all its forms, rejoicing in its successes, and acknowledged for creating the very framework in which logic may exist. It seems a long and somewhat unnecessary path ahead that might have been avoided if in about 628 AD, Maqauqas, the governor of Egypt, had not acquiesced to the demands from Mecca and sent two slave girls in tribute (one a Coptic Christian "Mary"). Once that initial conversion took place, the followers of that new faith were to send forth summonses that allowed for neither denial nor delay, or death would be the consequence. Truly, great roads sometimes start with the smallest of steps along the barren earth. However, back to the doctrine I believe we increasingly share; that Providence makes no mistakes and that it is the combination of free will and logic with faith which will ultimately allow a world culture to be created.

Each faculty member has been assigned duties for the fall festival, which is held on campus and includes everything from archery to quilting exhibits. As this is my first year, I volunteered for the duty that seemed to be least appealing to the other faculty members, the dreaded *"clean-up detail"*! They all seemed to be taken aback when I volunteered to not only oversee the process but to actively take part in it. Next year, I shall seek a job held by any departing faculty member, and I will probably not see any opposition due to what I have volunteered for this year. The objective of the festival of course is to raise additional funds for the college, which in this poor community is not easily accomplished.

If the general population becomes fully aware of the transient value of knowledge over the next several generations, it would seem logical that they will only pursue those occupations that have substantial barriers to entry and in that manner preserve the value of the knowledge through some period of time. The medical profession comes to my thoughts, for I have often admired how they have managed to limit the number of doctors by limiting the number of medical school positions available for students. The reason always given, that only the best and the brightest are suitable for the profession is well accepted by the consumers of medical services. By such method an artificial shortage is created that allows the profession to charge high fees and still claim that it is in the public interest to do so. This shrewd artificial shortage, coupled with the provision of company-provided health insurance after WWII, has guaranteed their success. I imagine that such niches of prolonged value in knowledge will become more difficult to create in the future. Even for the doctors, the fees necessary to maintain their lifestyles will eventually become too great for business to pay and remain competitive in the world markets. In that sequence, the poor will come to depend upon the government for some form of lesser quality care and the lengthening of the general lifespan will slow or even reverse itself.

Thank you for acquiring those two and one half acres of land adjoining the entrance lane to the family farm. I am simply unable to address such matters from a financial perspective at this time, yet I know that they must be done to preserve the long-term value for those who come after us. You spoke of the value of privacy in financial transactions, which I believe is true, but you should also be aware in this increasingly crowded world that raw, undeveloped land with naturally running streams, trees, and pastures also has the ability to create a feeling of personal privacy that may become even more valued in the decades ahead. I believe the family will benefit from our long-term perspective, just as we are in their debt for their efforts.

Chapter XXXX

Dear E,

This social responsibility focus of yours can be most disconcerting. Even I, who is now thought of as a somewhat heartless corporate employee took heed of your description of the poverty that exists in your current location and the extent to which you have embraced it in your personal surroundings. To that end I have decided to engage in a small amount of social contributions myself, by taking on a weekend teaching assignment for Columbus State University. The courses are on Saturday and Sunday afternoons, so they do not really interfere with my weekday responsibilities. The student body is the most unique I have ever worked with in a professional capacity. I am teaching business courses in the minimum-security prison near London, Ohio. The prison actually does not resemble the traditional idea of a prison, except for the minor factor of the tall exterior fences that are topped with razor wire.

I saw the advertisement for an instructor in a newspaper and was hired immediately upon my interview. Of course the compensation is not significant in the larger scheme of things, but it does provide some pocket money. The prison is entered through a building that also houses the visitation area for inmates. A guard escorts me through the entrance building, and then to the right and by the cafeteria, to the next building that houses the prison library and the classroom area. This weekend activity has not been discussed with my full-time employer, as it would not appear wholly rational from their perspective.

A prison guard remains outside the classroom, in the hall, during my class sessions. I have learned a little about what is the proper protocol in interaction with inmates. It is never seemly to inquire what an inmate is incarcerated for, as that leads to the inevitable question of guilt, and there apparently are no such individuals within the confines of this facility. Their quarters are not cells, since this is a minimum security situation, but instead they reside in what might be called large barracks, with about seventy-five inmates sleeping on beds in a large room. The guard is always on duty directly outside the sleeping area. It seems a bit odd to be teaching generally accepted accounting concepts to convicted felons, but it is probably a good use of their time. The state has a program that reduces the length of their sentence by a small amount for each college level course they complete with a grade of C or better. Due to this incentive, the students have always been well prepared and never cause any difficulties in class. It might serve the public well if others from the outside were to be exposed to these classroom conditions. They seem to apportion the quarters of the inmates into facilities according to the crimes they have been convicted of. This does not appear wise, for what good does it do to place a criminal with one who is better at his specific trade? For they will surely discuss their vocation, and I fear society will not benefit from this cross communication of skills.

You are correct about the corporate environment: it is stressful, and one is asked to do things that do not always assist one in obtaining a good night's rest. After one recent bank acquisition, I was asked to visit the local president and obtain his signature on a few documents. One document required that he turn over control of the investment portfolio to the holding company, a task he had previously performed himself. Another document required that all data processing and operations functions related to the production of customer statements also be turned over to the holding company. Of course, there was one transferring all asset/liability management functions from the local bank to the holding company. Although he should not have been surprised, yet another document transferred marketing responsibilities to the holding company. He asked what he was to do with his local marketing officer, and I explained to him that such matters were his decision, but that all that was budgeted was a local marketing clerk to handle small local issues. We then had a brief discussion on obtaining the annual profit budgeted for his bank. I simply said that I was unaware of any subsidiary where the same local president had failed to achieve his budgeted profit more than once. By the paleness of his face, I believe he fully comprehended the message behind my smiling face. It really was not much of an assignment, but the impact it had on this individual, who was clearly accustomed to making decisions, was disturbing. He seemed to suddenly realize he was now just an employee and not the ultimate figure of authority that he had been prior to the sale of his bank to our company. Yet I know we paid handsomely for the bank (of which he pocketed a large portion), so how can one truly feel sorry for someone who is very wealthy as a result of his own decisions?

As the consolidation of both the banking industry and American industry continues, I believe we are watching the removal of local expertise from smaller rural communities. By transferring operational functions that may be moved to some advantage through economies of scale, well-paying jobs are being transferred out of the smaller communities, and I do not believe they will be easily replaced. From an economic perspective, I know the greater good is served through the creation of a more efficient economy, but the personal losses that must be borne through the creative destruction of capitalism are not often discussed.

My fellow bankers are living the American illusion, oblivious to what most probably lies ahead. After a period of consolidation in the industry, lasting a number of decades, most of the efficiencies will have been wrested from the operational aspects of the industry. Small town banks will still exist in slow growth rural markets that cannot produce the return on investment required by the national capital markets. Larger banks will dominate the metropolitan areas through their pricing power.

A banker on the lending side of the industry seems to think that while those folks over in operations may be replaced through consolidation, his position is secure due to the analysis required for loan decisions. What he does not understand is that just as my bank has quantified the credit risks in the credit card business to such an extent that almost no human contact is required prior to the decision to extend credit, so may other, more complicated credit decisions be quantified through better computer applications. I believe this will transform the consumer lender and eventually even the commercial lender into little more than salesmen of money. The actual decision of whether to lend money, except in very large loans, will be transferred to an automated process based on credit ratings, cash flow, and assets available for collateral. This transition will allow commercial banks to gradually lower the higher prices paid for the labor of lenders. I believe the transition will occur first in the consumer lending area, for we have already shown the path through our successful unsecured credit card lending program. Note that this is consistent with the depression of wages for so-called skilled professional labor in the future and the transient value of knowledge if it is involved in a process that may be replicated by a computer. Original thought will retain value, but what one man may be trained for another less expensive man may also be trained, to the advantage of the employer.

Your vision of the future potential of improving the efficiency of college teaching is also another example of what probably lies ahead. Most post-secondary schools will be resistant to the change, as the college experience has been changed over the past century from the pursuit of education into a social swirl that merely includes academics as one portion of the equation. The combination of athletics, cultural arts, fraternal organizations, and tenured faculty argue for the continuation of the status quo in most places of higher learning. Only relatively new educational enterprises or smaller institutions without much in the way of athletics or cultural presentation will find it to their advantage to embrace what you have described as a more efficient way of delivering the educational product to the students. No, I do not fully disagree with your vision of the future in this respect, but I believe it will take longer (probably a number of decades) to achieve. As students discover that what they have learned is outdated within a decade or so, they will demand a more efficient way of obtaining sufficient knowledge for continued employment than going back to a college campus. It will seem odd that the very institutions that are supposed to push the advancement of knowledge will lag in their embrace of the consequences of it.

As you suggested, I will wait until the spring season to visit you in the mountains. Please do not do anything rash, such as marrying one of those female students for the sake of good cooking. If you are to relocate out of the mountains and back into the hills, remember that those significant cultural differences you wrote about could have a negative impact on a long-term relationship with any wife from such a remote background. Instead of visiting you, I have decided to use a week of my upcoming vacation to go back to the hills and try to get on better personal terms with our uncle. Yes, I did enjoy your description of your fall festival duties. I guess you are one of the better educated garbage men on any cleanup crew in the mountains. *As we were taught, there is always dignity in work, regardless of the type of work. Any indignity is reserved for those who cannot find some way to contribute to society or to the betterment of their families.* I trust your guarded personal nature will shield you from the more emotional types, but take care of your future.

I also agree with your general outline of the probable course of history for the species, but with a few caveats. The aspect of timing is where we have the greatest divergence of vision. You are correct about the probable success of the Middle Eastern culture with petroleum wealth, combined with a religion that supports the total destruction of opponents. I have not forgotten the small stir you caused in the family when your seventh-grade science project won that blue ribbon. Who else but you would have presented a model of the interior workings of an atomic bomb? At least you restrained yourself and did not go into the details of the more complicated hydrogen bomb. The point is, I am aware that if a reasonably intelligent junior-high student can understand the basics of how to build such a device, there will be those in the Middle East who will see it as a means to an end. Their culture has such a different perspective, I tend to forget the beginnings of it, and I thank you for reminding me of those fateful seventh-century events. Remember that it was only after his death that his followers collected those revelations they deemed proper to include into the holy book. The "suras's" references to Christ and the prophets should provide a bridge between the two cultures, if only ours had not taken such a secular turn. *Theirs is a religion of much value, such that it teaches to be humble in spirit, temperate, and just, and these facets must be appreciated.* It is only in the aspect of guiding toward charity and brotherly love—only to other Muslims—that I find much to reproach them for in their beliefs. Even this will pose little harm as long as their level of technology does not match the depth of conviction in their beliefs. It would have been a joy to see such devotion among Christians, but perhaps we did during the Inquisition and it did have some negative social impacts. The Prophet attempted to wrap the religion of Abraham into an understanding of Christ and incorporate beliefs that would gain support from the tribes of the noblest Arabs. Surely such an attempt for the betterment of mankind is likely to provide a positive and ever lasting contribution to the species.

In another local financial institution, executive management terminated a marketing director in a most unprofessional way. A junior executive was sent to his home in the evening and was asked to pick up his keys and any documents that might relate to the bank or customers, and arranged to have his company car driven back to the bank. He was told that his personal items in his office would be mailed to him. It would seem that in our Christian/secular culture, brotherly love is of little use when it comes to disposing of human factors of production.

What would you think about a crematorium on part of our property adjoining the family farm? As the population becomes more mobile and the nuclear family continues to break down, individuals will have a much more confusing choice of where any traditional burial should be held. If they have relocated for employment, cremation may become an appealing alternative in such a self-centered society. Your thoughts on this option would be appreciated.

Chapter XXXXI

Dear Y,

I am in disagreement with your crematorium idea and will not support the location of it in proximity to the family farm. It does not seem to be consistent with the preservation and restoration of the natural surroundings. Further, I fear that this culture is leaving far too little behind in the way of permanent features upon the landscape and placing far too much capital in technology that will not readily be traceable to our efforts. Cemeteries serve as a visual reminder of those who have built the society in which we reside, and the idea of obtaining greater efficiencies through the use of crematoriums does not leave much to show for the societies' efforts. Beyond that, we are only up to slightly more than 914 acres, and remember that it takes 640 acres to make up a square mile. To hide a crematorium from obvious view would require a considerable addition to the family farm. It would be grand if we could manage to consolidate two sections, 1280 acres under the protection of the family, but I believe it is simply too much for us to accomplish even working together in a single lifetime. Have you ever considered how fortunate we are to both follow the same general plan, with some minor deviations? If there was only one of us, I doubt whether the individual would have managed to accomplish even what we have to date.

It seems I may have taught one of my marketing classes a bit too well. Some of the local business types have approached me about doing an economic feasibility study on a state park type lodge facility on top of one of the local mountains. The state already owns the land, and the local business community seems to think a lodge would bring tourism to the area. One can hardly bear to not tell them that moving tourists and multitudes of coal trucks and trains through the same area makes for less than a totally scenic experience. I suppose I will need to participate to some degree in their discussions, but I will not appear to give my support to a project I know will end up costing the taxpayers money through an endless negative cash flow.

I had an interesting encounter with another faculty member. There seems to be a great number of committees faculty are expected to serve on in addition to our teaching duties. I am attempting to limit my participation to the minimum required. A young (about thirty years of age) female faculty member asked if I would like to take her place on a committee she has served on for the last two years. I simply looked her straight in the face and said "No!" You should have seen the expression on her face. I do not believe she is accustomed to being told "no" in such a direct manner, and she apparently thought she could dump another assignment on this newcomer. The alternative is that she is accustomed to having her way on campus, as she is the most physically attractive female faculty member. She was sorely disappointed, but I am not going to play the faculty game of trying to obtain tenure through politics. I believe the fact that I was willing to lead the cleanup crew for the fall festival may have given her the idea that I was an easy mark!

Did I tell you about my first paycheck? I cannot remember if I have shared the experience with you. We are paid once monthly, for a nine-month contract, with the option of summer teaching if the demand for the courses exists and if we are willing to teach. When I received my first paycheck, I honestly thought there had been some error and went down to the accounting office. They reminded me of my contractual compensation, and I really thought it was pretty humorous. The take-home pay is not all that different from the level paid for the Peace Corps task that we joke about. They were absolutely correct in their calculations.

I stopped at a small store on the way to Corbin, Kentucky, for a meeting, and the shopkeeper looked at me strangely. When I started to pay for my snack food, she asked me if I was that preacher she sees on Sunday television. After I assured her I was not the one seeking donations via the mass media and that she was mistaken, her words gave me pause for thought. Would not the calling of the ministry be a worthwhile attempt to quell the rush of secular culture toward the probable dismal outcome that awaits us? Apparently, I look the part to such an extent that people believe I am a preacher when they first meet me. It is a noble profession, providing comfort to the population, and the Christian faith dwells on the mission of faith beyond the material world that surrounds us. Yes, I know about the problems with the math, the universal constant is not really constant over time (just a fudge factor), but these matters need not be raised when matters of faith are for the betterment of all concerned. As for that seventh-grade science project of decades ago, please burn all documents if anything ever happens to me. This might be yet another career path twist and one I am far from ready to embrace, but it does have the allure of perhaps providing a greater benefit to my fellow travelers than teaching them to be better capitalists. On this matter, your thought would be appreciated, if you would please temper them with understanding that I feel the passing of the years. It would not be an economic burden, for my compensation is already below that which is enjoyed by any pastor of moderate success. I also do not believe that we have ever had a preacher in the family, at least not since our arrival in 1698. This all may be just a way I am trying to connect with a larger social group in order to replace the family I have not been successful in forming. Sometimes looking inward at my own thoughts, biases, and reasons for choices is far more challenging than any academic endeavor.

On business issues that relate to our personal lives, I have noticed something in these mountains. Remember that academic thought about how employees internalize their salaries and just as quickly any monetary raises they receive, so that little marginal incentive to productivity is actually provided as the employee believes the compensation is their due anyway? I believe the very same process exists in non-business personal relationships! When I look back on all the money and time I have lavished on female relationships, I realize there is not a single one of them who would take the time to engage in a pleasant conversation with me at present. The economic benefits they derived from their personal relationship with me were what they believed were just and fair compensation for their companionship. Never do I remember any one of them saying, "No, you have spent too much on me and it must stop." Rather, I believe every one of them would have allowed me to spend myself into penury and simply thought the process was their due. I now believe there is a possibility that such an eventuality may even exist in some marriages, although I prefer to think we both will avoid such a fate.

Now transfer that thought of internalizing the material things given to those who are emotionally significant in our lives, noting that there is little long-term emotional return on our material investments. When I have done something that has cost me little or nothing in the way of monetary burden, such as the cleanup detail at the fall festival, folks go out of their way to express their appreciation. These are individuals with whom I hardly have any personal relationship at all. In a similar manner, if I take but a little time outside of class to help some slightly confused student see exactly how an accounting problem may be solved, they are much more appreciative than the A student who attends class and believes the time I take to prepare a class presentation is fully their due (even if they appear to not be interested in the content at all). Small acts of assistance, even of the non-monetary type, garner much more personal satisfaction for me than any of the expensive gifts I have bestowed on individuals whose affections I have actively sought.

There appears to be an almost inverse correlation between the degree of personal connection to the other individual and the satisfaction derived from providing him or her with some small personal assistance in his or her life. I believe this is almost a theorem, for in the general society, family members seldom express appreciation for the efforts it takes the breadwinner to provide sustenance for the table and shelter for the body; they simply believe it is their due. They have internalized the vast personal sacrifices that most individuals engage in to maintain the family unit through participating in the economic process to generate cash flow. Obviously I see little common sense in this rubbish about finding fulfillment in work, for it is the need to provide substance to our families that drives most of the participation in the workforce. Single individuals may say they are working solely for themselves, but if one weighs how much of their cash flow is actively or indirectly used to engage in social experiences, I daresay they are mistaken.

Based on these observations, I now believe the greatest personal satisfaction may be obtained by providing small amounts of assistance (both monetary and otherwise) to individuals with whom we have little if any personal relationships, if the assistance is limited to an almost random and unexpected basis. In these instances, the individuals have not had time to internalize the value of our assistance and genuinely express appreciation for what we have done. If you think I am wrong, cousin, try to remember the last time anyone you have had a close personal relationship of any significant duration with did anything for you that was unexpected and generous. Should you find such an individual, marry her immediately! I may not have entered a monastery in these mountains, but the spiritual and personal enlightenment I am garnering is something close to that experience. So even if this twist in my career does not provide sufficient monetary reward to justify the journey, I believe it has already provided me with a better understanding of my fellow "man" (yes, the Greek interpretation of encompassing all of humanity, rather than the Roman emphasis on only the male gender).

Recently, I had a driving experience I hope to never replicate. A fellow business instructor at another community college in Virginia, on the other side of Black Mountain, asked me to meet with him to discuss a business opportunity. I thought he might actually have a thought about how to make money in these mountains outside of the realm of coal or tourism. It turned out that he has a relative who is trying to put investors together for a dinner-tour-boat operation in Guam! It was one of those trips where you listen politely and sadly indicate that due to personal financial constraints, there will not be any possibility of participating in the venture. Just as I started back to Kentucky over Black Mountain, it began to snow. Initially it was just a nuisance, but it consistently became more challenging to drive up the mountain. There are not any guardrails on the Virginia side of the mountain, but there are any number of very impressive sheer drop-offs. Shortly after, I went around a sharp hairpin corner, and steering to the left, I lost control of the vehicle on the snow-covered road. The car turned around 360 degrees in the road, and I ended up heading in the correct direction up the mountain, but I felt white as a ghost and my hands seemed to be locked to the steering wheel.

It was interesting to watch the scenery go by in a manner like one of those 360 degree murals; at least I did not do anything totally stupid like applying the brakes. When I finally made it to the top of the mountain, I pulled over and a fellow driving behind me stopped and asked if I would like to ride down the Kentucky side with him back to Cumberland (he had front wheel drive, truly a modern advantage in these mountains). He had been behind me when the spinout occurred and was most amazed I was still alive. I thanked him for his kind gesture but declined the offer and literally inched the vehicle down the Kentucky side through the snow to my humble abode in Cumberland. There was hardly any snow down in the valley, so it really makes you think about the impact of a few thousand feet in elevation on the immediate climate.

The entire experience also made me think about the magnificent uncertainty in our daily lives. We live as if we are immortal, with such grand long-term plans, and yet the slightest mistake or unforeseen event may erase our very existence. I remember hearing that "the events of the future are but our dreams of today," but increasingly I am aware that perhaps more focus should be placed on the aspect of living for today.

The entire topic of altruism seems more of a rational allocation of capital. If I am correct, the unselfish interest in the welfare of others has a far greater return to us (in a non-economic sense) than any financial investment. This would seem to be at odds with the doctrine of the rational man we preach in our economics classes. Another example would be the personal interactions within most families. While I know that in ours we go out of the way to never speak in a negative fashion toward anyone else in the clan, such behavior is apparently not the norm in this country. Within the context of most family units, it is seemingly common for individuals to speak to each other in tones and phrases they would not dream of using in a more public setting, or with individuals with who they are less acquainted. The obvious exception is a great deal of the northeast, but as those are Yankees, I exclude them from our definition of "normal" behavior. Again, note that society condones a less gentlemanly conduct within the family and home than is permissible outside the family unit. To me, this conduct is akin to a façade we maintain for the benefit of the outside world, while the American family is most likely to see the true nature of the individuals.

On the topic of the future, let me pose another option of possible development that may predispose the eventual calamity we see in the clashes of the cultures. As the secular side advances and becomes more efficient, it must tie more of the world together ever more closely to achieve the very efficiencies that drive capitalism. This is entirely reasonable within the context of the so-called rational economic man and will undoubtedly continue to develop. The flaw in the civilization is that the more interconnected the individuals become, the specialization that raises the standard of living will leave them more exposed to the risk of a sudden downward spiral if anything disrupts the efficient system that has developed. Again, the question should be whether the risk is worth the reward to the individual and not just decided by the net gain to the society. Look at the question of water alone. While we still have the old well out on the family farm and are capable of obtaining water with relative ease (even if it probably should be boiled prior to drinking it), look at the risk borne by the greater whole of society without any apparent knowledge. If anything major disrupted the flow of electricity in this country, to such an extent that it would not be available for a period of weeks, the vast majority of the population would not be capable of availing themselves of the necessary water to carry on their existence.

The very interconnectivity that raises the standard of living in our society to such a height never before seen in the history of mankind is also its greatest weakness and the greatest risk to the survival of the individual who places all his faith on the continuation of the great endeavor. I know you dislike it when I reference Biblical context, but does not the situation remind you of that tower incident in the Old Testament? Their extensive connectivity allowed them to attempt something that had never been done, but when someone disrupted their ability to communicate, every individual suffered to the extent to which they had carried their specialization of endeavor. So the greatest risk to the individual may not be from the clash of the cultures at the margin but from any major disruption in the interconnectivity of the economic process that will become a worldwide process to use all resources (human and other) to the most efficient means possible. The focus on culture hides the risk that increases daily from this growing interdependence. Perhaps we should plan to reopen that fireplace our uncle has closed off, as heat is another factor in which self-reliance and independence seems to have a definite advantage in mitigating personal risk.

I much enjoyed your sharing of the teaching experience in the state prison and note that you seem to obtain as much enjoyment from the experience as you do from the business environment that pays you so well. The state does seem to be enlightened in allowing incarcerated individuals the opportunity to pursue education. I only hope it does not simply provide the individuals with even greater long-term frustration, as one does have to wonder how many employers will ever allow a convicted felon to use the academic business skills they acquire within the prison. The entire concept of punishment within our society is so unique. If an individual does not commit a crime, but is destitute, we will not as a society provide the person with food, shelter, or even medical assistance in many cases. Yes, I know the welfare system is designed to assist individuals during sustained gaps in their employment. Compare though, cousin, if that same person commits a crime of minimal magnitude, he or she may be assured of regular food, housing, medical care, and perhaps even education. Should we not provide the honest man the same standard of living (and some dignity from work) as the criminal receives during his confinement?

I hope your vacation in the hills went well and that you have reached a better understanding with our uncle. I also hope you are enjoying that surplus cash flow from your banking job. Please spend some of it on yourself, for life is ever so short and should be enjoyed to such extent as is reasonable.

Chapter XXXXII

Dear E,

You appear to have found your calling in those mountains. As you do not have any personal responsibilities at the moment, it would seem that you are free to stay as long as you are happy. If those fleeting moments of happiness associate themselves with being of assistance to those less fortunate, either mentally or materially, perhaps this is the essence of an enlightened lifestyle. I do agree with you that it far better to be generous with those who know us either only slightly, or even better, not at all. For I too have found that the more familiar people are with one another, the greater freedom to inflict emotional distress is presumed by at least one if not both parties. You joke about the monastery in the mountains, but did not the life of some medieval monks celebrate the piety of little if any verbal communication and the helping of one another in the community? If only they had taken better care to defend themselves, perhaps that way of life could have persisted on a large scale for a longer period of time. To be blunter, cousin, never forget that you should be prepared to defend yourself, for those you try to help are also those most likely to inflict harm upon you. Please remember our past: Carmichael is nothing but a modern translation of Michael's fortress, and it would not have been necessary if those longboats had not pulled ashore in the ninth century. Were it not for that fortress, all trace of generosity and Christianity would have been swept from those hard-won shores on the North Sea. Take care that your personal life does not become too entangled with the families of those mountains, for neither monks' robes nor academic attire has proven any shield from the irrationality of emotional types.

My mini vacation to the hills went both well and less than totally acceptable. On the real estate front, I spent some time reviewing county land maps and located a twenty-acre parcel adjacent to the north side of the family farm. It is located a quarter mile further down Clifty Creek from the large sixty-acre parcel you purchased. It is a full quarter of a mile long, running east to west, but only one eight of a mile wide. The parcel is fully landlocked, with no road access, but it has the benefit of having old growth hardwood on it that does not appear to have been cut since the first settlers in the 1850s. The forest is not only hardwood; it is, better yet, of the white oak type. The family farm ends at the north edge of the hill, and this parcel encompasses land from the edge, down the nearly sheer face of the hill and about halfway across the valley. I had to make connections in Memphis to find the owner, and I mistakenly asked our uncle to oversee something I wanted done in my absence. More on that mistake later but suffice to say that once again I have learned the limitations of getting things done as an absentee owner. The owner of the twenty-acre parcel turned out to be an elderly lady in a nursing home, and her family was only too glad to unload what they viewed as a worthless parcel of mostly vertical hillside for only $200 per acre. For a total price of only $4,000 for the twenty acres, I simply put it on my credit card. I believe it fits with the larger puzzle, for now together we own three quarters of a mile of free-flowing stream along Clifty Creek, arranged in such a manner as to prevent most development by city folks seeking a spot for a cabin in the woods. I am an open preservationist, even though it will simply delay the development process, for I am sure that those who come after us will not fail to see the potential for financial gain our purchases have created (when combined with the family land). May we both have long, prosperous lives!

On the topic of our uncle, I asked him to oversee the construction of a new brick pump house over the well for the cattle. The old pump house had definitely seen its better day, as it was made of wood. Being only about three feet or so in height and six feet square, it was made so the roof could be lifted off by two fellows in order to work on the pump. My thought was that I would have a concrete floor poured and build six-foot walls from concrete blocks covered with a brick façade. The idea is to gradually improve the appearance of the place. It seemed such a simple idea. When I returned, there was a beautiful pump house, with a new roof and shingles as well. Then I walked around it to admire the work and noticed there was no door! You would have been pleased, for I did not express dissatisfaction overtly but merely inquired how one was supposed to enter this facility. I was told, with not a trace of a smile, that it would take two fellows to have a ladder on each side and together lift off the roof (five feet by seven feet). I just mentioned that this might be a bit of a problem if the pump needed working on in the middle of winter, with only one person present. The original and simple idea was to have a small place to work shielded from the elements. Instead, I paid for the smallest fortress ever constructed. You need to remember to pull a ladder into the pump house after you get the roof off in case I am not there, otherwise getting out of the structure may be a problem. There will be a need later to have another contractor put a door in the structure, but I did not have the time or the good humor to correct the situation during this trip. I have decided to name the pump house after our uncle in later years, to remind me always that he was forever building walls for us to scale and never providing a door. Of course I paid for this most unique construction myself and will count it as a capital improvement that will hopefully never be replicated.

In banking, I continue to enjoy the intellectual opportunity to promote change and detest the daily interaction with those who have a vested interest in maintaining their employment through the status quo. There is a significant and material cost advantage of using electronic processing of transactions versus paper checks. Such a vast opportunity awaits anyone who can quickly persuade customers to always try to use plastic rather than paper, you would think bankers would be tripping over themselves to push customers in that direction. Instead, the industry seems content with seeking ways to make check processing more efficient.

To me, a customer who pays off his balance on the credit card every month generates three streams of revenue, or cost reduction. First is the merchant rebate, a small amount that varies according to the merchant's activity, but which in the aggregation of all merchants is material. Second is the annual fee that is charged to the user of the plastic. This may be waived if the customer has sufficient transactions so the merchant discount fee is adequate to replace the revenue from this source. The third and most important revenue stream is what I have the greatest difficulty in getting bankers beyond our bank to realize as important. As ever more of our merchants are on electronic transmission, we have replaced the paper check with the electronic transmission. The cost savings are simply huge! Most bankers seem to think I am grossly overstating the cost savings, because a good portion of plastic transactions take place out of the market area of their banking operations. Such are the perspectives of individuals who see only the present and do not have a clear vision of the future. As we have discussed, the consolidation of this industry will eventually lead to a relatively small number of large institutions controlling the majority of the national banking market, with small rural segments and non-growth areas divided between a substantial number of smaller commercial banks. They simply cannot see that if we are successful, our commercial banking operation will grow to sprawl across this land and take their business away from them. If we already have the customer biased toward plastic, we will have a tremendous efficiency advantage over the smaller local institutions whose customers are still using paper checks. Frankly, I believe the industry should be willing to share some of the short-term marginal gains from the switch to plastic with the customer in order to speed the process along. However, as public companies need to focus on the improvement of results on a quarterly basis, I doubt the idea will ever sell. The reality is that stock prices are driven by quarterly earnings, and I must realize the industry focus on immediate results. Occasionally I slip into a long-term government employee perspective, which I must try to bury in my past. It would require a large, closely held financial institution with no immediate stockholder demands to pursue the advantage of plastic over paper to the extreme I believe is necessary. I am simply most fortunate to work for Banc One, with their emphasis on efficiency and plastic.

Another banker in our community may have lost his bearings, or at least is more eccentric than I can imagine having as a boss. Word is that he called a staff meeting and appeared in a gorilla suit. To me this cries out as an individual in desperate need of attention. Purportedly he used this tactic because he believed his staff was not paying enough attention to his directives. What ever happened to decorum in the office? Word about town is that he also met with his professional level staff and told them he expected them to work at least one day each weekend, but that he really did not care which day. Remember when the five-day workweek existed a generation ago? I suspect this fellow will need to replace a number of his professional staff members during the next year, as who would stand to be treated in such a demeaning manner in a so-called staff meeting? In defense of this individual, who I do not know personally, the pressure to seek new ways to enhance revenue or reduce expenses in this industry is immense, and his superiors may be pushing him for more in the way of results than he has been able to deliver. If such is the case, he may simply be transferring the pressure downward. I still would not recommend this as a management tactic, for this poor fellow will forever be known as the guy who wore a gorilla suit to a business meeting.

I had a small problem with my home, but problems are to be expected with older homes. While sitting in the den, I smelled smoke and located it originating at the base of a radiator. It turned out that a small leak had developed and the water had seeped into an electrical connection and caused a short circuit. The fire department responded quickly, and no real damage was done with the exception of a little smoke, and that was minimized due to the location in the entrance hall (I just opened the door to air out the smoke). It seemed the fire crew was there within just a few minutes of my call. Timing is everything in life, and I am aware that had I not been home, everything might have gone up in smoke. The only thing I own of significant and material value is a solid teak bedroom suite from Sweden. The remainder of my belongings I fear look the part of belonging to a corporate migrant worker who has been on the road far too long. I, as you, am beginning to feel that I am not twenty-one years of age anymore.

A potential romantic attachment has developed, which I will probably regret, for your analysis of most personal attachments rings disturbingly true. To narrow it down to perhaps a hundred million individuals, her last name is Ho, and she is from Hong Kong. With a British mother and a Chinese father, she is intelligent and striking in appearance. A fellow banker by trade, it is appealing to discuss reality with another individual who shares a similar frame of reference. Even though she is from southern China, she speaks Mandarin, rather than some obscure local dialect. The only problem is that she is obviously better suited for some older and wealthy individual than for such a modestly successful individual as myself. Excuse this reference to personal details that we tend to avoid, but when fate is kind to an individual in a land far from home, the event deserves mentioning, even if it is probably short-lived.

With the addition of the new twenty acres, our combined total is now 122 and one half acres. Combined with the family farm of 812 acres, the total under our direct and indirect control is now a more respectable 934 acres. This is close to one and one half square miles of what most folks would describe as worthless hill country. As there are more than fifty-three thousand square miles in our home state, it would seem but a dent in an area of such magnitude, but remember that fully a quarter of the state is under government control of some type (national forest, state park, or public lakes). From that perspective, our portion is a significant amount since it is all contiguous. I suspect we will begin to have the problem of externalities as individuals become aware of the different names we are operating under and discover the potential advantage of locating close to what is really a substantial private holding that will not be developed. I trust you understand that I am not opposed to selective logging, but I will resist any large-scale clear cutting. I may not have mentioned, but we now have a new species of animal life on the place—armadillos— which have migrated from the south. They dig large holes, which are dangerous to cattle and humans alike, but appear too numerous to exterminate. The snakes also seem to be becoming more numerous; copperheads and the occasional rattlers are the greatest nuisance.

Do try to have some fun. An individual recently inquired whether I ever really had any fun, and I truthfully had to answer that I could not remember any recent such event and it would take a little thought to recall the last time "fun" occurred. If moments of happiness are rare, perhaps the occurrences of actual gleeful fun are rarest of all. I always try to remember Aristippus, who taught that true temperance is not the absolute abstaining from all pleasure but in being moderate in its enjoyment. As I neither drink nor smoke, it is perhaps too easy a lesson for me to remember. It always springs into my thoughts when I would rather enjoy a second helping of some food or a scandalous dessert, and I remember that particular student of Aristotle who spoke best in matters of moderation in all things good in life. Do you find yourself so jaded with the commonplace that you wonder how any of it can be fun? If it was not for the wonderful gift of free thought, I surely would not find any pleasure in remaining in this world for any duration beyond what I have already endured. The necessary interaction with so many members of the public in matters of business simply grates upon my temperament. I do remember the advice of our grandfather in matters of public endeavor. He thought that it is best to limit speaking to any group to no more than once or twice—more for the benefit of the speaker than the group. If they cannot comprehend the message within that timeframe, they are unlikely to do so, and frustration will likely develop on both sides of the podium. Grandfather is an individual I sorely miss. Yes, I am aware that every individual's apparent perfection increases with each year after their death, but we both agree that he was a rare individual of high moral and intellectual character.

You have not spoken of your health recently, so I am trusting that it is at least none the worse. You are not exactly in the best location for modern medical care if you should need it quickly. Have you considered a community college somewhat closer to a larger city?

I had a bat flying through my living room recently, so wildlife does seem to exist even in this semi-urban environment. It apparently came in via the chimney, and that avenue of entry has now been modernized and closed effectively. It was a bit of exercise to assist the little mammal in exiting the house through an open door by the use of a broom. If any of the neighbors saw me, they probably have confirmed their thoughts on the state of my sanity.

Chapter XXXXIII

Dear Y,

You have made such good progress with the land acquisition program that I must express my appreciation. Even if the pace of the land additions does need to slow somewhat due to financial limitations, we now have sufficient road access to make it clear that we are no longer the folks who live behind everyone else. Your pump house construction endeavor was most entertaining, but it reminds me of the general level of quality I had almost forgotten about in rural construction. Again, the problem is that once beyond the city limits in our home state, not only is there not any zoning, but there are no construction regulations. This results in contractors, who are at least licensed, to build according to their interpretation of what quality construction might be, without regard for any building inspectors.

I agree, a door might be a nice touch on your structure, and I support the naming of it after our relative.

The winter has been a bit harsh in the mountains, but compared to Alaska, it has practically been a long spring. They simply do not have adequate financial resources to move the snow off the roads quickly and we have ended up missing a few days of school. The administration is tacking it onto the end of the spring term, so it really does not matter. I have taken your suggestion and put my name in for an open business teaching position at a University of Kentucky system community college in western Kentucky, near Henderson. It is a much larger city, with better medical facilities, and a good four-hour drive west of these mountains. I have already been in for an interview, and it looks promising. The administration at my present school is not pleased and has offered me a $1,000 raise if I will stay. The prospective new employer is willing to match their offer, so I believe I will head west. It is remarkable that my prospective raise in compensation is about what I once spent on parking in larger cities. Note that in this academic environment there is no compensation for moving expenses. There are some reasons to miss the financial rewards of the banking industry (but not all that many). I plan to relocate my meager belongings myself, rather than engaging a moving company.

In a small campus, the students soon hear about every development, and word of my probable departure spread quickly. At lunch one day, my accounting students got together and arranged a surprise appreciation party for me, complete with a small plaque from the whole group of them. It was a potluck affair with the students supplying the food themselves. I will always appreciate that plaque, from a poor group of students (about twenty), far more than the awards I have received from previous employers. As I am departing the school, they did not have to do anything for me, for they need not fear having to take classes from me next year. Instead, it was simply something they decided to do on their own. Some of them are not even taking classes from me this spring term but were in my class during the fall term. There are good people back in these hills. Again, it was that national college teaching publication that led me to the open position at the other school in Kentucky. It was readily available in our college library, not the greatest idea for the expenditure of resources by the administration, but certainly a great help to me.

The upcoming graduation ceremony will be the first in which I have participated since I graduated from Vanderbilt. At long last I will get to use the master's hood over my academic gown in the ceremony and sit among the faculty. It seems like such a small thing, of no monetary significance, yet it seems to solidify the upcoming completion of a successful academic year. As an adjunct facility (part-time) at other colleges and universities, I was never invited to participate in the graduation exercises as a faculty member (which always made me feel somewhat like a second-class citizen).

I have made no attachments with the opposite gender that would hinder the relocation, but it is odd that perhaps I might have if I had been so inclined. It seems that in these mountains there remains a respect for simple education, which has grown lacking in most of the so-called civil society in which I have been previously employed. I doubt, in western Kentucky, whether I will find the same respect accorded to educated individuals, as there will be far more of them relative to the general population.

As to my health, what can you say when you find yourself residing inside a facility that probably should be condemned? It functions, but there are continual technical difficulties. Calcium deposits on my knees, which I have had since a young man, make the pace of my walk slower than most, and significant stairs are something to avoid if possible. The vertigo remains an issue and my driving is slower as I deal with the feeling of falling forward while driving. I also thought, until this year, that shingles was a disease of old age, when I learned it was a reactivation of the chicken pox virus I had as a child. I would not recommend the shingles experience, due to the discomfort (only a doctor who has not experienced the affliction would not call it pain). Even more interesting is that I am told it might arise again at some later point in my life, so who says there are not things to look forward to in later life?

I have a tip for you that might be considered for next year. Our uncle has informed me that another neighbor has approached him and wishes to sell some of their property. I believe another twenty acres might be available, which would include another three hundred feet of Clifty Creek, along with an equal amount of county road frontage. It is not a large parcel, and our uncle has already indicated to me that he does not believe it is worth the money. This means that if you wait some months, and if the property is still available, you might be able to add it to your holdings. As to the owner, let me simply say that it is adjacent to some property that you already own, and I believe you will know the parcel and potential seller. Waiting for a couple of months or more would also lower the possibility of any conflict with our uncle. It is yours for the consideration of the matter. The property is somewhat oddly shaped, but it would join the family farm for a quarter of a mile on a steeply sloped hillside. The hillside is second growth hardwood that has not been cut in nearly a century. This acquisition would result in our combined property adjoining the outer boundary of the family farm for a total of more than a mile and make us the neighbor with the most adjacent property. I still do not know what it takes to get any respect from our uncle in this matter, but I know that Grandfather would appreciate the long-term plan to build on what he most ably established. I suspect that you will have to pay more than the $200 per acre you were lucky enough to pay on that other twenty acres, perhaps several times more. In this case the total acreage is again about twenty.

On the matter of the animal life, I was not aware of the armadillos. Some of our cousins have informed me that we now have coyotes and deer, neither of which existed on the farm when I was young. It seems that what was once similar to a rural park land is now turning into something of a wildlife preserve. Our uncle has informed me that the State Game and Fish department even released a number of wild turkey onto the place due to the remote location and unique topography, which restricts the number of likely trespassers or hunters. I do not know whether the turkeys will survive, but the diversity of wildlife has definitely increased.

Your observation on the issue of "fun" is interesting. I seem to have forgotten even the topic with all the other ongoing developments in life. When I did have excess financial resources and a little time, what passed for fun was actually spent on trying to make other people (of the opposite gender) happy. A foolish endeavor, as we both agree that happiness either exists within the individual or it does not. It is not something that another person can create out of the ether. About the closest thing to fun that I can remember is a walk along a beach more than a decade ago, with the smell of the ocean wind. Today I do not even try for fun but would be pleased with just some few moments of happiness from time to time. Since I have removed myself from the daily conflict of business life, the change in perspective probably could best be described as a certain tranquility. Without the need to continually press for improvements in profitability, I have more time to think and contemplate the societal developments. It is almost like being able to watch the stream from onshore, without having to dive in and expend all energy in the constant swimming against the current. I now have a much greater respect for the force of the current and the degree to which it drove my life, but I also believe I now have a far better perspective of where the entire stream is headed that could not have been gained from my earlier business positions.

Concerning cattle and the family farm, please consider that commodity prices of livestock should not be anticipated to keep pace with inflation in the decades ahead. The continuing improvements in the efficiency of raising poultry and pigs should drive down their relative prices compared to the general price level. Because of the ability to easily move from beef to these other meats; the consumer is likely to shift their tastes to the more economical choices. This will effectively place a pricing restraint on beef prices and gradually remove the economic profit available to the small cattle producer. In this matter, we will either need to consider becoming significantly larger—a minimum of two hundred fifty head of cattle, I believe—to garner the necessary economies of scale or exiting the business. The problem of growing the cattle aspect of the family business is that it is relatively labor intensive, with daily challenges from fencing to weaning, and we both know that rural farm labor is becoming scarce. This is not of immediate concern, as our uncle does not really raise the cattle for money but for something to occupy the time of his retirement years. If he does decide to retire from the fields at some future time, we will then need to decide whether we can afford the luxury of non-economic cattle wandering the hills for the sake of the scenic addition they add to the place.

You seem to be getting the hang of this management discipline. By promoting change and aligning yourself with executive management, you effectively become their instrument in helping guide their business. By always challenging those who resist change, you effectively manage the process by always pressing the offensive. It is far easier to win from that position than being on the defensive, as those who resist change often discover from experience. It is recommended that you send out a memo on issues you want to guide along, with a "cc" showing that that a copy has obviously been forwarded to your chairman. If he does not disagree, the other recipients of the memo will believe that you are acting on his advice and directives. This will build your status in the corporation and reduce resistance to the changes you wish to deploy. The appearance of power is often just as if not more important than the actual power itself. As long as your initiatives are aligned with the wishes of the chairman, he is likely to support your efforts and take credit for any thoughts you originate. This will be to your long-term advantage. Always take the time to add all members of executive management to your annual Christmas card list. It is a subtle way of reminding everyone of the attention to detail and at the same time appear to be of good seasonal spirits. It is also one of the few times of the year when we can all get away with a little personal advertising, while spreading a few words of good cheer that might not be well received during other portions of the year. In addition, always send seasonal greetings to any and all who oppose you in the corporation and who have caused you any grief during the past year. They should find this action somewhat disquieting and be unsure of how to respond, and keeping the opposition guessing about your intentions is always a good tactical move.

Ongoing management seems to be a combination of the daily tactical grind within the corporation, managing the process, combined with the necessity of looking at the long-term strategic objective of shareholder wealth maximization by guiding the corporation through the market and general economy. I believe you have successfully made the transition from public servant to corporate manager, and your success is likely to continue. Remember that I have always been somewhat paranoid about the internal competition within the corporation, trusting no individual, and publicly discussing only those factors that serve my vision of the future. While blind trust of others is something I do not support, aligning yourself with individuals you enjoy mutual respect with may be to your advantage and to the advantage of the entire corporation, as groups of individuals are created who share the same vision of shareholder wealth maximization. Do not hesitate to eliminate those with different perspectives, for peaceful coexistence is not really an alternative. Darwin could have saved himself a long journey if he had just had an opportunity to study survival of the fittest within modern corporations.

I will be at the present address for only about a month (presuming the new job is offered) prior to making the next jump to my new location. I do not plan to teach summer school this year and will instead just take a break from this semi-retirement of teaching and settle into the new community.

One more student story, if you will indulge me, for this one is very unusual. This year, one of my female students has dressed much better than the typical student, and I have resisted inquiring about her background. If I was going to remain on this campus, such curiosity would not be appropriate. Now that I am planning to depart, I felt that I might get away with speaking directly with her after one of my classes. This lady is in her late twenties and intelligent. I mentioned to her that she did not seem to be in the same financial duress as most students and wondered if I might inquire what her employment had been prior to coming back to school, for it appeared she must have been very successful. She was polite and indicated her previous success was a result of a joint effort between her and her husband. They had decided they wanted to have a home paid for in its entirety prior to attending college, and they accomplished their objective. I stated that I was impressed with their foresight and planning at such a young age. At that point, I inquired about their successful business and the area they owned it and whether they were still engaged in the endeavor. She replied that they had retired from business and were pursuing college full time, with her husband at another school about fifty miles away. It seems they had purchased beer and alcohol in bulk in a wet county some distance away and transported it to the dry county where they reside. They then sold the product out of their back door for a number of years at a substantial markup. They viewed it as a community service, for individuals did not have to drive long distances over mountain roads to obtain alcohol, thereby reducing the possibly of accidents occurring by drunk drivers on their way home after procuring the beer. It was one of those moments when you truly do not know what to say.

Enjoy Ohio; I have heard the art museums in Cincinnati are very impressive.

Chapter XXXXIV

Dear E,

It seems that the mountain culture in rural America differs from the urban environment more than one would imagine. I suspect that the story you told of one of your successful students is just a continuation of the mountain heritage of being polite to the "revenuers," but just going about their business as usual. There are of course not enough law enforcement officers in the country to enforce all the laws, and yet the legislative bodies insist on passing more with each of their sessions. If we cannot even enforce our borders from illegal aliens, little else that occurs should surprise any of us. It would seem that so-called "dry" counties may simply serve as central watering holes, or points of product dispersion. As we have discussed, you should not hope to legislate morality; it is something that must be taught in the homes, honored in the communities, and treasured in the society for much progress to be made in the delicate nature of human relationships.

Our bank is continuing to grow and become one of the leading banks in the Midwest; I am pleased to just have the opportunity to be a small part of it. The acquisition mode has now extended from Ohio into Indiana, Kentucky, and Wisconsin. The solid balance sheet of this organization, coupled with its great profitability, enables us to use the currency of our stock to acquire other banks. The acquisitions allow the bank to use the excess liquidity the smaller banks typically have to fund continued growth in our credit card portfolio and other commercial loans. The local banks continue to serve the needs of their local markets, while the redeployment of their excess liquidity simply adds to the greater profitability of the combined organizations. This is truly one of those programs in which there are a lot of winners and few (if any) losers that I am aware of in the process. Shareholder wealth maximization is achieved, greater efficiency is reached through the combining of the operational aspects of the organizations, and a wider diversity of financial products at better cost is offered to the consumer. Viewing the process from the outside, it is certainly a money-making machine. Working for such an employer gives one almost the same feeling as going to an upscale private school, for you know that the organization is developing a positive reputation throughout the banking industry.

On a personal level, I am responsible, along with my staff, for managing the interest rate risk of this growing business. Along with guiding deposit pricing, we use interest rate swaps to shift the risk of significant movements in interest rates away from the bank. All an interest rare swap actually causes is an exchange of a series of payments between the two parties to the swap. One party pays a variable series of interest rates on a specific amount for a specific period of time, while the other party pays a series of fixed interest rates on the same amount for the same period of time. Notice that the actual amount on which the interest is paid (you would call it the principal) is never paid off by either party. It just allows each party to balance their interest rate risk. We have about $3+ billion of interest rate swaps on the books, for an organization with more than $20 billion in assets, so it is a significant tool in balancing the interest rate risk. With the risk balanced, the earnings flow of the bank should be relatively unaffected by either upward or downward movements in interest rates. If it is not, then I have not done my job correctly. Of course the staff has other tasks, but I view this as the most important portion of the overall department responsibilities.

Smaller financial institutions are at such a disadvantage as they usually try to simply use their investment portfolios to balance interest rate risk (coupled with deposit pricing). You notice them running so-called "specials" with higher rates for particular deposit maturities, which they must need to balance their risk. It is a much more difficult task for the smaller financial institution. From the perspective of a small bank, the best economic environment is a prolonged period of relatively steady interest rates, or if rates must move, it is hoped that the movement will be gradual so the bank can adjust to them with the internal tools it has available. You must respect small bank managements, for they are more akin to sailors tacking into the wind, which is a task requiring much skill and a delicate touch on the wheel. Those of us at larger banks, who feel comfortable with interest rate swaps and other off balance sheet techniques, are more like the crew on a modern cruiser, with a complicated engine at our disposal to overcome any shortfalls in our manual sailing abilities. The additional specialization that a larger staff allows simply makes the process easier.

Thank you for the tip on the land back in the hills being available for acquisition. It will have to wait until after my annual bonus, but as you probably have foreseen, I will pursue it at the earliest moment my personal financial condition permits. It we are successful with yet another acquisition, I believe it will bring our total up to 142 and one half acres adjacent to the family property of 812 acres, for a total of 954 and a half acres. Better yet, it will add another separate area of county road frontage, bringing to four the number of access points we will have added to the core farm. Yes, I believe Grandfather would approve of the process. I think we will also be one of the few farms in the valley to successfully transition to a fourth generation and maintain continuity of ownership for well past the century mark.

On the matter of wildlife, I could probably do without the State Game and Fish department placing the wild turkeys on the place, as I suspect it will increase our challenges with trespassers and potential hunters. Another relative indicated that the state has released elk into the northern part of the state, so perhaps we are just lucky that deer and turkey are the only game animals that we have to deal with at this time. Again, it is a wonder that state government can apparently change the natural habitat in any way they please, under the guise of restoring the environment to the condition it was before the state was settled. The unfortunate fact is that the climate was changing then and it is continuing to change, and the environment for the animals is also changing. There is no better example of this than the pine plantation venture our uncle has led us into on the farm. When we were young, the winters were much cooler, and large pine plantations were limited to southern areas of the state. Today, as the climate warms, the pine plantations are moving northward, along with such far southern wildlife as those armadillos. They are trying to recreate something that is increasingly out of synch with the reality of the environment that exists today and is likely to exist over the next century.

Congratulations on that going-away party your students threw for you! It is something to be appreciated in this day and age. As you say, it is often those with whom we have little personal relationships who seem to appreciate our efforts. In the business culture of this country, I am noticing fewer and fewer such affairs as going-away parties or even small celebrations of individuals reaching such events as twenty years of service for an organization. Even more disturbing, I have even seen divorce parties but fewer such events to celebrate long-term marriages. The focus is increasingly on the individual and not on their long-term contribution or connection with either an organization or family. I do envy your daily access to a college library and perhaps the time to simply indulge yourself in reading whatever you may find interesting. Of course we both always have found the time to read the daily national financial publications, but I do not have ready access to a library or the ability to easily shift the focus of my thoughts from work to the general pursuit of knowledge that we both learned from our liberal arts background.

It would seem you have found your calling in this teaching devotion, with the option of two institutions in which to teach during the next school year. Your decision to pursue the school in western Kentucky is a wise one, for it sounds like a larger community college. It would also place you closer to several larger public universities, just in case you decide to go after that doctorate degree. Yes, I know a doctorate cannot be justified on economic grounds when one considers the lost wages of the years devoted to the education. However, there are some few things that should be considered to have an intrinsic value in life that stands above the daily economic battle in which we engage. With no family responsibilities, and neither of us growing any younger, it would appear to be well timed to at least consider the option. Do not worry about the family farm, as we seem to have the venture well underway, and I believe that the appropriate amount of acreage may be acquired by the time we are both ready to relocate back home. I regret that the academic community does not pay for your relocation; for I know that it cannot only be a personal bother but an unbudgeted expense. All consideration given, the relocation still seems like a net gain, both in location and in the small additional amount of marginal compensation.

As a bonus, your new location will only be about five hours from the family farm, so perhaps you will be able to keep a closer eye on our uncle and his unending series of ventures. The word from a relative is that he now seems to be on a constant mission of bush hogging the fields with another one of his elderly friends. They apparently both go out in the mornings and take turns riding the tractor and mowing the bushes with the tractor and bush hog. Of course, it is dangerous for even a young man to be hauling around a machine with a six foot cutting swath and no front guard if one was to be thrown from the tractor. This does not even consider the added danger from a live PTO connecting the bush hog to the tractor, but such things do not seem to concern him in the least.

We are also securitizing bank card debt, to get it off the balance sheet while still retaining a handsome fee for managing the process. Capitalism is grand! It is a neat way to avoid the restraints of deposit growth.

Enjoy your remaining days in the mountains; such scenery does not exist in western Kentucky. I believe it is more of a rolling sort of country, more similar to our hills back home.

Chapter XXXXV

Epilogue

Dear reader and friend,

It should suffice to say that life is inherently unfair. With each day in which we live and enjoy the fullest bounty of life that is made available to each of us, we all also suffer a slight death in both our spirits and bodies. At some point, it may be argued, there reaches a point of balance between the bounty of daily life and the cumulative burden of the daily death by a million small incidents or perhaps a few large ones. I believe that it is at those points of balance in which we are at the most precarious perches above the ravine of death stretching beneath each of us. If we are most fortunate, we find solace in another individual. As we both anticipated, cancer took E away, as is expected within our family.

Some of us even reach into religion, as my cousin often did, knowing that the continuity and development of beliefs stretching from Zoroastrianism through Christianity must have some purpose. He chose to believe it was a divine purpose, and I certainly hope he was correct. He often said that God may be seen in pure math, which does not contain errors and that all individuals, regardless of faith, race, sexual preference, or nationality were put here for a purpose, and to question the purpose was to question existence itself. He was a much more benevolent individual than I will ever hope to become. His belief that the physical logic of the creator must prevail over the apparent chaos of human existence was based on the understanding that mankind is simply part of the grand design. To question any single event or even the history of the species was as alien to him as questioning why any particular atom or molecule behaved as it does. Yet the understanding of event sequences allowed us to prevail against formidable odds to escape the narrow mental confines of our youth. The logic of math allowed us to peer within the physical universe, but only the utmost respect for the creator permitted sanity in daily life. However, I believe it may be said that over the fifteen-year period of our correspondence, we both became more enlightened and much more understanding of the wide variations that exist within mankind.

It can be said that my cousin became one with the mountains of Kentucky, and that his life was one of both occasional physical and spiritual bounty. His journey led him back and forth across this continent and touched many lives, but with few actually getting to know him. I trust that our correspondence, edited to such few letters that tell the general story of our existence, may provide some understanding of how we and the nation we treasured grew and prospered financially, emotionally, and spiritually through the years. I know that I speak for him in saying that we both are deeply appreciative of all those individuals who provided us insights into the human nature that was the real exploration expressed in our correspondence. Having been reared in a sheltered environment, where harsh words were never heard, the actual savagery of the world expressed in interpersonal dealings was a constant source of amazement, and, initially, bewilderment, to each of us. We learned much too late that it is no longer he who has the best sword and logic of attack who wins, but rather the combination of the best logic and lawyers is the order of attack for victory today. We both recognized that diversity in thought is similar to a diversified financial portfolio; it reduces risk in a society. May your personal risk be minimized and all changes be positive in the fulfillment of reasoned thought.

For those who wonder over the details, the period of this correspondence was from the mid 1970s to the late 1980s. Our uncle still lived throughout the period of these letters, but one of us did manage to survive beyond the years of his reach. During the late 1980s, the family farm project continued, and I believe our grandparents would be pleased to know the details. More than eight thousand new metal fence posts and countless new gates were added to update the facilities for the cattle. Land was continually added in almost every year to add value for future generations. There were many setbacks yet to endure, such as the tornado and treachery in business dealings, but my cousin would still recognize the general plan of which he was the chief architect. Yet the pine trees still grow and the deer have multiplied like rabbits. We have even been fortunate enough to survive life within another corporation and find a member of the opposite gender who expressed interest in us when they thought we were nearly destitute. It was a moment to be forever cherished but best included in the next volume of this review.

Si vis pacem, para bellum! ("If you wish for peace, prepare for war!")